REA's
VERBAL
TUTOR®
for the SAT

(Also known as
the **SAT I**)

Staff of Research and Education Association
Dr. M. Fogiel, Chief Editor

Research and Education Association
61 Ethel Road West
Piscataway, New Jersey 08854

REA's VERBAL TUTOR® for the SAT

Printed in the United States of America

Library of Congress Control Number 00-110150

International Standard Book Number 0-87891-963-5

THE HIGH SCHOOL TUTOR is a registered trademark of Research & Education Association, Piscataway, New Jersey 08854

CONTENTS

ABOUT RESEARCH & EDUCATION ASSOCIATION

Research & Education Association (REA) is an organization of educators, scientists, and engineers specializing in various academic fields. Founded in 1959 with the purpose of disseminating the most recently developed scientific information to groups in industry, government, high schools, and universities, REA has since become a successful and highly respected publisher of study aids, test preps, handbooks, and reference works.

REA's Test Preparation series includes study guides for all academic levels in almost all disciplines. Research & Education Association publishes test preps for students who have not yet completed high school, as well as high school students preparing to enter college. Students from countries around the world seeking to attend college in the United States will find the assistance they need in REA's publications. For college students seeking advanced degrees, REA publishes test preps for many major graduate school admission examinations in a wide variety of disciplines, including engineering, law, and medicine. Students at every level, in every field, with every ambition can find what they are looking for among REA's publications.

Unlike most test preparation books—which present only a few practice tests that bear little resemblance to the actual exams—REA's series presents tests that accurately depict the official exams in both degree of difficulty and types of questions. REA's practice tests are always based upon the most recently administered exams, and include every type of question that can be expected on the actual exams.

REA's publications and educational materials are highly regarded and continually receive an unprecedented amount of praise from professionals, instructors, librarians, parents, and students. Our authors are as diverse as the subject matter represented in the books we publish. They are well-known in their respective disciplines and serve on the faculties of prestigious high schools, colleges, and universities throughout the United States and Canada.

ACKNOWLEDGMENTS

We would like to thank Dr. Max Fogiel, President, for his overall guidance, which brought this publication to completion; Larry B. Kling, Quality Control Manager of Books in Print, for supervising revisions; Ariana Baker, Editorial Assistant, for coordinating revisions; and Marty Perzan for typesetting the manuscript. We are also grateful to these contributors: Claire Adas; Suzanne Coffield, M.A.; Anita Price Davis, Ed.D.; Joseph D. Fili, M.A.T.; Marilyn B. Gilbert, M.A.; Bernice E. Goldberg, Ph.D.; Jennifer Kovacs; Gary Lemco, Ph.D.; and Richard C. Schmidt, Ph.D.

HOW TO USE THIS BOOK

WHAT THIS BOOK IS FOR

For as long as the SAT I has been administered, students have found this test to be difficult and challenging. Despite the publication of hundreds of test preparation books intended to provide improvement over previous guides, students continue to remain perplexed.

In a study of the problem, REA found the following basic reason underlying students' difficulties with taking the SAT I:

Students need systematic rules of analysis which they may follow in a step-by-step manner to solve the usual questions and problems encountered.

This book is intended to aid students in studying for the Sentence Completion, Analogies, and Critical Reading sections of the SAT I and overcoming the difficulties described, by supplying detailed explanations which may not be apparent to students. In using this book, students may review and study the illustrated questions at their own pace; they are not limited to the time allowed for explaining questions on the board in a class.

To meet the objectives of this book, we have selected question types usually encountered on the SAT I examination, and have solved each problem meticulously to illustrate the steps which are difficult for students to comprehend.

To Learn and Understand a Question Type Thoroughly

This book is set up such that each chapter is dedicated to one of the types of verbal questions which will appear on the SAT I. Chapter 1 reviews Sentence Completions, Chapter 2 covers Analogies, and Chapter 3 is dedicated to Critical Reading questions.

Each chapter begins with a review which briefly explains the strategies you should use in attacking the different question types. These reviews are followed by questions and their solutions, which illustrate the points made over the course of the review material. All questions which follow the review material are representative of the questions on the actual SAT I, and will prove to be an excellent source of practice in studying for the exam.

Be sure to spend extra time on the question types which pose the most difficulty to you, although for maximum benefit, all chapters of this book should be studied.

1. Locate the question type you are looking for by referring to the "Table of Contents" in the front of this book.

2. Refer to the review material pertaining to the question type. You should become acquainted with the material discussed there.

3. Review the questions following the review material, in the order given. The questions are arranged in order of complexity, from the simplest to the more difficult.

4. To learn and understand a question type thoroughly and retain its content, it will generally be necessary for students to review the questions several times. Repeated review is essential in order to gain experience in recognizing how to answer the different questions types.

To Find a Particular Problem

To locate one or more problems related to a particular question type, refer to the index. In using the index be certain to note that the numbers given there refer to question numbers, not to page numbers. This arrangement of the index is intended to facilitate finding a question more rapidly, since two or more questions may appear on a page.

If a particular type of question cannot be found readily, it is recommended that the student refer to the "Table of Contents" in the front pages, and then turn to the chapter which is applicable to the question being sought. By scanning or glancing at the material that is boxed, it will generally be possible to find questions related to the one being sought, without wasting considerable time. After the questions have been located, the explanations can be reviewed and studied in detail. For the purpose of locating questions rapidly, students should acquaint themselves with the organization of the book as found in the "Table of Contents."

ABOUT THE SAT I

Who Takes the Test and What is it Used For?

The SAT I is usually taken by high school juniors and seniors. College admissions officers use the test as a way to fairly judge all the students that apply to their school. Because high schools often have many different grading systems, the officers use SAT I scores to put applicants on equal ground. Your SAT I score, along with other information provided by you and your high school, helps colleges predict how well you will do at the college level.

The SAT I is usually a requirement for entering college, but if you do poorly, it does not automatically mean you cannot get into college or that you will not do well once you are there. A score on the SAT I that does not match your expectations does not mean you should change your plans about attending college. There are several other criteria by which admissions officers judge applicants, such as grade point average, extracurricular activities, and course levels taken in high school.

Who Administers the Test?

The SAT I is developed and administered by the Educational Testing Service (ETS) and involves the assistance of educators throughout the country. The test development process is designed and implemented to ensure that the content and difficulty level of the test are appropriate.

When Should the SAT I Be Taken?

You should try to take the test early in your junior or senior year so that you will have another opportunity to take it if you are not satisfied with your performance.

When and Where is the Test Given?

The SAT I is administered seven times a year in most states. It is given at hundreds of locations throughout the country, including high schools. The usual testing day is Saturday, but the test may be taken on an alternate day if a conflict, such as a religious obligation, exists.

For information on upcoming administrations of the SAT I, consult the *SAT I Registration Bulletin,* which may be obtained from your guidance counselor or by contacting:

Educational Testing Service
P.O. Box 6200
Princeton, NJ 08541-6200
Phone: (609) 771-7600
Fax: (609) 734-5410
E-mail: etsinfo@ets.org
Website: www.collegeboard.com

Is There a Registration Fee?

To take the SAT I, you must pay a registration fee. A fee waiver may be granted in certain situations. To find out if you qualify, or to register for the waiver, contact your guidance counselor.

FORMAT OF THE SAT I

The following chart summarizes the verbal format of the SAT.

Section	Question Type	Number of Questions
Verbal (Skills covered: Vocabulary, Linear Thinking, and Reading)	Sentence Completions Analogies Critical Reading	19 multiple-choice 19 multiple-choice 40 multiple-choice

There are three types of verbal questions on the SAT I:

- Sentence Completion (19 questions): A sentence will be given with either one or two words omitted. You will be required to choose the word or words which best fit the meaning of the sentence.

- Analogy (19 questions): These questions test your ability to identify the relationship between two words and choose a pair that shows a similar connection.

- Critical Reading (40 questions): There are four reading passages on the SAT I, including one double passage consisting of two related selections. The questions are designed to test your critical reading skills, such as analyzing and synthesizing material.

Chapter 1
Sentence Completions

CHAPTER 1

SENTENCE COMPLETIONS

Regardless of the verbal SAT I section in which one is working, all problem-solving techniques should be divided into two main categories: skills and strategies. This chapter will present skills and strategies that are effective in helping the test-taker successfully answer Sentence Completions. These techniques include the recognition of a context clue, a knowledge of the levels of difficulty in a Sentence Completion section, the application of deductive reasoning, and familiarity with the logical structure of sentence completions. You will encounter 19 Sentence Completion questions, which appear in two different sections, on the SAT I.

ABOUT THE DIRECTIONS

The directions for Sentence Completion questions are relatively straightforward.

DIRECTIONS: Each sentence below has one or two blanks, each blank indicating that something has been omitted. Beneath the sentence are five lettered words or sets of words. Choose the word or set of words that BEST fits the meaning of the sentence as a whole.

Example:

Although the critics found the book _____, many of the readers found it rather _____.

(A) obnoxious . . . perfect

(B) spectacular . . . interesting

(C) boring . . . intriguing

(D) comical . . . persuasive

(E) popular . . . rare

(A) (B) ● (D) (E)

ABOUT THE QUESTIONS

You will encounter two main types of questions in the Sentence Completion section of the SAT I. In addition, the questions will appear in varying difficulties which we will call Level I (easy), Level II (average), and Level III (difficult). The following explains the structure of the questions.

Question Type 1: One-Word Completions

One-Word Completions will require you to fill in one blank. The one-word completion can appear as a Level I, II, or III question depending on the difficulty of the vocabulary included.

Question Type 2: Two-Word Completions

Two-Word Completions will require you to fill in two blanks. As with the one-word completion, this type may be a Level I, II, or III question. This will depend not only on the difficulty of the vocabulary, but also on the relationship between the words and between the words and the sentence.

The remainder of this review will provide explicit details on what you will encounter when dealing with Sentence Completion questions, in addition to strategies for correctly completing these sentences.

ANSWERING SENTENCE COMPLETION QUESTIONS

Follow these steps as you attempt to answer each question.

| STEP 1 | Identifying context clues is one of the most successful ways for students to locate correct answers in Sentence Completions. Practicing constantly in this area will help you strengthen one of your main strategies in this type of word problem. The Sentence Completion below is an example of a Level I question. |

Pamela played her championship chess game _____ , avoiding all traps and making no mistakes.

(A) hurriedly

(B) flawlessly

(C) prodigally

(D) imaginatively

(E) aggressively

The phase "avoiding all traps and making no mistakes" is your context clue. Notice that the phrase both follows *and* modifies the word in question. Since you know that Sentence Completions are exercises seeking to test your vocabulary knowledge, attack these problems accordingly. For example, ask yourself what word means "avoiding all traps and making no mistakes." In so doing, you discover the answer flawlessly (B), which means perfectly or without mistakes. If Pamela played hurriedly (A), she might well make mistakes.

Difficult words are seldom the answer in easier questions; therefore, prodigally (C) stands out as a suspicious word. This could be a magnet word. However, before you eliminate it, ask yourself whether you know its meaning. If so, does it surpass flawlessly (B) in defining the context clue, "making no mistakes"? It does not.

Imaginatively (D) is a tempting answer, since one might associate a perfect game of chess as one played imaginatively; however, there is no connection between the imagination and the absence of mistakes. Aggressively (E) playing a game may, in fact, cause you to make mistakes.

Here is an example of a Level II Sentence Completion. Try to determine the context clue.

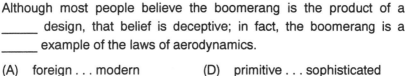

Although most people believe the boomerang is the product of a _____ design, that belief is deceptive; in fact, the boomerang is a _____ example of the laws of aerodynamics.

(A) foreign . . . modern   (D) primitive . . . sophisticated

(B) symbolic . . . complex   (E) faulty . . . invalid

(C) practical . . . scientific

The most important context clue in this sentence is the opening word "although," which indicates that some kind of antonym relationship is present in the sentence. It tells us there is a reversal in meaning. Therefore, be on the lookout for words which will form an opposite relationship. The phrase "that belief is deceptive" makes certain the idea that there will be an opposite meaning between the missing words.

Primitive . . . sophisticated (D) is the best answer, since the two are exact opposites. "Primitive" means crude and elementary, whereas "sophisticated" means refined and advanced.

Foreign . . . modern (A) and symbolic . . . complex (B) have no real opposite relationship. Also, "complex" is a magnet word that sounds right in the context of scientific laws, but "symbolic" is not its counterpart.

Practical . . . scientific (C) and faulty . . . invalid (E) are rejectable be-

5

cause they are generally synonymous pairs of relationships.

The following is an example of a Level III question:

The weekly program on public radio is the most _____ means of educating the public about pollution.

(A) proficient   (D) capable

(B) effusive   (E) competent

(C) effectual

The context clue in this sentence is "means of educating the public about pollution." Effectual (C) is the correct answer. Effectual means having the power to produce the exact effect or result. Proficient (A) is not correct as it implies competency above the average—radio programs are not described in this manner. Effusive (B) does not fit the sense of the sentence. Both capable (D) and competent (E) are incorrect because they refer to people, not things.

| STEP 2 | Since the verbal SAT I is fundamentally a vocabulary test, it must resort to principles and techniques necessary for testing your vocabulary. Therefore, certain dynamics like antonyms (word opposites) and synonyms (word similarities) become very useful in setting up a question or word problem. This idea can be taken one step further. |

Another type of technique that utilizes the tension of opposites and the concurrence of similarities is *word values*. Word values begin with the recognition that most pivotal words in an SAT I word problem can be assigned a positive or negative value. Marking a "+" or "−" next to choices may help you eliminate inappropriate choices. In turn, you will be able to more quickly identify possible correct answers.

Dealing with Positive Value Words

Positive value words are usually easy to recognize. They usually convey a meaning which can be equated with gain, advantage, liveliness, intelligence, virtue, and positive emotions, conditions, or actions:

The ability to recognize positive and negative word values, however, will not bring you very far if you do not understand how to apply it to your advantage in Sentence Completions. Below you will find examples of how to do this, first with a study of positive value Sentence Completions, then with a study of negative value Sentence Completions. The following is an example of a Level I question:

An expert skateboarder, Tom is truly __+__ ; he smoothly blends timing with balance.

(A)   coordinated   (D)   supportive

(B)   erudite   (E)   casual

(C)   a novice

As you know, the context clue is the clause after the word in question, which acts as a modifier. Naturally, anyone who "smoothly blends" is creating a *positive* situation. Look for the positive answer.

An expert skateboarder, Tom is truly _____ ; *he smoothly blends timing with balance.*

+(A)   coordinated   +(D)   supportive

+(B)   erudite   –(E)   casual

–(C)   a novice

Coordinated (A), a positive value word that means ordering two or more things, fits the sentence perfectly.

Erudite (B) is positive, but it is too difficult to be a Level I answer.

A novice (C) in this context is negative.

Supportive (D) and casual (E) don't fulfill the definition of the context clue, and casual is negative, implying a lack of attention. Notice that eliminating negatives *immediately reduces the number of options from which you have to choose.*

This raises the odds of selecting the correct answer. (One of the analytic skills you should develop for the SAT I is being able to see the hidden vocabulary question in any exercise.)

A Level II question may appear as follows:

Despite their supposedly primitive lifestyle, Australian aborigines developed the boomerang, a __+__ and __+__ hunting tool that maximizes gain with minimum effort.

(A)   ponderous . . . expensive   (D)   sophisticated . . . efficient

(B)   clean . . . dynamic   (E)   useful . . . attractive

(C)   dangerous . . . formidable

In this case, the context clues begin and end the sentence (in italics below).

Despite their supposedly primitive lifestyle, Australian aborigines developed the boomerang, a _____ and _____ hunting *tool that maximizes gain with minimum effort.*

−(A) ponderous . . . expensive   +(D) sophisticated . . . efficient

+(B) clean . . . dynamic   +(E) useful . . . attractive

−(C) dangerous . . . formidable

The first context clue (*despite*) helps you determine that this exercise entails an antonym relationship with the word primitive, which means simple or crude. The second context clue offers a definition of the missing words. Since the meaning of primitive in this context is a negative word value, you can be fairly confident that the answer will be a pair of positive word values.

Sophisticated . . . efficient (D) is positive *and* it satisfies the definition of the latter context clue. This is the best answer.

Ponderous . . . expensive (A) is not correct.

Clean . . . dynamic (B) is positive, but does not meet the definition of the latter context clue.

Dangerous . . . formidable (C) is negative.

Useful . . . attractive (E) is positive, but it does not work with the latter context clue.

Here is a Level III example:

When a physician describes an illness to a colleague, he must speak an __+__ language, using professional terms and concepts understood mostly by members of his profession.

(A) extrinsic   (D) esoteric

(B) inordinate   (E) abbreviated

(C) ambulatory

Looking at this question, we can see an important context clue. This appears in italics below.

When a physician describes an illness to a colleague, he must speak an _____ language, *using professional terms and concepts understood mostly by members of his profession.*

+(A) extrinsic   +(D) esoteric

−(B) inordinate   −(E) abbreviated

+(C) ambulatory

This clue gives us a definition of the missing word. Begin by eliminating the two obvious negatives, inordinate (B) and abbreviated (E). This leaves us with three positives. Since this is a Level III exercise, at first you may be intimidated by the level of vocabulary. In the section on etymology you will be given insights into how to handle difficult word problems.

For now, note that esoteric (D) is the best answer, since it is an adjective that means *inside* or *part of a group.*

Ambulatory (C) is positive, but it is a trap. It seems like an easy association with the world of medicine. In Level III there are *no* easy word associations.

Extrinsic (A) is positive, but it means *outside of,* which would not satisfy the logic of the sentence.

Dealing with Negative Value Words

Here are examples of how to work with negative value Sentence Completion problems. The first example is Level I.

Although Steve loves to socialize, his fellow students find him __+__ and strive to __+__ his company.

(A) generous . . . enjoy   (D) sinister . . . delay

(B) boring . . . evade   (E) weak . . . limit

(C) altruistic . . . accept

The context clue (in italics) tells us that a reversal is being set up between what Steve thinks and what his fellow students think.

Although Steve loves to socialize, his fellow students find him __−__ and strive to __−__ his company.

+(A) generous . . . enjoy   −(D) sinister . . . delay

−(B) boring . . . evade   −(E) weak . . . limit

+(C) altruistic . . . accept

Boring . . . evade (B) is the best answer. The words appearing in Level 1 questions are not overly difficult, and they satisfy the logic of the sentence. Generous . . . enjoy (A) is positive. Altruistic . . . accept (C) is not only positive but contains a very difficult word (altruistic), and it would be unlikely that this would be a Level I answer. The same is true of sinister . . . delay (D), even though it is negative. Weak . . . limit (E) does not make sense in the context of the sentence.

This next example is Level II.

Because they reject _____ , conscientious objectors are given jobs in community work as a substitute for participation in the armed services.

(A) labor

(B) belligerence

(C) peace

(D) dictatorships

(E) poverty

Essentially, this example is a synonym exercise. The description of conscientious objectors (in italics) acts as a strong context clue. Conscientious objectors avoid ("reject") militancy.

Because they reject __−__ , conscientious objectors *are given jobs in community work as a substitute for participation in the armed services.*

+(A) labor

−(B) belligerence

+(C) peace

−(D) dictatorships

−(E) poverty

Since we are looking for a negative word value (something to do with militancy), labor (A) is incorrect since it is positive. Belligerence (B) fits perfectly, as this is a negative value word having to do with war. Not only is peace (C) a positive value word, it is hardly something to be rejected by conscientious objectors. Dictatorships (D), although a negative word value, has no logical place in the context of this sentence. The same is true of poverty (E).

Here is a Level III example:

Dictators understand well how to centralize power, and that is why they combine a(n) __−__ political process with military __−__.

(A) foreign . . . victory

(B) electoral . . . escalation

(C) agrarian . . . strategies

(D) domestic . . . decreases

(E) totalitarian . . . coercion

Totalitarian . . . coercion (E) is the best answer. These are difficult words, and both have to do with techniques useful in the centralizing of power by a dictator. *Totalitarian* means centralized, and *coercion* means force.

Dictators understand well how to *centralize power,* and that is why they combine a(n) __−__ political process with military __−__.

+(A) foreign . . . victory

+(B) electoral . . . escalation

+(C) agrarian . . . strategies   +(D) domestic . . . decreases

−(E) totalitarian . . . coercion

Foreign . . . victory (A) are not only easy words, they do not appear to be strictly negative. Remember that easy word answers should be suspect in Level III. Agrarian . . . strategies (C) is positive. Domestic . . . decreases (D) is a positive combination. Since you are searching for two negatives, this answer is incorrect. There will be more about this in the next section.

Dealing with Mixed Value Words

In examples with two-word answers so far, you have searched for answers composed with identical word values, such as negative/negative and positive/positive. However, every SAT I Sentence Completion section will have exercises in which two-word answers are found in combinations. Below you will find examples of how to work with these. Here is a Level I example:

Despite a healthy and growing environmental _____ in America, there are many people who prefer to remain _____ .

(A) awareness . . . ignorant   (D) crisis . . . unencumbered

(B) movement . . . enlightened   (E) industry . . . satisfied

(C) bankruptcy . . . wealthy

The context clue *despite* sets up the predictable antonym warning. In this case, the sentence seems to call for a positive and then a negative value word answer.

Despite a healthy and growing environmental __+__ in America, there are many people who prefer to remain __−__ .

+/−(A) awareness . . . ignorant

+/+(B) movement . . . enlightened

−/+(C) bankruptcy . . . wealthy

−/+(D) crisis . . . unencumbered

+/+(E) industry . . . satisfied

Awareness . . . ignorant (A) is the best answer. These are logical antonyms, and they fit the meaning of the sentence. Notice that the order of the missing words is positive, *then* negative. This should help you eliminate (C) and (D) immediately, as they are a reversal of the correct order. Furthermore, industry . . . satisfied (E) and movement . . . enlightened (B) are both identical values, and so are eliminated. Practice these techniques until you confidently can recognize word values *and* the order in which they appear in a sentence.

Here is a Level II example:

Prone to creating characters of ___+___ quality, novelist Ed Abbey cannot be accused of writing ___–___ stories.

(A) measly . . . drab	(D) sinister . . . complete
(B) romantic . . . imaginative	(E) two-dimensional . . . flat
(C) mythic . . . mundane	

The best answer is mythic . . . mundane (C). Measly . . . drab (A) does not make sense when you consider the context clue *cannot,* which suggests the possibility of antonyms. The same is true for sinister . . . complete (D), romantic . . . imaginative (B), and two-dimensional . . . flat (E).

Prone to creating characters of ___+___ quality, novelist Ed Abbey *cannot* be accused of writing ___–___ stories.

–/–(A) measly . . . drab

+/+(B) romantic . . . imaginative

+/–(C) mythic . . . mundane

–/+(D) sinister . . . complete

–/–(E) two-dimensional . . . flat

Notice that the value combinations help you determine where to search for the correct answer.

Here is a Level III example:

Reminding his students that planning ahead would protect them from _____ , Mr. McKenna proved to be a principal who understood the virtues of _____ .

(A) exigency . . . foresight

(B) grades . . . examinations

(C) poverty . . . promotion

(D) deprivation . . . abstinence

(E) turbulence . . . amelioration

The best answer is exigency . . . foresight (A). The first context clue tells us that we are looking for a negative value word. The second context clue tells us the missing word is most likely positive. Furthermore, exigency . . . foresight is a well-suited antonym combination. Exigencies are emergencies, and foresight helps to lessen their severity, if not their occurrence.

> Reminding his students that planning ahead would *protect them* from
> ___–__ , Mr. McKenna proved to be a principal who understood the
> *virtues* of __+__ .
>
> –/+(A) exigency . . . foresight
>
> 0/0(B) grades . . . examinations
>
> –/+(C) poverty . . . promotion
>
> –/–(D) deprivation . . . abstinence
>
> –/+(E) turbulence . . . amelioration

Grades . . . examinations (B) are a trap, since they imply school matters. Furthermore, they are neutrals. There will be more on this below. Poverty . . . promotion (C) is an easy word answer and should be immediately suspect, especially if there are no difficult words in the sentence completion itself. Also, this answer does not satisfy the logic of the sentence. Turbulence . . . amelioration (E) is a negative/positive combination, but it does not make sense in this sentence. Even if you are forced to guess between this answer and exigency . . . foresight (A), you have narrowed the field to two. These are excellent odds for success.

Dealing with Neutral Value Words

There is another category of word values that will help you determine the correct answer in a Sentence Completion problem. These are neutral word values. Neutral words are words that convey neither loss nor gain, advantage nor disadvantage, etc. Consider the example above, once again:

> Reminding his students that planning ahead would *protect them* from
> ___–__ , Mr. McKenna proved to be a principal who understood the
> *virtues* of __+__ .
>
> –/+(A) exigency . . . foresight
>
> 0/0(B) grades . . . examinations
>
> –/+(C) poverty . . . promotion
>
> –/–(D) deprivation . . . abstinence
>
> –/+(E) turbulence . . . amelioration

Notice that grades . . . examinations (B) is rated as neutral. In fact, in this case, both words are considered of neutral value. This is because neither word conveys a usable value. Grades in and of themselves are not valued until a number is assigned. Examinations are not significant until a passing or failing value is implied or applied.

Neutral word values are significant because they are *never* the correct answer. Therefore, when you identify a neutral word or combination of words, you may eliminate that choice from your selection. You may eliminate a double-word answer even if only one of the words is obviously neutral.

Neutral words are rare, and you should be careful to measure their value before you make a choice. Here is another example from an exercise seen previously (Note: The answer choices have been altered.):

> *Dictators* understand well how *to centralize power,* and that is why they combine a(n) ___–___ political process with military ___–___.
>
> 0/+(A) foreign . . . victory
>
> 0/+(B) electoral . . . escalation
>
> 0/+(C) agrarian . . . strategies
>
> 0/0(D) current . . . jobs
>
> –/–(E) totalitarian . . . coercion

Here, current . . . jobs (D) is an obvious neutral word combination, conveying no positive or negative values. You may eliminate this choice immediately. There is no fixed list of words that may be considered neutral. Rather, you should determine *from the context* of a word problem whether you believe a word or word combination is of a neutral value. This ability will come with practice and a larger vocabulary. As before, the correct answer remains totalitarian . . . coercion (E).

| STEP 3 | Another way to determine the correct answer is by using etymology. Etymology is the study of the anatomy of words. The most important components of etymology on the SAT I are prefixes and roots. SAT I vocabulary is derived almost exclusively from the etymology of Greek and Latin word origins, and that is where you should concentrate your study. In this section, you will learn how to apply your knowledge of prefixes and roots to Sentence Completion problems.

Etymological skills will work well in conjunction with other techniques you have learned, including positive/negative word values. Furthermore, the technique of "scrolling" will help you understand how to expand your knowledge of etymology.

Scrolling is a process whereby you "scroll" through a list of known related words, roots, or prefixes to help you discover the meaning of a word. As an example, consider the common SAT I word *apathy.* The prefix of apathy is *a.* This means *without.* To scroll this prefix, think of any other words that may begin with this prefix, such as *a*moral, *a*typical, *a*symmetrical. In each case, the meaning of the word is preceded by the meaning *without.*

At this point, you know that *apathy* means without something. Now try to scroll the root, *path,* which comes from the Greek word *pathos.* Words like pathetic, sympathy, antipathy, and empathy may come to mind. These words all have to do with feeling or sensing. In fact, that is what *pathos* means: feeling. So apathy means without feeling.

With this process you can often determine the fundamental meaning of a word or part of a word, and this may give you enough evidence with which to choose a correct answer. Consider the following familiar Level I example:

An expert skateboarder, Tom is truly __+__ ; he smoothly blends timing with balance.

+(A) coordinated   +(D) supportive

+(B) erudite   −(E) casual

−(C) a novice

As you should remember, the correct answer is coordinated (A). The prefix of this word is *co,* meaning together, and the root is *order.* Something that is "ordered together" fits the context clue perfectly. Combining that with the knowledge that you are looking for a positive value word certifies coordinated (A) as the correct answer.

Here is a Level II example:

Because they reject ____−__ , conscientious objectors *are given jobs in community work as a substitute for participation in the armed services.*

+(A) labor   −(D) dictatorships

−(B) belligerence   −(E) poverty

+(C) peace

From working with this example previously, you know that the correct answer is belligerence (B). The root of this word is *bellum,* Latin for war. Belligerence is an inclination toward war. Other words that may be scrolled from this are bellicose, belligerent, and antebellum, all of which have to do with war. Study your roots and prefixes well. A casual knowledge is not good enough. Another root, *bellis,* might be confused with *bellum. Bellis* means beauty. Is it logical that a conscientious objector would reject beauty? Know when to use which root and prefix. This ability will come with study and practice.

Here is a Level III example:

When a physician describes an illness to a colleague, he must speak an __+__ language, *using professional terms and concepts understood mostly by members of his profession.*

+(A) extrinsic   +(D) esoteric

−(B) inordinate   −(E) abbreviated

+(C) ambulatory

Recalling this example, you will remember that the context clue defines the missing word as one meaning language that involves a special group of people, i.e., "inside information." The correct answer is esoteric (D). *Eso* is a prefix that means *inside.* The prefix of extrinsic (A) is *ex,* which means *out,* the opposite of the meaning you seek. Inordinate (B) means *not ordered.* In this case, the prefix *in* means *not.* This is Level III, so beware of easy assumptions! The root of ambulatory (C) is *ambulare,* which means *to walk.* Abbreviated (E) breaks down to *ab,* meaning *to,* and *brevis,* Latin for brief or short.

In many Level III words you may not be able to scroll or break down a word completely. However, often, as in the example above, a partial knowledge of the etymology may be enough to find the correct answer.

Now, take what you have learned and apply it to the following questions.

> **DIRECTIONS**: Each sentence below has one or two blanks, each blank indicating that something has been omitted. Beneath the sentence are five lettered words or sets of words. Choose the word or set of words that BEST fits the meaning of the sentence as a whole.

• PROBLEM 1–1

_____ swept the crowd when the natural _____ suddenly occurred.

(A) Infirmary . . . dispensation

(B) Pandemonium . . . catastrophe

(C) Vehemence . . . iodides

(D) Rectification . . . cravenness

(E) Turbulence . . . atmosphere

SOLUTION:

(B) The way that the word "when" is used in this sentence produces a cause-and-effect relationship. We must choose the two nouns that are related in such a way that the occurrence of one will directly cause the other to happen. Choice (B) is the best answer because "pandemonium" (a wild uproar) will sweep a crowd when a natural "catastrophe" (great disaster) occurs.

Choice (A) is incorrect because the noun "infirmary" (a clinic for sick people) does not make sense followed by the active verb "swept."

Choice (C) is incorrect because although "vehemence" (great force) can sweep a crowd, "iodides" (a chemical term) not only does not relate to the meaning of the entire sentence, but is also awkward followed by the active verb "occurred."

Choice (D) is incorrect because "rectification" (to make or set right) is semantically meaningless in a cause-and-effect relationship with the noun "cravenness" (cowardliness).

For the same reason, choice (E) is wrong, because although "turbulence" (violence or disturbance) may sweep a crowd, it would not be caused by "atmosphere."

• PROBLEM 1–2

The family left their country to _____ to Utopia and escape _____ because of their beliefs.

(A) immigrate . . . prosecution

(B) peregrinate . . . extortion

(C) emigrate . . . persecution

(D) wander . . . arraignment

(E) roam . . . censure

SOLUTION:

(C) In this cause-and-effect sentence, we are looking for a verb whose action is caused by a noun with a negative connotation. (C) is the correct answer because to "emigrate" (leave a place to settle elsewhere) is synonymous with the action described earlier in the sentence, "left their country," and people often experience "persecution" (constant affliction for reasons of religion, race, etc.) because of their beliefs.

Choice (A) is wrong because "immigrate" (come into a foreign country) does not work as well with the word "left," and it would be unlikely for a family to be "prosecuted" (served with a law suit) because of beliefs rather than actions.

Choice (B) is wrong because although "peregrinate" (to travel) fits into the sentence, "extortion" (drawing something from someone by force) does not, as it is commonly used to describe a means of gathering money or material possessions and would be unrelated to a family's beliefs.

Choices (D) and (E) are incorrect because both "wander" and "roam" imply movement with no fixed destination, and we know that the family went specifically to Utopia.

• PROBLEM 1–3

The _____ was _____ .

(A) desert . . . pudding   (D) condiment . . . stew

(B) dessert . . . parfait   (E) compliment . . . pastry

(C) hors d'oeuvre . . . ice cream

SOLUTION:

(B) The sentence calls for two nouns which are related as a category and a member of that category. Choice (B) is correct because "dessert" is a category of food and "parfait" (a frozen dessert of rich cream and eggs) is a type of dessert, and therefore fits into that category.

Choice (A) is incorrect because to describe a "desert" (an area of dry, arid land) as "pudding," makes no sense. This option was probably included in order to call attention to the similar spellings of "dessert" and "desert."

Choice (C) is incorrect because it is unlikely that "ice cream" would be served as an "hors d'oeuvre" (an appetizer before the main course).

Choice (D) is wrong because "stew" is not used as a "condiment" (a seasoning or relish, as pepper, mustard, etc.).

Choice (E) does not make sense because a "compliment" (something said in praise) is verbal, and "pastry" (pies, tarts, etc.) is a material object.

• PROBLEM 1-4

The _____ associated with drug abuse and alcoholism are often _____ .

(A) outgrowth ... impromptu

(B) consequences ... grave

(C) compensation ... inconsequential

(D) fruit ... malnutrition

(E) benefit ... illumination

SOLUTION:

(B) To complete this sentence it is necessary to choose a plural noun and an adjective to describe it. The correct answer is (B) because "grave" (serious) is an appropriate description of the "consequences" (results) associated with drug abuse and alcoholism.

Choice (A) is incorrect because "outgrowth" (product), being singular, does not agree with the plural verb "are" and because "impromptu" (spur of the moment) does not make sense in the sentence.

In choice (C), "Compensation" (reward) is inappropriate to speak of in relation to drug and alcohol abuse, and, being singular, it does not agree with the plural verb.

The same applies to "fruit" (D), and "malnutrition" does not work because it is a noun and not an adjective. The same reasoning applies once again to option (E); not only is it inappropriate to speak of "benefit" (improvement, advantage) in relation to drug and alcohol abuse, but it is a singular noun, and "illumination" is a noun where an adjective is needed.

• PROBLEM 1-5

The _____ of the situation warranted _____ measures.

(A) gravity ... extreme   (D) levity ... crass

(B) importance ... pompous   (E) uniqueness ... wonted

(C) significance ... piquant

SOLUTION:

(A)   In this sentence, the correct answer must contain a noun and an adjective which describes the action taken as a result of the noun. Choice (A) is correct because a situation with "gravity" (seriousness, weight) would be important enough to require "extreme" (very great, drastic) measures in response.

The word "pompous" (B) (unnecessarily showy) has negative connotations of excess, and it is unlikely that any situation would "warrant" (authorize, as by law) something negative, especially if that situation was "important."

This is also true of option (C), in which "significance" fits the sentence, but "piquant" (power to whet the appetite or interest through tartness) is inappropriate to describe warranted measures.

Option (D) is a bad choice because "levity" (frivolity) does not fit with a word as weighty as "warranted," and it does not necessarily result in "crass" (grossness of mind precluding delicacy) actions.

(E) is wrong because "uniqueness" (having the quality of being without like or equal) would require the opposite adjective of "wonted" (customary or accustomed).

• PROBLEM 1-6

The phenomenon called the "self-fulfilling prophecy" occurs when one holds and acts on a belief that is not true; for example, parents who believe a child is destined to turn out "no good" and treat the child as if he were no good, often have their worst fears realized: false _____ becomes _____ .

(A) belief . . . reality

(B) fear . . . truth

(C) anxiety . . . fact

(D) presumption . . . certain

(E) dread . . . proven

SOLUTION:

(A)   The statement after the colon in this sentence paraphrases what was set forth in the example and relates it back to the idea set forth in the beginning of the sentence. Option (A) is correct because "belief" connects to "a belief" and "parents who believe," while "reality" connects to "fears realized." The rest of the options may work semantically, but only option (A) exactly mirrors the words of the beginning of the sentence.

• PROBLEM 1-7

The _____ speaker moved the audience to _____ .

(A) apprehensive . . . solitude

(B) enthusiastic . . . action

(C) vulnerable . . . adversity

(D) authentic . . . tranquility

(E) scrupulous . . . complacency

SOLUTION:

(B) Option (B) is the correct answer because it is the choice in which the noun is most clearly caused by the specific adjective in the beginning of the sentence. It is extremely likely that an "enthusiastic" (intensely eager) speaker could move an audience to "action." (B) also makes the most sense because the verb "move" implies activity or "action." In the rest of the options, although they could make sense in unusual contexts, the noun does not follow as inevitably after the adjective.

Choices (A) "solitiude," (D) "tranquility," and (E) "complacency" (contentment) are all quiet, passive words which do not make sense with the verb "moved." It would be as illogical as to say that someone was moved to stillness. "Moved" also implies self-motivated, and (C) "adversity" (misfortune) usually comes from outside forces.

• PROBLEM 1-8

The student's request for early graduation was _____ until all the grades were processed.

(A) denied   (D) ratified

(B) prohibited   (E) obscured

(C) deferred

SOLUTION:

(C) The word "until" suggests that the first part of this sentence is conditional upon the second part, and that a passage of time is necessary before the conditions are met. For this reason, (C) is the best choice. "Deferred" (to postpone or delay) also implies that a certain amount of time must pass before a decision is reached.

(A) "Denied," (B) "prohibited," (D) "ratified" (confirmed), and (E) "obscured" (not easily understood) are all very fixed states which are unlikely to change over time or in the very light of new evidence.

• PROBLEM 1-9

Winston Churchill was such a(n) _____ and _____ speaker that listeners from around the world would postpone whatever they were doing to hear his speeches on the radio.

(A) gullible . . . deliberate

(D) provocative . . . prosaic

(B) impartial . . . obscure

(E) eloquent . . . mesmerizing

(C) incoherent . . . pious

SOLUTION:

(E) In this sentence we are looking for two adjectives which positively describe the noun "speaker." We know that the adjectives imply that the speaker was good and captivating because the second half of the sentence tells us that people would interrupt their actions to listen to him speak.

Choice (E) is the only one in which both adjectives are complimentary, and therefore the correct answer.

Many of the other choices, (A) "deliberate," (B) "obscure" or (D) "prosaic," although they may describe an appropriate form of speaking for a teacher or lecturer suggest a tedious and even boring style, and could not describe a man who commanded attention all over the world. Someone who speaks in an (E) "incoherent" (not logically connected) style is not pleasant to listen to at all.

• PROBLEM 1-10

After he lost 20 pounds with healthy food choices and exercise, he found that his body responded with more _____ than before.

(A) frivolity

(D) vitality

(B) lethargy

(E) tranquility

(C) diligence

SOLUTION:

(D) This sentence tells us that a person lost weight by eating healthy food and by exercising. We know that this person is healthy and that his body will "respond" in a positive way. So we are looking for a noun that is related to the adjective "healthy." (D) "vitality" (having energy) is the best choice.

(A) is incorrect because although "frivolity" (fun) is a positive word, it does not relate semantically to a healthy body.

(B) is wrong because "lethargy" (lazy, passive) is not related to a healthful way of life.

(C) "diligence" (hard work) is related to having a healthy body, because it takes hard work to do so, but it does not tell us how the body responds.

(E) "tranquility" is incorrect because a healthy body is not usually described as responding in a "peaceful, still, or harmonious" manner.

• PROBLEM 1-11

The sales associate tried to _____ trade by distributing business cards.

(A) elicit   (D) elliptic

(B) solicit   (E) conciliate

(C) illicit

SOLUTION:

(B)   To complete this sentence we must find a verb related to money and business. (B) is the best answer because "solicit" (to pursue business or legal affairs) connects to "sales" and "business cards."

(A) "elicit" (to draw forth) although it may seem to make sense, is not as good an answer because it does not carry the association with money and business.

(C) "illicit" and (D) "elliptic" are incorrect because, not only do they not make sense semantically, they are also both adjectives where a verb is required.

(E) "Conciliate" (to win over or smooth) does not make sense because it usually is used in relation to people or animals and not to an impersonal noun such as "trade."

• PROBLEM 1–12

In order to express his reservations without offending anyone, the professor _____ his statements.

(A) lengthened

(D) warranted

(B) formed

(E) qualified

(C) constructed

SOLUTION:

(E) Judging from the context of this sentence, it is obvious that the professor is aware that his statements are potentially offensive. Since he wishes to express them anyway, the word chosen must imply a balance that will make his statements less likely to anger anyone. (E) "qualified" (to moderate, soften) expresses this balance.

Choice (A) "lengthened" is incorrect because if his statements were likely to be upsetting, the longer they were, the more upsetting they would be.

"Formed" (B) and "constructed" (C) do not work because they are both too neutral to reflect the negative connotations associated with the professor's reservations.

(D) "warranted" (guaranteed or authorized) would make more sense if the professor was sure his audience would agree with his statements and wanted to solidify them.

• PROBLEM 1–13

A storm of _____ swept over the country when _____ at the highest levels of government became common knowledge.

(A) indignation . . . corruption

(D) uncertainty . . . graft

(B) protest . . . cooperation

(E) indifference . . . actions

(C) praise . . . dedication

SOLUTION:

(A) This sentence involves a cause-and-effect relationship in which some action of the government caused a reaction among the people. The words "storm" and "swept" imply that the people reacted to a negative action. For this reason (A) is the best answer. "Corruption" (evilness, depravity, dishonesty) in the government would be certain to raise "indignation" (righteous anger) in the citizens of a country.

Both (B) and (C) contain words, "cooperation," "praise," "dedication," with positive meanings which don't fit into the negative atmosphere of the sentence. Likewise, the words, "uncertainty," "indifference," "actions," from (D) and (E), are too neutral and impassive to carry the meaning of the sentence.

• PROBLEM 1–14

He knew that all available evidence indicated the invalidity of the theory in question; nevertheless, he personally _____ it.

(A) researched

(D) explored

(B) repudiated

(E) investigated

(C) supported

SOLUTION:

(C) The semicolon and the word "nevertheless" in the middle of this sentence indicate that the second half of the sentence contains information which is contrary to that presented in the first half. Therefore, since the beginning of the sentence suggests a negative attitude towards the "evidence," the rest of the sentence must be more positive. The most positive of the options is choice (C) "supported" (to advocate).

Choices (A) "researched," (D) "explored," and (E) "investigated" are too neutral to contradict the thought presented in the first part of the sentence.

Choice (B) "repudiated" (to disavow) is incorrect because it mirrors the negative attitude towards the evidence expressed in the first half of the sentence instead of contradicting it.

• PROBLEM 1–15

Perhaps one reason for the lesser number of female writers is that women traditionally have lacked the _____ independence and the _____ necessary to permit them to concentrate their efforts on writing.

(A) literary . . . talent

(B) intellectual . . . ability

(C) social . . . reputation

(D) emotional . . . intelligence

(E) financial . . . leisure

SOLUTION:

(E) For this sentence, rather than look for grammatical clues, it is necessary to find the words which cause the sentence to make the most sense in the whole sentence. All of the pairs fit in the first part of the sentence, but only one takes into account the key phrase, " . . . in order to focus her attention on writing" which finishes the sentence.

• PROBLEM 1–16

The mayor stated that it was _____ knowledge that a campaign should _____ the election.

(A) ordinary . . . supersede

(B) familiar . . . persecute

(C) popular . . . prosecute

(D) common . . . precede

(E) vulgar . . . proceed

SOLUTION:

(D) This question relies on your knowledge of campaigns and elections. The easiest way to answer it is to look at the second choice. The best answer is (D). A campaign should "precede" (come before) the election.

Choice (A) is incorrect because a campaign doesn't "supersede" or take the place of an election.

Choices (B), (C) and (E) are wrong because they are semantically impossible. A campaign cannot "persecute" (afflict constantly), "prosecute" (serve with a law suit), or "proceed" (carry on), only people or groups of people can do these things.

• PROBLEM 1-17

I admire his ability; it's just his manner that I find _____ .

(A) appealing   (D) lacking

(B) interesting   (E) compelling

(C) hard

SOLUTION:

(D) The semicolon in this sentence divides two opposing thoughts. The word "just" means that there are reservations attached to this person's "manner." Thus, we are looking for a word that would describe his "manner" in a negative way, in contrast to "admire . . . ability." The best choice is "lacking" (D).

Choice (A) "appealing," choice (B) "interesting," and choice (E) "compelling" all have positive connotations and are therefore incorrect. Choice (C) is wrong because it would be unusual to use the word "hard" to describe someone's "manner."

• PROBLEM 1-18

She was _____ into the prestigious club despite her _____ .

(A) excepted . . . qualifications

(B) accepted . . . reputation

(C) enjoined . . . popularity

(D) inaugurated . . . fame

(E) rejected . . . notoriety

SOLUTION:

(B) The meaning of this sentence hinges on the word "despite." Something will happen that is contradictory to what is expected. (B) is the best answer because although "reputation" has a neutral denotation, it often has a negative connotation, and it is therefore contradictory to "accept" someone because of their reputation.

Choice (A) is incorrect because "excepted" (taken out) does not work with the word "into," which implies that something was put in. The word is semantically meaningless in the sentence.

Choice (C) "enjoined" and "popularity" do not make any sense because it would mean that she was commanded into the club despite her popularity; these words are not contradictory.

Choice (D) is wrong because "inaugurate" means to "put into office with ceremony" and this would not happen "despite" fame, but rather because of it.

Choice (E) is wrong because she would be "rejected" because of "notoriety," which means ill-fame, and not "despite" it; once again, the result is not the opposite of what one would expect.

• PROBLEM 1-19

After reading the letter, she unhappily _____ that the manager was attempting to _____ a contract with her.

(A) implied . . . abrogate   (D) concluded . . . nullify

(B) inferred . . . negotiate   (E) surmised . . . research

(C) imposed . . . analyze

SOLUTION:

(D)   To complete this sentence, we must assume the subject wanted a contract with the manager, and choose a verb which suggests that she was made unhappy because the manager did not want a contract with her. The words which best convey this meaning to the sentence are in option (D). She unhappily "concluded" (decided) that the manager was trying to "nullify" (cancel out) the contract.

Although "abrogate" (annul, revoke) fits into the sentence, (A) is not as fitting an answer because "unhappily" does not work as well as an adjective for "implied" as it does for "concluded."

(B), (C), and (E) do not work because if the woman wanted a contract, she would not be unhappy if the manager wished to "negotiate" (confer to arrive at a settlement), "analyze" (examine), or "research" (investigate) a contract with her.

• PROBLEM 1-20

Teenagers in part-time jobs today are relatively well paid: _____ workers in the fast-food segment of the work force can earn up to $5.00 per hour.

(A) additionally

(B) however

(C) therefore

(D) because

(E) for example

SOLUTION:

(E) "For example" is correct. The second part of this sentence gives supporting information in the form of an example for the assertion made in the first part of the sentence.

(A) "additionally" is wrong because the second part of the sentence does not add new information or another assertion.

(B) "however" is wrong because this word would be followed by information which contradicts or in some way contrasts with the assertion made in he first part of the sentence.

Choices (C) "therefore" and (D) "because" are wrong because they are both used to signal cause-and-effect relationships, and the second part of the sentence is neither a cause nor an effect of the first part of the sentence.

• PROBLEM 1-21

The grant was _____ because the budget was _____ .

(A) denied . . . obvious

(B) approved . . . infinite

(C) rejected . . . truculent

(D) reassessed . . . diffident

(E) allocated . . . finite

SOLUTION:

(E) The way that the word "because" is used in this sentence gives it a cause-and-effect relationship. The first blank calls for a predicate adjective which is caused by the quality of the budget described by the adjective used in the second blank. The correct answer is (E) because a grant will be "allocated" (assigned) if the budget is "finite" (has a definite ending), or has a specific number value.

Although all verb forms in the choices are possible answers, the predicate adjectives pose some problems.

Choice (A) is incorrect because it is not logical that a grant would be "denied" because of an "obvious" (evident) budget.

Choice (B) is also incorrect because a grant would not be "approved" if the budget was "infinite" (never ending). Most grants ask for a complete, detailed budget.

Choices (C) and (D) are wrong because both "truculent" (fierce or threatening) and "diffident" (shy or lacking in self-confidence) are adjectives used to describe people or animals, and are ridiculous when applied to an inanimate object such as a budget.

• PROBLEM 1-22

The prisoner finally _____ that he drank to _____ on the night he committed the murder.

(A) acceded . . . access

(B) conceded . . . excess

(C) exceeded . . . extreme

(D) eluded . . . escape

(E) alluded . . . abundance

SOLUTION:

(B) There are few clues to help the reader decide which pair of words is most appropriate in the sentence. It is necessary to simply decide by a process of elimination, which two words complete the sentence in such a way that it makes the most sense.

Saying that the prisoner finally "conceded" (yielded) that he drank to "excess" (too much) on the night of the murder is a perfectly logical sentence; (B) is the best answer. Saying that a prisoner "acceded" (agreed with) the fact that he drank to "access" (availability) on a murder night is not logical; therefore, (A) is not the best selection.

A prisoner who "exceeded" (surpassed) is not a clear thought; therefore, (C) is not the best answer.

Choice (D) is incorrect because one would not say that the prisoner finally "eluded" (escaped from) that he drank to "escape" on the night of the murder.

The word "alluded" (E), which means "made a reference to," might fit the first part of the sentence well, but not when coupled with "abundance."

• PROBLEM 1-23

Living out the ____ consequences of choices made, he realized the meager nature of his existence: his life was not to be so _____ as he had once assumed it would be.

(A) surprising . . . intricate

(B) unexpected . . . exciting

(C) inevitable . . . full

(D) boring . . . predictable

(E) happy . . . unusual

SOLUTION:

(C) Because the man's nature is "meager" (poor, inadequate) which is a negative term, we can assume that the man's life will be described with another negative term. The "not" after the semicolon, however, when applied to the second blank, turns it to its opposite, so that a positive term is needed there. The only pair of words which fit this pattern is (C).

In the context, "inevitable" (unavoidable) has negative connotations, while a "full" life is desirable. In the remainder of the choices, the two words are too similar in their connotations, and would only work if the word "not" was removed from the sentence.

• PROBLEM 1-24

Although the legislative body is sometimes described as lethargic, it can sometimes act in a _____ manner, especially in an emergency.

(A) vigorous

(B) prudent

(C) indolent

(D) elusive

(E) virulent

SOLUTION:

(A) The word "although" suggests that the word which would be most appropriate for this sentence is the opposite of "lethargic"; and that word would be "vigorous" (A).

"Prudent" (B) (wise, careful) might be considered as a possibility, especially in light of the phrase "in an emergency," but not within the context of the sentence where we are looking for a word opposite in meaning to "lethargic."

Choice (C) is incorrect because "indolent" is synonymous with "lethargic."

Choice (D) doesn't apply because "elusive" is not an antonym of "lethargic," nor would the legislature act in an elusive manner in an emergency.

Choice (E) "virulent" is not appropriate because a legislature hopefully wouldn't act in a malicious manner, under any circumstances, and certainly not in an emergency

• PROBLEM 1-25

Faced with a limited budget and many attractive choices, Michael had to _____ the merits of each possibility so that he didn't encounter any debt.

(A) concede

(D) waive

(B) denounce

(E) assess

(C) refute

SOLUTION:

(E) Because the phrase "limited budget" is semantically juxtaposed with "many attractive choices," we must choose a term which suggests a balance between these things. (E) "assess" (judge the worth) is just such a word because judging implies weighing or balancing.

The rest of the options, (A) "concede" (acknowledge), (B) "denounce" (condemn), (C) "refute" (disprove), and (D) "waive" (give up possession) are all too definite and fixed and do not carry this sense of making a decision.

• PROBLEM 1-26

Although the topic embarrassed him, he spoke _____ about his bankruptcy and financial situation.

(A) vainly

(D) bitterly

(B) rapidly

(E) candidly

(C) cryptically

SOLUTION:

(E) The key word here is "although," which tells us to interpret the sentence as follows: even though the topic was embarrassing to the speaker, he spoke in a way that didn't show his embarrassment. The best choice for this sentence is (E) "candidly" (truthfully, sincerely).

Choice (A) is wrong because "vainly" futilely, unsuccessfully) does not suggest the opposite of embarrassment.

Choice (B) "rapidly" is a possibility, but doesn't convey the essence of the meaning of the sentence as well as (E).

Choice (C) "cryptically" (meant to be puzzling) is not meaningful in the sentence.

• PROBLEM 1–27

In spite of the fact that the professor was _____ , his lecture was so _____ that few students understood him.

(A) articulate . . . abstract   (D) illuminating . . . deliberate

(B) arrogant . . . austere   (E) affable . . . derogatory

(C) taciturn . . . superficial

SOLUTION:

(A) The clue here is "in spite of the fact," which means that regardless of the quality that described the professor, the quality of the lecture would have to be contradictory to it. The fact that "few students understood" the lecture is negative, and therefore the adjective to describe the professor must be positive. We can conclude that few students would understand a lecture that is "abstract" (vague, having no clear definition), even though the professor is "articulate" (well-spoken). Therefore, (A) is the best choice.

In choice (B), although "arrogant" (haughty) is a possible way to describe the professor, "austere" (harsh, strict, severe) is also a negative term and does not contradict the quality described in the first part of the sentence.

Choice (C) is incorrect because "taciturn" (reserved, quiet) and "superficial" (cursory, shallow) are also both negative.

Choice (D) is incorrect because although the professor might be "illuminating" (make understandable), students would understand a "deliberate" (carefully considered) lecture. This does not go with "in spite of the fact."

Choice (E) "affable" (friendly, amiable, good natured) is a positive way of describing the professor, and "derogatory" (belittling, uncomplimentary) is negative, which is the contradictory relationship we are looking for. This is not the best answer, however, because "derogatory" describes the content of the lecture and not whether or not it was understandable.

• PROBLEM 1-28

Tile manufacturers need high-quality clay; this is why brickyards are invariably located in places where high-quality clay is _____ and can be readily _____ .

(A) present . . . verified

(B) evident . . . procured

(C) nearby . . . obtained

(D) abundant . . . accessed

(E) visible . . . utilized

SOLUTION:

(D)   The first part of this sentence establishes a need, and the second part shows how those needs are met. Therefore, we must find two words which describe a condition of "high-quality clay" which would help tile manufacturers fill their need for it. The best answer is (D); the need can best be met if the clay is "abundant" (plentiful) and can be readily "accessed" (easily obtained).

All of the remaining choices, (A) "present . . . verified" (proven true), (B) "evident . . . procured" (obtained), (C) "nearby . . . obtained," and (E) "visible . . . utilized," make sense within the context of the sentence, but they are not the best answers. Although they maintain that the clay is present and obtainable, choice (D) adds the important connotations that the clay is plentifully present and easily obtainable.

•PROBLEM 1-29

People who drive when they are drunk put themselves and others on the road in _____ .

(A) guile

(B) discord

(C) jeopardy

(D) distress

(E) dissonance

SOLUTION:

(C)   It should be common knowledge that many drunk driving accidents result in the death of many of the people involved. Therefore, we should look for a word which suggests a threat to life. (C) "jeopardy" (great danger or risk) is just such a word. The implication of this sentence is that drunk drivers are a menace on the road; therefore, if they drive while they are under the influence of alcohol, they put people's lives in "jeopardy" (danger).

(A) "guile" (slyness, deceit), (B) "discord" (disagreement, lack of harmony), and (E) "dissonance" (harsh contradiction) are incorrect answers because they do not fit into the semantic context of the sentence.

Choice (D) "distress" (pain, anguish) is a possibility, but is not the best answer, because it is not as strongly negative a word. It describes pain or suffering, but not possible death.

• PROBLEM 1-30

Although the explorers often felt _____ , they managed to _____ the desert.

(A) defeated . . . achieve   (D) relentless . . . finish

(B) elated . . . survive   (E) withdrawn . . . subject

(C) exhausted . . . conquer

SOLUTION:

(C)   The key word in this sentence is "although," which indicates that the second half of the sentence must contradict the expectations established in the first half. (C) is the correct answer because "exhausted" explorers couldn't normally "conquer" the desert.

Although in choice (A), "defeated" and "achieved" are contradictory, you could never say that someone "achieved" the desert. This is not semantically correct.

Choice (B) is incorrect because "elated" and "survive" do not relate back to "although." They are not contradictory ideas.

"Relentless" explorers (D) would manage to "finish" the desert, but again, this does not make sense with the conditional word "although" in the sentence.

It is possible that the explorers might have felt "withdrawn" (E), but the word "subject" has no meaning in the sentence.

• PROBLEM 1-31

A great _____ remained after the tornado completely _____ the population of the small town.

(A) devastation . . . overwhelmed   (D) windfall . . . invaded

(B) fallout . . . covered   (E) vacancy . . . augmented

(C) detachment . . . broke

SOLUTION:

(A)   The meaning of this sentence hinges on your knowledge of the consequences of a tornado. Knowing that a tornado is destructive, the only possible choice is (A) "devastation." A tornado has no relation to (B) "fallout," (C) "detachment," (D) "windfall," or (E) "vacancy."

• PROBLEM 1-32

Young people who have never experienced serious illness or harm often have an exaggerated sense of _____ that leads them to believe that the really bad things in life only happen to other people.

(A) judgment   (D) well-being

(B) happiness   (E) concern

(C) life

SOLUTION:

(D)   The correct answer is (D) "well-being," because people who have never been sick or experienced harm do not really believe that illness or bad things could ever happen to them.

Choice (A) "judgment" is incorrect because it has no bearing on the topic of the sentence.

Choice (B) "happiness" is wrong because people who believe that bad things happen only to other people don't have an exaggerated sense of happiness.

Choice (C) is wrong because "life" has no meaning in the sentence. The same applies to choice (E), "concern."

• PROBLEM 1-33

The crushing _____ suffered by the soccer team left the fans feeling _____ with the bragging goalie.

(A) blow . . . overwhelmed   (D) defeat . . . disenchanted

(B) failure . . . indecisive   (E) loss . . . placid

(C) defense . . . angry

SOLUTION:

(D) The word "crushing" in the first sentence should indicate that something bad has happened, and that the fans would be feeling very negative towards the "bragging goalie" who has nothing to brag about.

Choice (D) "defeat" and "disenchanted" (disillusioned) are the best words to meet these conditions.

Choice (A) is only partially correct. Although "blow" (unexpected calamity) would fit into the first part of the sentence, "overwhelmed" would not.

Choice (B) "failure" is appropriate for the first part of the sentence, but "indecisive" is incorrect for the second part as it has neutral rather than negative connotations.

Choice (C) "defense" is inappropriate for the first part of the sentence, so although "angry" fits into the second part, choice (C) is the incorrect answer.

Choice (E) is only partially correct. "Loss" fits in semantically but "placid" is, once again, too neutral a term to convey the negative reactions of the crowd.

• PROBLEM 1-34

Since the calendar year originally contained only 355 days, an extra month was occasionally _____ .

(A) contingent   (D) superadded

(B) introduced   (E) intercalated

(C) incident

SOLUTION:

(E) The word "since" creates a cause-and-effect relationship. The second half of the sentence must be caused directly by the information provided in the first half. The word "occasionally" further informs us that the action must be capable of repetition. The correct choice is (E) because "intercalculated" (inserted among existing elements) relates to the original information and can be frequently repeated.

Choice (A) "contingent" and choice (C) "incident" imply chance.

Choice (B) "introduced" (to bring forth for the first time) and choice (D) "superadded" (to add to something already complete) are both too finite to happen "occasionally."

• PROBLEM 1-35

The acquisition of exact knowledge is apt to be _____ , in that it is time-consuming to check for accuracy; but it is essential to every kind of excellence.

(A) wearisome   (D) amorphous

(B) equable   (E) eccentric

(C) erratic

SOLUTION:

(A)   The phrase "in that it is" is an important clue that the correct word will be synonymous or closely related to whatever immediately follows it. In this case the idea is "time-consuming," and the option closest in meaning is (A) "wearisome."

The remainder of the words, (B) "equable" (fair), (C) "erratic" (unpredictable), (D) "amorphous" (having no shape), and (E) "eccentric" (odd, peculiar), have little or no connection to "time-consuming" and make no sense in the sentence.

• PROBLEM 1-36

There was something _____ about the old house. In many ways one was made to feel that ghosts and demons existed there.

(A) ominous   (D) celestial

(B) tutelary   (E) mythical

(C) attractive

SOLUTION:

(A)   The best answer is (A) "ominous" (foretelling evil, threatening). The context of the sentence tells us that ghosts and demons existed there, and as a result, the adjective that would best describe the "old house" should reflect the feeling of something scary.

(B) "tutelary" (acting as a guardian) has no relationship to the context of the sentence as it does not imply anything frightening.

(C) "attractive" is the opposite of what the sentence context implies and is the wrong answer.

(D) "celestial" (heavenly, divine) is an antonym of the contextual implications in this sentence. As are looking for a word that describes a house with "demons and ghosts."

(E) "mythical" (legendary narrative that is related to the beliefs of a people or explains a practice or natural phenomena) is not appropriate to the context of the sentence.

• PROBLEM 1-37

The _____ policy of the Defense Secretary was regarded by the army as a national humiliation.

(A) pliant

(B) impartial

(C) pacific

(D) malleable

(E) histrionic

SOLUTION:

(C)   A country establishes an army because of a real or implied threat by foreign or domestic agents. Therefore, anybody who joins an army would be willing to fight to eliminate this threat. The most humiliating quality for a Defense Secretary or his policy would be the opposite of "wanting to fight." Therefore, (C) is the best answer because a "pacific" (peaceful) policy would be inappropriate for a military man.

(A) "pliant" (flexible), (B) "impartial" (fair), and (D) "malleable" (adaptable) would be possible answers. However, none of these words implies the opposite of the desirable quality for the Defense Secretary as well as "pacific" and therefore are not the best choices. (E) "histrionic" (relating to the theater) does not relate to the subject of the sentence.

• PROBLEM 1-38

Her constant stealing of lunch money from others in the class _____ her teacher.

(A) annoys

(B) irritates

(C) exasperates

(D) delectates

(E) inconveniences

SOLUTION:

(C) Choice (C) is the best answer because we are looking for a very strong word that illustrates or describes the negative feelings associated with stealing lunch money.

Choice (C) is the extreme feeling of vexation and irritation.

Choice (A) "annoys" is a mild feeling compared to "exasperates."

Although choice (B) "irritates" is a stronger emotion than "annoys," it is a lesser one than "exasperates."

"Delectates" (D) (delight), is not correct, because the teacher would not be delighted about "her stealing lunch money."

Choice (E) "inconveniences" (causes a lack of comfort) is a possibility, but is incorrect because it is not an emotionally strong word.

• PROBLEM 1-39

Typically a wedding is a _____ occasion, not a _____ one.

(A) superfluous . . . pious

(B) reprehensible . . . caustic

(C) private . . . stagnant

(D) solemn . . . comic

(E) futile . . . tedious

SOLUTION:

(D) This sentence needs an adjective to describe a wedding, and another one that tells you what a wedding is not. So we are looking for two words that are opposite in meaning. The only choice that fits both conditions is (D).

A wedding is "solemn," but it is not "comic."

Choice (A) is not appropriate because a wedding is not a "superfluous" (exceeding what is sufficient or necessary) situation. In addition, a wedding *is* a "pious" time, so it is inaccurate to say that it is *not* such a time.

Choice (B) is incorrect because a wedding is not "caustic," nor can it be described as "reprehensible" (deserving blame or censure) because this word can only be used to describe people or their actions.

Choice (C) is only partially correct. A wedding may or may not be a "private" occasion but "stagnant" (foul from lack of movement) is inappropriate to describe a wedding, and is not the opposite of "private."

Choice (E) is incorrect. A wedding is not usually considered a "futile" or "hopeless" occasion.

• PROBLEM 1-40

Rather than trying to _____ , one should try to _____ .

(A) abolish . . . destroy

(D) hurt . . . harm

(B) instigate . . . temper

(E) console . . . comfort

(C) demolish . . . enhance

SOLUTION:

(C) The word "rather" implies a contrast of words within the sentence. So we are looking for two words which are the opposite of each other. (C) "demolish . . . enhance" is the only choice that meets this condition. "Demolish" means "to tear down" and "enhance" means "to improve."

Choice (A)'s words are synonyms of each other: "abolish" and "destroy" mean the same thing.

Choice (B) is incorrect because "instigate" means "to provoke" and is not the opposite of "temper," which means "to modify." "Hurt" and "harm" are synonymous words, and therefore choice (D) is incorrect. Likewise, "console" and "comfort" are close in meaning, and not antonyms; therefore, choice (E) is incorrect.

• PROBLEM 1-41

The frightened mother _____ her young daughter for darting in front of the car.

(A) implored

(D) reproved

(B) extorted

(E) abolished

(C) exhorted

SOLUTION:

(D)   A key word in this problem is "for." It is important to find the option which works the best with this word, as well as making the most sense semantically in the sentence. To fit both of these qualifications, "reproved" is the best choice.

One "reprimands . . . " for, but typically, one "implores . . . " to, "extorts . . . " from, "exhorts . . . " to, and "abolishes . . . " from. Furthermore, a frightened mother would reprimand her daughter for disobeying street rules and running in front of a car. The mother would not (A) "implore" (beg) her daughter for doing a dangerous action. This makes no sense. Nor would the mother (B) "extort" (obtain by force) her daughter in this situation. (C) "exhorted" (urge, advise) and (E) "abolished" (to do away with) are not semantically correct in the sentence.

• PROBLEM 1-42

The doctoral candidate was _____ as she sought to make the results of her research _____ to her committee.

(A) objective . . . lucid   (D) hypocritical . . . flagrant

(B) disdainful . . . complacent   (E) candid . . . subtle

(C) discerning . . . obscure

SOLUTION:

(A)   There is a cause-and-effect relationship in this sentence. The first blank needs an adjective to describe a manner of speaking, and the second blank needs an adjective to describe the effect that this manner of speaking has on an audience. The best answer is (A) "objective . . . lucid." The best way way to describe the candidate would be "objective" (dealing with facts without personal feelings or prejudices), which would have the effect of making her research "lucid" (easily understood) to the committee.

Choices (B) "disdainful" (to look down upon), (C) "discerning" (distinguishing one thing from another), and (D) "hypocritical" (two-faced, deceptive) are not appropriate to the context of the sentence. Choice (E) "candid" (honest, truthful, sincere) is a possibility, but candidness could not cause "subtlety" (understatement, sophistication, cunning).

• PROBLEM 1-43

The computer is a(n) _____ tool, for if one neglects to save a file, it cannot be recalled.

(A) ominous

(B) complicated

(C) essential

(D) difficult

(E) unforgiving

SOLUTION:

(E)   The way the word "for" is used in this sentence makes it synonymous with the word "because" and creates a cause-and-effect relationship. Some quality of a computer causes the effect described in the second half of the sentence. Furthermore, the second half of this sentence cites an example to support the assertion made in the first part of the sentence. The computer is "unforgiving" (E), because if one neglects to save a file, that file is lost. It cannot be recalled.

(A) "ominous" (threatening), (B) "complicated," (C) "essential," and (D) "difficult" do not express the idea of no reprieve for a mistake as does (E) "unforgiving."

• PROBLEM 1-44

Even though the dog seemed _____ , it was actually _____ .

(A) furtive . . . eloquent

(B) stoic . . . auspicious

(C) prodigious . . . innocuous

(D) benign . . . prodigal

(E) servile . . . peripheral

SOLUTION:

(C)   The key words in this sentence are "even though the dog seemed" which means that the speaker perceived the dog a certain way, but that was not the way it actually was. Therefore, (C) is the best answer. A "prodigious" (enormous) dog is not usually perceived as "innocuous" or "harmless."

Choices (A), (B), (D), and (E) are wrong because they all contain words which would be unusual if used to describe an animal. "Eloquent" (forceful in speech) and "prodigal" (extravagant) are only used to describe people, and "auspicious" (positive) and "peripheral" (unimportant) can only be used to describe ideas or inanimate objects.

• PROBLEM 1-45

To _____ the action required _____ from an official of the company.

(A) rescind . . . enigma

(B) refute . . . colophon

(C) defer . . . permission

(D) facilitate . . . ineffectiveness

(E) solicit . . . apathy

SOLUTION:

(C)   We are looking for a verb to describe an "action" and a noun upon which it is conditional. (C) is the best answer because "to defer" (put off until another time) an action already in service might require "permission" from someone in authority ("an official of the company").

Choice (A) is wrong because "to rescind" (repeal, cancel) an action would not require an "enigma" (a puzzle).

(B) is incorrect because "to refute" (prove to be false) would not require a "colophon" (a small design or inscription). (D) is not right because "to facilitate" (bring about) an action does not require "ineffectiveness," but rather effectiveness.

Choice (E) is wrong because to take the initiative to "solicit" (try to bring about) an action does not indicate "apathy" (unconcern), but rather concern.

• PROBLEM 1-46

John's _____ only _____ the problem of the impending deadline.

(A) immunity . . . derided

(B) indolence . . . augmented

(C) stanza . . . mitigated

(D) virtue . . . hackneyed

(E) incessance . . . disparaged

SOLUTION:

(B)   A person's "indolence" (laziness) would certainly serve to "augment" an impending deadline. (B) is the best answer.

(A) "immunity" (safety) and "derided" (ridiculed) have no meaning when substituted into the sentence.

(C) "stanza" (a section of a poem) does not fit well into the sentence, although "mitigated" (made milder) might belong if the first answer were appropriate. The way the sentence is worded, (C) is the wrong answer.

(D) "virtue" (moral excellence) might fit the sentence, but "hackneyed" (banal, overused) is not appropriate. John's "incessance" (E) or "never stopping" might be a good choice for the first part of the sentence, but it is clear that "disparaged" (speak badly of) does not fit well.

• PROBLEM 1–47

The gold-studded costume appeared _____ when compared to the _____ of the flannel suit.

(A) chaste . . . gaudiness

(B) laconic . . . opulence

(C) reserved . . . savoir-faire

(D) ornate . . . simplicity

(E) feudal . . . raucousness

SOLUTION:

(D) The phrase "when compared to" suggests that we are looking for two words which describe opposite qualities. Certainly a flannel suit is in many ways opposite to a gold-studded costume. The best answer is (D) "ornate" (elaborately decorated) is the most effective way of describing a "gold-studded costume," and "simplicity" (lack of complication) is a good way of describing a "flannel suit," especially when compared to a "gold-studded costume."

(A) "chaste" (virtuous, pure) is an incorrect description of something that is "gold-studded," and "gaudiness" (garishness, flashiness) is not an appropriate choice to describe a "flannel suit."

(B) "laconic" (terse) is an inappropriate way to describe a suit; "laconic" is used to describe people, so (B) is incorrect.

(C) "reserved" (restrained in actions or words) is not the way to compare a "gold-studded costume" to the "savior-faire" (knowing how to act) of a "flannel suit." (C) makes no sense when substituted into the sentence.

(E) "feudal" (having the characteristics of feudalism) is a meaningless choice in the sentence.

• PROBLEM 1-48

He had a blind temper. He _____ fights over _____ remarks.

(A) enjoyed ... valid

(B) refuted ... plausible

(C) assessed ... benign

(D) initiated ... innocuous

(E) provoked ... provocative

SOLUTION:

(D)   The first sentence describes a person who does not intelligently control his temper ("blind temper"). Choice (D) is the best answer because someone who "initiates" (starts) fights over "innocuous" (innocent) remarks is not rational. In all choices, the adjective is appropriate for the sentence; therefore, we are concerned with the verb assigned to "fights."

Choice (A) is wrong because although the verb "enjoyed" is plausible, someone with a bad temper wouldn't necessarily fight over a "valid" remark.

Choice (B) "refuted" (prove false by argument) is not something someone with a "blind temper" would do.

Choice (C) is incorrect because "assessed" (evaluated) is a word associated with a rational person.

Choice (E) is possible because a man who can't control his temper might "provoke" fights, but it is also possible that any mild tempered person might fight over a "provocative" (aggravating) remark.

• PROBLEM 1-49

In contrast to her _____ personality, she was known to vacillate on certain important issues.

(A) tranquil

(B) austere

(C) determined

(D) conspicuous

(E) provocative

SOLUTION:

(C)   The key phrase here is "in contrast to." This means we are looking for an adjective that is the opposite of "vacillate." The best answer is (C) "determined" (firm, resolute), which is contrary to "vacillate" (to incline first to one course or opinion and then another, waver). The meaning of the sentence would be clear: In contrast to her determined personality, she was known to change her mind on certain issues. The remainder of the adjectives, (A) "tranquil" (peaceful, harmonious), (B) "austere" (harsh, strict), (D) "conspicuous" (easy to see, noticeable), and (E) "provocative" (tempting, irritating) are incorrect, because they do not contradict "vacillate."

• PROBLEM 1–50

After carefully evaluating the painting, the art critics unanimously agreed that the work had been done by a _____ and should be _____ .

(A) progeny . . . refurbished

(B) charlatan . . . repudiated

(C) neophyte . . . qualified

(D) prodigal . . . nullified

(E) fanatic . . . purchased

SOLUTION:

(B)   We are looking for two words which are compatible—a noun and a verb which are related in a meaningful cause-and-effect way. (B) is the most logical choice. If a "charlatan" (imposter) paints a painting, then it should be "repudiated" (rejected), because the painting would have no value.

(A) has little meaning, because if a "progeny" (talented child) paints a painting, then why should it be "refurbished" (made new)?

(C) is incorrect because a "neophyte" (beginner) may paint a painting, but then it would be unusual for art experts to examine it, and there would be no reason for them to "qualify" it.

(D) is obviously incorrect in the context of the sentence, because of "prodigal" (someone lavish and wasteful) probably would not spend time painting, or doing anything meaningful.

(E) is also incorrect because a "fanatic" is an extremist and art experts would not necessarily recommend "purchasing" (buying) a painting from such a person.

• PROBLEM 1–51

The _____ of the companies was inevitable since neither could profit without the assets of the other. This showed _____ behavior on the part of the owners.

(A) merger . . . prudent

(D) hiatus . . . monotonous

(B) pivot . . . exemplary

(E) diversity . . . fundamental

(C) antagonism . . . beneficial

SOLUTION:

(A) The first sentence must provide an example which proves the quality set forth in the second sentence. The best answer is (A) "merger . . . prudent." The companies had to "merge" (combine, unite) because they needed each other's profits. This showed "prudent" (foresighted, sensible) behavior.

Choice (B) "pivot" (a fixed pin on which something turns) . . . "exemplary" (commendable) is incorrect, because although "exemplary" is an appropriate choice, "pivot" is semantically incorrect.

Choice (C) "antagonism" (hostility) . . . "beneficial" (helpful, advantageous) is also wrong, because the words "neither could profit without the assets of the other" imply that the companies needed each other, therefore "antagonism" is not semantically correct within the context of the sentence.

(D) "hiatus" (break, lapse in continuity) . . . "monotonous" (one-tone, boring) has no meaning when inserted into the sentence.

(E) "diversity" (variety) . . . "fundamental" (basic) are incorrect, because they do not fit into the context of the sentence.

• PROBLEM 1–52

He was eagerly interested and wanted to participate in the experiment; but he was ultimately _____ on account of his age.

(A) dissuaded

(D) acclimated

(B) accommodated

(E) resigned

(C) reconciled

SOLUTION:

(A) The semicolon followed by the word "but" in this sentence suggests that the second half of the sentence will somehow contradict the first. Since we know he was eager to participate, we must choose the word which means that he was NOT encouraged to do so. Therefore, "dissuaded" (persuaded not to do something) is the best choice for the context of the sentence.

(B) "accommodated" and (C) "reconciled" are synonyms referring to bringing into agreement. These two words are not appropriate within the sentence because they are not contextually accurate with the use of "but."

Both (D) "acclimated" (to accustom to a new climate or situation) and (E) "resigned" (to give up) do not make any sense when inserted into the sentence.

• PROBLEM 1-53

Some people believe that flying saucers exist. As far as Jaclyn is concerned, this theory is a (an) _____ and has to be proven.

(A) obituary   (D) kaleidoscope

(B) travesty   (E) enigma

(C) irony

SOLUTION:

(E) To choose a correct answer for this question, we would have to find a noun that describes something that "has to be proven." An "enigma" (mystery, secret, perplexity) is something that is unknown and has to be proven, just like the existence of flying saucers mentioned in the first sentence.

Choices (A) "obituary" (notice of a person's death), (B) "travesty" (parody, burlesque), and (C) "irony" (something contradictory, sarcastic) do not need to be proven, and so do not fit logically into the sentence.

(D) "kaleidoscope" (an instrument or toy that forms patterns through the use of mirrors) is the worse choice because as a material object it can never be "proven."

•PROBLEM 1–54

Eric felt _____ after his _____ remark, but it was too late to retract it.

(A) respite . . . inadvertent

(B) irrational . . . incautious

(C) remorse . . . disparaging

(D) tentative . . . extravagant

(E) insensitive . . . premeditated

SOLUTION:

(C)   The best answer is "remorse" (regret for one's actions) . . . "disparaging" (degrading, belittling). We have to find a verb and an adjective that would fit the context of the sentence. What was Eric's feeling about his remark and what kind of remark was it that would cause him to want to "retract" (take back) what he said? That Eric felt "remorse" for a "disparaging" remark is the best choice for the sentence.

(A) "respite" (temporary delay) and "inadvertent" (heedless, unintentional) is an incorrect choice; although "inadvertent" is a fitting adjective, "respite" has no semantic integrity in this sentence.

(B) "irrational" (incapable of reasoning) and "incautious" (not careful) is incorrect. Although "incautious" would be a good choice, "irrational" makes no sense in the sentence.

(D) "tentative" (hesitant, uncertain) and "extravagant" (excessive) is incorrect. Both words are not logical for inclusion in the sentence.

(E) "insensitive" (not caring) and "premeditated" (carefully planned) are wrong. If Eric's remark was "premeditated," he would not want to retract it, even if it was "insensitive."

• PROBLEM 1–55

Residents of the town, who normally wouldn't agree on anything, now _____ to _____ the construction of a wood-fired power plant which would cause air pollution.

(A) proceeded . . . defend

(B) dispersed . . . hamper

(C) assembled . . . endorse

(D) alternated . . . establish

(E) mobilized . . . resist

SOLUTION:

(E)   The combination "normally . . . now" suggests that the present situation is opposite to a habitual one. Since the residents normally don't agree, the correct answer would have the residents of the town agreeing on something. Furthermore, since air pollution is something negative, the verb would suggest opposition to it. Choice (E) "mobilized . . . resist" is the only answer that satisfies both conditions.

Choice (A) is not correct because although the first word satisfies the conditions, the residents of the town would not "defend" air pollution.

Choice (B) is not correct because although the residents might normally "disperse" (break up) on this issue, we are looking for the opposite now.

Choice (C) is wrong because although "assembled" satisfies the condition for the residents getting together, they wouldn't "endorse" air pollution in their town.

Choice (D) is incorrect because the residents of the town wouldn't "alternate" (take turns) getting together or "establish" a construction which causes air pollution.

• PROBLEM 1–56

Zane Gray was able to _____ fictionalize the life of western cowboys even though he lived thousands of miles away in New York and probably never visited these western locales.

(A) benevolently

(B) authentically

(C) prosaically

(D) frivolously

(E) incoherently

SOLUTION:

(B)   The phrase "even though" in this sentence tells us that the state described in the second half of the sentence exists despite its contradictory relationship to something mentioned in the first half. Since the fact that Grey lived far away would imply that he would NOT be able to write about the West, we must look for a word that suggests the opposite, or that he wrote WELL about it. Therefore, (B) "authentically" (realistically) would be the best choice.

Choice (A) "benevolently" is incorrect; although Gray could describe cowboys in a kind way, that does not fit the context of the sentence where we are looking for a word that signifies the opposite of knowing little about a subject.

Choice (C) "prosaically" (in an ordinary way) is incorrect because it does not fit into the context of the sentence.

Choice (D) "frivolously" put into the sentence would mean that Gray made fun of the cowboys, and that is not implied in the sentence. Choice (E) "incoherently" is wrong because it would mean that Gray did not know what he was writing about, and the sentence implies that the opposite was true.

• PROBLEM 1-57

The scientist was horrified when all the new data he compiled for his experiment _____ his previous results.

(A) nullified

(D) validated

(B) suppressed

(E) consecrated

(C) instigated

SOLUTION:

(A) Horrified is a very strong adjective describing negative emotions. We are looking for a word to fit into the second half of the sentence which would cause this extreme emotion. "Nullified" (cancelled) is correct because if all the scientist's data was "nullified" by the new data, then the results of his experiment would be incomplete. This is a good reason to be "horrified" (appalled, dismayed).

(B) is a possibility because having data "suppressed" (held back) is bad for a scientist, but not as terrible as having it cancelled, and since the scientist is described as being "horrified," this is not the best answer.

(C) "instigated" (provoked) is wrong because the word makes the sentence meaningless.

(D) is incorrect because if the new data "validated" (made acceptable) the old data, then the scientist would be thrilled, not horrified.

Choice (E) is wrong because "consecrated" (make sacred) is not a word associated with a scientific experiment.

• PROBLEM 1-58

She took a _____ first step onto the unstable ladder.

(A) skeptical

(B) tentative

(C) limber

(D) haggard

(E) wanton

SOLUTION:

(B) We are looking for an adjective to describe what kind of step she would take to climb an "unstable ladder." The best answer is "tentative" (B) (hesitant, uncertain). Certainly, one would only climb something unstable in a hesitant or uncertain way.

Choice (A) is wrong because "skeptical" (doubtful) relates more to an attitude than an action.

Choice (C) "limber" (flexible, pliant) is obviously wrong in the context of the sentence. No one in their right mind would climb in a limber way up an unstable ladder.

Choice (D) is wrong because "haggard" (tired looking, fatigued) describes how a person feels, not the way he would climb a ladder. It is used to describe an emotion not an action.

Choice (E) "wanton" (unruly, excessive) is not contextually accurate, because it does not describe how a person would climb a ladder.

• PROBLEM 1-59

Facsimile or fax machines became common equipment in offices because they were _____ and more _____ than express mail and telex.

(A) faster . . . efficient

(B) trivial . . . supported

(C) effusive . . . salutary

(D) valid . . . impeccable

(E) sporadic . . . torpid

SOLUTION:

(A) The best answer is (A) "faster . . . efficient," because we are looking for two adjectives that describe why fax machines replaced express mail and telex.

(B) "trivial" (minor importance) and "supported" do not make any sense in the sentence.

(C) "effusive" (gushing) and "salutary" (beneficial) are not appropriate as reasons why fax machines replaced mail and telex.

(D) "valid" (true) and "impeccable" (faultless) do not logically fit into the sentence.

(E) "sporadic" (happening occasionally) and "torpid" (lacking vigor, dull) are negative adjectives, and if placed in the sentence would mean that fax machines ran on an occasional basis and were dull. This makes little sense.

• PROBLEM 1-60

In ancient Greek mythology, the gods and goddesses would _____ before they came to Earth. Sometimes they would appear as animals, and at other times, as plants.

(A) rant

(B) metamorphose

(C) venerate

(D) articulate

(E) saunter

SOLUTION:

(B)   The clue to completing this statement is the information given in the second sentence: "Sometimes they would appear as animals, and at other times, as plants."

Choice (B) "metamorphose" (change form) is the answer that describes this condition. "Rant" (to speak in a loud, pompous manner) is possible, but doesn't address the conditions in the second sentence.

Therefore, (A) is incorrect. (C) "venerate" (revere) is wrong, because one must venerate something and there is no object for this verb in this sentence.

(D) "articulate" (to speak distinctly) is logically incorrect when substituted into the sentence.

(E) "saunter" (walk at a leisurely pace, stroll) may describe how the gods and goddesses would walk before they came to Earth, but it does not relate to the conditions set up in the second sentence.

• PROBLEM 1-61

A notary public is sometimes hired by a lawyer to _____ the _____ of certain signatures.

(A) constrain . . . watermarks

(D) efface . . . consonance

(B) disdain . . . sanctity

(E) abrade . . . matrix

(C) verify . . . veracity

SOLUTION:

(C)   For this sentence, one must simply choose the words which make the most logical sense in the sentence based on knowledge of the function of a notary public, as well as two words which are directly related to one another. For these reasons, the best choice is (C). "Verify" and "veracity" have the same latin root word meaning "true," and it makes sense to say that a notary public is hired to "verify" (authenticate, confirm) the "veracity" (truthfulness) of signatures.

The remainder of the options (A) constrain . . . watermarks, (B) disdain . . . sanctify, (D) efface . . . consonance, and (E) abrade . . . matrix, make no sense when substituted into the sentence.

• PROBLEM 1-62

The waitress was _____ because her _____ attitude insured that she would not receive a tip from the diners.

(A) lethargic . . . cryptic

(D) contrite . . . insolent

(B) nostalgic . . . esoteric

(E) antagonistic . . . prudent

(C) fortuitous . . . incongruous

SOLUTION:

(D)   The key words in this sentence are "not receive a tip from the diners." This means that we have to find a word which describes a negative quality in a waitress which would displease the customers enough that they would not tip her, and then a word to describe how she felt "because" (cause/effect) she did not get tipped due to her own actions. "Contrite" (regretful, sorrowful) and "isolent" (rude, disrespectful) fit these qualifications, so (D) is the best answer.

(A) "lethargic" (lazy), (B) "nostalgic" (homesick), and (C) "fortuitous" (fortunate) are not appropriate to describe how the waitress felt about not receiving a tip.

(E) "antagonistic" (hostile) is a possible way of describing how the waitress felt towards the diners when they didn't leave her a tip, but "prudent" (wise) is not the kind of attitude that would cause this situation. Had the waitress acted in a prudent manner, she probably would have received a tip.

• PROBLEM 1-63

The sociologist interpreted _____ as being socially shared ideas about what is right and _____ as specific moral rules of behavior for a surrounding environment.

(A) culture . . . laws

(B) mores . . . technologies

(C) class . . . caste

(D) sanctions . . . folkways

(E) values . . . norms

SOLUTION:

(E)   This sentence is essentially a definition of the two nouns we are searching for, so the correct answer would be the two nouns which fit the definition provided. "Values" (socially shared ideas about what is right) in a particular environment, and "norms" (specific moral rules of behavior in a particular environment) are therefore the best answer. (A) "culture" (the thoughts and behaviors within an environment that are handed down from generation to generation), means more than just "shared ideas" and is therefore incorrect. "Laws" are norms which have been enacted through the formal process of government, and all "moral rules" are not "laws." (B) is incorrect because the words do not fit into the sentence definitions. "Mores" are strongly sanctioned norms, and "technologies" are practical solutions.

(C) "class" is a social level defined by economic factors such as occupation, income, and wealth. "Caste" is a social level into which people are born and where they must remain for life. These words do not fit into the definitions provided in the sentence.

(D) "sanctions" are rewards and punishments for adhering to or violating behaviors designated; and "folkways" are rules of behavior which are less strongly sanctioned. Thus, (D) is wrong because the words do not fit the definitions.

• PROBLEM 1-64

The general was _____ ; he considered disagreement with any of his ideas _____ .

(A) provocative ... euphonic   (D) intangible ... reticent

(B) elusive ... compatible   (E) dogmatic ... heretical

(C) fallacious ... austere

SOLUTION:

(E) This sentence demands two words which are logically related. Any word which describes the general will have to semantically relate to how he "considered disagreement with any of his ideas." The best answer is (E) "dogmatic" (positive in stating matters of opinion) ... "heretical" (dissent from a dominant opinion or theory). The general is forthright in stating his opinion, and anyone who disagrees is dissenting with the dominant opinion.

The remainder of the options, (A) "provocative" (tempting, irritating) ..."euphonic" (pleasant sounding), (B) "elusive" (hard to catch, difficult to understand) ..."compatible" (harmonious), (C) "fallacious" (misleading) ..."austere" (harsh, severe, strict), and (D) "intangible" (immaterial) ..."reticent" (silent, reserved, shy) are illogical choices for the context of the sentence.

• PROBLEM 1-65

The westward _____ from the Midwest to California in the 1930s created a large population of _____ workers on the Western produce farms.

(A) influx ... wandering   (D) highways ... hopeful

(B) movement ... incapable   (E) exodus ... migrant

(C) expansion ... lackadaisical

SOLUTION:

(E) This is a cause-and-effect sentence in which the action described in the first half of the sentence caused the quality of the workers described in the second half. Furthermore, the phrase "from the Midwest to California" should indicate that the first word shows movement out of an area. The word that fits this definition is "exodus"; therefore, (E) is the best choice. An exodus would cause a large incidence of migrant workers.

Choices (A) "influx" and (D) "highways" would not be appropriate answers.

Choice (B) "movement" is possible, but "incapable" is not meaningfully related to the rest of the sentence.

Choice (C) "expansion" would fit into the first part of the sentence, but "lackadaisical" (lacking spirit or zest) is not connoted by the sentence.

• PROBLEM 1–66

Police officers often face _____ situations where they must maintain their _____ .

(A) inhospitable . . . agility

(B) impossible . . . gallantry

(C) unequivocable . . . sternness

(D) perilous . . . composure

(E) extraordinary . . . strength

SOLUTION:

(D) The first part of the sentence asks for an adjective that describes the type of situation faced by a police officer. The second part of the sentence requires a word that describes a quality the police officers must maintain in the face of the chosen situation. The best answer is (D). Police officers often face "perilous" (dangerous) situations where they must maintain their "composure" (calmness).

Choice (A) is incorrect because although "inhospitable" (not fit for normal living) might be appropriate to the context, "agility" (ability to move quickly) is not a word used with "maintain," nor is it considered a quality of a person's character.

Choice (B) "impossible" is a possible choice for the first part, but "gallantry" is not meaningful to the context.

Choice (C) "unequivocable" (leaving no doubt, clear) is not an appropriate choice for the first part of the sentence. Police officers often face situations which call for judgments because they are not clear-cut.

Choice (E) is a possible answer, but not the best choice. Although police officers face "extraordinary" situations, they don't have to maintain their "strength" at all times.

• PROBLEM 1-67

The reason that restaurants have their personnel introduce themselves by their first names is that the _____ of familiarity may _____ the customer's inclination to be critical of the service rendered or the meal received.

(A) appearance ... reduce

(B) affliction ... retard

(C) reality ... prohibit

(D) growth ... limit

(E) pleasure ... deny

SOLUTION:

(A)   The correct answer is (A) "appearance ... reduce." The persons in question remain strangers to each other but on the surface they share a first-name basis, which might reduce the customer's inclination to complain about the service or the food.

Choice (B) "affliction" (to cause pain and torment) is incorrect because it makes no sense that familiarity would cause affliction.

Choice (C) "reality" also has no semantic value when added to the sentence, and makes the ideas meaningless.

Choice (D) "growth" implies that the customer and the personnel will become friends and there is nothing in the context of the sentence that supports this.

Choice (E) "pleasure" may fit the sentence, but it is not possible for "pleasure" to "deny," only people can "deny."

• PROBLEM 1-68

The heavy spring rains caused the rivers to rise and _____ the surrounding fields.

(A) imbibe

(B) sedate

(C) impugn

(D) inundate

(E) acerbate

SOLUTION:

(D)   The word "caused" should make us instantly aware of the cause-and-effect relationship in the sentence. We must think logically what would happen as a result of the action described in the first part of the sentence. It makes sense that rising rivers would (D) "inundate" (cover with a flood) the surrounding fields. The word "inundate" is basically a synonym for flood in this case.

(A) "imbibe" (drink, absorb), (B) "sedate" (quiet and dignified), (C) "impugn" (to attack by words or arguments), and (E) "acerbate" (irritate, exasperate) are not words that would be used to describe what excessive water would do to surrounding fields.

• PROBLEM 1-69

_____ is a key variable in relation to achievement; talent, support, effort, and practice are all important, but the fact remains: those who _____ to succeed go the furthest.

(A) Potential . . . need   (D) Training . . . struggle

(B) Desire . . . want   (E) Education . . . hope

(C) Heredity . . . train

SOLUTION:

(B) The best choice is "Desire . . . want." The first blank identifies a key variable in relation to achievement, and the second blank requires you to find a synonym of the word in the first blank. The key phrase here is "but the fact remains," which tells you that what follows will be a reiteration of the first sentence. All of the other choices [(A), (C), (D), and (E)] have potentially correct first words; it is the second word that we must consider.

(A) "need" is not a synonym for "potential," and is therefore incorrect.

(C) "train" has no relation to "heredity," and would be an incorrect choice for the context of the sentence.

(D) "struggle" is not an appropriate choice because it is not a synonym for "train." "Hope" is not correct because it is not contextually related to "education" in the sentence.

• PROBLEM 1-70

The _____ of the young student gave way to _____ as the semester progressed.

(A) provinciality . . . anarchy   (D) insecurity . . . confidence

(B) animosity . . . amity   (E) beneficience . . . profundity

(C) resignation . . . coalescence

SOLUTION:

(D) We are looking for a word that describes a student's initial feelings in the first part of the sentence. The second word would be an antonym because the sentence says that the initial feelings "gave way . . . as the semester progressed." The best answer is (D). The student was "insecure" (uncertain, shaky) in the beginning of the semester, but became "confident" (self-assured) as the semester progressed.

(A) "provinciality" (narrow in ideas, confined to a region) and "anarchy" (a social structure without government) is incorrect. The words are contextually inaccurate in this sentence.

(B) "animosity" (ill will, resentment) and "amity" (friendship) meet the criteria of being antonyms, but do not fit into the meaning of the sentence. It is unlikely that a student will start a semester feeling resentful; it is more credible that he/she will begin by feeling insecure about the courses, professors, etc.

(C) "resignation" (give up deliberately) and "coalescence" (merging, blending) are meaningless when inserted into the sentence.

(E) "beneficience" (beneficial quality) and "profundity" (deep intellectual insights) have no relationship to the meaning of the sentence.

• PROBLEM 1-71

The bitter root, when properly cooked, was converted into a _____ and nutritious food.

(A) palatable   (D) appealing

(B) dissonant   (E) decorous

(C) delightful

SOLUTION:

(A) The best answer is (A) "palatable" (agreeable to the taste). The sentence implies that the "bitter root," when cooked, converts (changes) into a food that is then agreeable, not bitter. The key word here is "converted" which implies that something changed to its opposite, so we are looking for the antonym of "bitter."

(B) "dissonant" (discord) is not appropriate to the meaning of the sentence.

(C) "delightful" is not a word that is the opposite of "bitter" with regard to food.

(D) "appealing" (to arouse a sympathetic response) might be considered a possibility, but "palatable" is the most likely antonym of "bitter."

(E) "decorous" (proper, seemly, correct) has no meaningful relationship to food.

• PROBLEM 1-72

The home team fans greeted their players with _____ , but treated their rivals with _____ .

(A) arrogance . . . urbanity

(B) reverie . . . defamation

(C) complacency . . . maliciousness

(D) alacrity . . . derision

(E) valor . . . discord

SOLUTION:

(D) The home team players will be "greeted" by a positive adjective, and the rivals will be "treated" with a negative adjective; therefore, the best answer is (D). The home team fans greeted their players with "alacrity" (enthusiasm, fervor), and the rivals were treated with "derision" (scorn, ridicule).

Choice (A) is incorrect because the fans would not greet their home team with "arrogance" (conceit).

"Reverie" (daydream) is not an appropriate word for the answer, so (B) is a bad choice.

(C) "complacency" (self-satisfied, smug) is not an adjective that describes how fans would greet their home team.

(E) "valor" (personal bravery, heroism) is not an appropriate choice for this sentence. It doesn't make any sense when added to the text.

• PROBLEM 1–73

As the city grows and more suburbs are annexed, its parks will become _____ for its needs; therefore, land should be purchased to provide _____ parks in the outlying suburbs.

(A) insufficient ... updated   (D) important ... new

(B) depleted ... more   (E) inadequate ... additional

(C) deficient ... larger

SOLUTION:

(E) The sentence implies that the city is growing. Under this circumstance, there will not be enough parks for the amount of people; therefore, more land should be purchased in the suburbs that will provide room for more parks. The best word choice that meets the context of the sentence is (E) "inadequate" to describe the amount of parks, and "additional" to tell that many parks will be provided "in the outlying suburbs."

(A) "insufficient" (not sufficient) is a possibility, but "updated" does not work because we are told that there won't be enough parks, not that those that exist are out of date.

(B) "depleted" (exhausted) implies that the amount of parks will be used up and is not appropriate to the context of the sentence.

(C) "deficient" (lacking in something necessary) is an appropriate word to describe the parks, but "larger" does not fit the context because the sentence tells us that more parks are needed, not necessarily larger ones.

(D) "important" is not a proper choice for the context of the sentence, because the parks were important to the city even before growth occurred.

• PROBLEM 1–74

The use of a pen with indelible ink will _____ a student's ability to _____ at a later time.

(A) preclude . . . erase   (D) deplete . . . digress

(B) hinder . . . slander   (E) enhance . . . ameliorate

(C) nullify . . . desecrate

SOLUTION:

(A)   The key word here is "indelible." An indelible pen is one that has permanent ink which can never be erased; therefore, the use of such a pen will "preclude" (make impossible) a student's ability to "erase" at a later time. (A) is the best choice.

(B) "hinder" (interfere) is possible, but whether or not a student uses an indelible pen does not effect the ability to "slander" (defame).

Choice (C) "nullify" (cancel, invalidate) is possible, but not when coupled with "desecrate" (violate a holy place).

Choice (D) "deplete" (reduce, empty) is not meaningful in the sentence.

"Enhance" (improve), choice (E), and "ameliorate" (to make better) are not semantically logical choices for the sentence.

• PROBLEM 1–75

Committees are ineffective when they cannot agree upon what to do or just how to go about accomplishing it; this situation is a(n) _____ of faulty _____ of committee responsibility.

(A) factor . . . acceptance   (D) part . . . knowledge

(B) cause . . . guidelines   (E) example . . . direction

(C) result . . . specifications

SOLUTION:

(C)   The two parts of this sentence, although divided by a semicolon, are joined together in a cause-and-effect relationship. The first part states a problem, and the second shows how that problem was caused. In fact, the first blank calls for a verb which shows that this is a cause-and-effect sentence. Such a verb is "result," which suggests that one condition causes another. Since the stated problem is "ineffectiveness," we must choose a word which would fit into the sentence to describe a condition which would cause this. If the committee did not know their responsibilities, it is likely that they would be ineffective, therefore, "specifications" (a description of work to be done) is the best word for the sentence.

Choices (A) "factor," (D) "part," and (E) "example" are incorrect because the situation described affects the whole committee all of the time, and not just part of it or on certain occasions. (B) "cause" is incorrect because the situation is a result, not a cause of the faulty specifications.

• PROBLEM 1-76

After winning the award, her once pleasant personality altered. She was now consistently _____ and _____ .

(A) arrogant . . . authoritative   (D) depraved . . . holy

(B) ambivalent . . . determined   (E) erratic . . . organized

(C) skeptical . . . gullible

SOLUTION:

(A)   This sentence requires you to find two adjectives which are the opposite of "pleasant personality." The key words are "once" and "altered." The best answer would be "arrogant" (acting superior to others, conceited) and "authoritative" (demanding obedience), because, being negative, these are opposite to a "pleasant" personality. Somebody who was once pleasant might win an award and become arrogant and authoritative.

Choice (B) "ambivalent" (undecided) makes no sense in relation to the context, even though "determined" (being single-minded in purpose) is possible.

Choice (C) "skeptical" (doubtful) and "gullible" (easily fooled) are not correct. "Depraved" (morally corrupt) and "holy" (D) make absolutely no sense in the context of the sentence.

Choice (E) "erratic" and "organized" are not correct choices. Although "erratic" (unpredictable, strange) is possible, "organized" is a poor choice.

• PROBLEM 1-77

The weekly program on public radio is the most _____ means of educating the public about pollution.

(A) proficient

(D) capable

(B) effusive

(E) competent

(C) effectual

SOLUTION:

(C) To find the correct word for this sentence, you must agree that public radio is the best way to reach a large audience. If that is true, then the word which logically fits is the one that supports this idea. "Effectual" (having the power to produce the exact effect or result) is the best choice.

(A) "proficient" (competency that is above average), (B) "effusive" (too emotional), (D) "capable" (able to produce results), and (E) "competent" (capable, fit, qualified) are words that refer to people and would not be used to describe the effects of a radio program.

• PROBLEM 1-78

The board members _____ the organization for the _____ measures it had adopted to save money during the recession.

(A) extolled . . . hedonistic

(D) denounced . . . exhaustive

(B) censured . . . expedient

(E) lauded . . . stringent

(C) revered . . . frivolous

SOLUTION:

(E) The best answer is (E) "lauded" (praised) and "stringent" (strict, severe). The most effective way of answering the question would be to look at the second part of the sentence and ask which word fits best with "measures it had adopted to save money during the recession." "Stringent" is the correct choice, because if the organization took "stringent measures" and saved money during a bad economy (recession), then the board would "laud" them.

(A) "extolled" (praised, commended) is correct for the first space, but "hedonistic" (pleasure seeking) does not fit the context of the sentence.

(B) "censured" (criticized or disapproved of) and "expedient" (speed up, make easier) do not fit into the sentence. The board would not "censure" the committee for "expedient" measures to save money.

(C) "revered" (worshipped) is an incorrect choice for the sentence. It is semantically meaningless.

(D) "denounced" (condemned) is an inappropriate choice if the committee tried "exhaustive" (thorough, complete) measures to save money.

• PROBLEM 1-79

Although her bedroom at home was always in disarray, her office work space was _____ .

(A) aloof (D) diligent

(B) meticulous (E) insipid

(C) viable

SOLUTION:

(B)   "Meticulous" (exacting, precise) is the best answer because the context of the sentence asks for a word that is opposite in meaning to "disarray" (to be out of order, disorganized). The key word here is "although," which implies that whatever follows the first thought will be contradictory in meaning.

(A) "aloof" (distant in interest, reserved) is incorrect because this is an adjective that is usually used to describe a person, not a work area.

(C) "viable" (capable of maintaining life, possible) is an inappropriate word choice as an antonym for "meticulous."

(D) "diligent" (hard-working) is a word which describes a person's characteristics, and is not a good choice for the sentence.

(E) "insipid" (uninteresting, bland) is not an adjective that meets the conditions of the sentence, as it is not a word that is opposite in meaning to "meticulous."

• PROBLEM 1-80

The pitcher tried to _____ the wounded catcher through increased

_____ .

(A) tarry . . . spending   (D) divulge . . . repugnance

(B) offset . . . concentration   (E) alleviate . . . preparation

(C) mediate . . . dedication

SOLUTION:

(B)   The best answer is "offset" (balance, compensate for) and "concentration." The sentence tells us that the catcher is wounded, and therefore the pitcher (who works as a team with the catcher) has to make up for this deficiency. "Offset" tells us that the pitcher will compensate for the catcher's injury by improving his own performance through "concentration."

(A) "tarry" (to delay) and "spending" make no sense when substituted into the context of the sentence.

(C) "mediate" (acting as an intermediary to settle a dispute) and "dedication" are not meaningful. The pitcher's increased dedication does not mediate a wounded catcher.

(D) "divulge" (reveal, disclose) is not an appropriate choice because it makes no sense when put into the sentence.

(E) "alleviate" (to make easier) is not the correct choice because "alleviate" is used in conjunction with a symptom or a circumstance, not a person.

• PROBLEM 1-81

Despite the fact that they believed in different political philosophies, the politicians agreed to _____ on issues when their goals were

_____ .

(A) digress . . . ambivalent   (D) demur . . . provocative

(B) concede . . . controversial   (E) collaborate . . . compatible

(C) dissent . . . viable

SOLUTION:

(E) The phrase "Despite the fact ... " suggests that the results of the situation described in the sentence will be different than one would normally expect. The second part of the sentence, after the word "when," shows the specific conditions necessary for this unexpected condition to occur. Therefore, (E) is the best answer, because politicians from different political parties wouldn't normally "collaborate" (cooperate) with each other, but they might only do so if their goals were "compatible" (in agreement).

Choice (A) "digress" (stray from the subject) and "ambivalent" (undecided) do not make any sense when substituted into the sentence.

(B) is only partially correct in that "concede" would fit in, but then "controversial" would not. Politicians wouldn't agree if their goals were controversial.

Choice (C) is incorrect because it is rare that people, even politicians, agree to "dissent," or disagree, especially on issues that are "viable" (workable).

(D) is a possibility because politicians may agree to "demur," or object, to "provocative" issues, but it is not the best answer. We are looking for a word which is a strong synonym for "agree" and that word is "collaborate."

• PROBLEM 1–82

The poet's _____ style caused the publisher to _____ its contract with her.

(A) sycophantical ... coil

(B) slipshod ... renew

(C) uninspired ... cancel

(D) enduring ... acclaim

(E) prosaic ... praise

SOLUTION:

(C) The word "caused" in this sentence is an immediate indication that the sentence contains a cause-and-effect relationship. We are looking for an adjective that describes the poet's style and a verb that tells how the publisher was affected by that style. Therefore, the words must mirror one another. If the style is described negatively, the publisher must take negative actions, or vice versa. The best answer is (C), because an "uninspired" (not arousing) style is a negative quality for a poet and might provoke a publisher to "cancel" a contract.

Of the remaining options, (B) and (E) don't work because they are antithetical, one word is negative and the other is positive. (A) and (D) don't work because it is impossible either to "coil" or to "acclaim" a contract.

• PROBLEM 1–83

American words and phrases have been added to the lexicon of French and Japanese cultures despite the displeasure of politicians and the _____ of purists.

(A) concession

(D) resolution

(B) neutrality

(E) denunciation

(C) endorsement

SOLUTION:

(E)   The correct answer is "denunciation," because we are looking for a word which supports "displeasure." The key word here is "and" between the phrase "displeasure of politicians" and "purists." This means that the attitude of the purists is similar to that of the politicians.

(A) is incorrect because "concession" (give in) is the opposite of displeasure.

(B) is wrong because "neutrality" suggests that the purists won't take a stand; however, the sentence tells us that the purists hold the same attitude as the politicians.

(C) "endorsement" is wrong because it is the opposite in meaning to "denunciation," and we are looking for a word that has a parallel connotation.

(D) is wrong because "resolution" (determination) is not logical to the context of the sentence.

• PROBLEM 1–84

Evan is five feet five inches tall and inclines towards stoutness, but his erect bearing and quick movements tend to _____ this.

(A) emphasize

(D) camouflage

(B) conceal

(E) disavow

(C) denigrate

SOLUTION:

(D) The word "but" in this sentence means that something will turn out differently than the originally described situation might lead us to expect. From the description of Evan as relatively short and large, it is a surprise that he is "quick" and that he has an "erect bearing." The word we are looking for is a verb which causes this disparity. (D) "camouflage" (disguise in order to conceal) is the best answer, because it implies that things are not as they seem or as we expect them to be.

"Emphasize" (A) (to stress), is wrong because it would have the opposite effect to that described in the sentence.

"Conceal" (B) (to remove from view) might be considered as a possibility, but it is not the best choice. His bearing and movements do not "hide" his appearance; they only disguise him.

(C) "denigrate" and (E) "disavow" are synonyms meaning "to deny." Evan's movements and bearing do not "deny" his appearance; they disguise him.

• PROBLEM 1-85

Some people say that fashion is _____ . What is in style today is outdated tomorrow.

(A) illicit

(B) capricious

(C) benign

(D) circuitous

(E) idiosyncratic

SOLUTION:

(B) The second sentence acts as a definition for the word which fits into the blank. "Capricious" (changing suddenly) is the best choice. "What is in style today is outdated tomorrow" means that fashion trends can change suddenly, or from day to day and this is described by the word "capricious."

(A) "illicit" (not licensed) and (D) "circuitous" (not being forthright or direct in language or action) are inappropriate choices.

(E) "idiosyncratic" (peculiar tendency of a person) and (C) "benign" (kindly) are words used to describe people not things.

• PROBLEM 1-86

Although they tried to implicate him, they could not. He stated _____ and unequivocally that he was not involved in the crime.

(A) categorically

(D) fallibly

(B) contritely

(E) ignominiously

(C) elatedly

SOLUTION:

(A) "Categorically" (absolutely, unqualified) is the best choice. We are looking for a word that is related as a synonym to "unequivocally" (leaving no doubt, clear) because of the key word "and" which joins the word in the blank with the word "unequivocally." The sentence context implies that the man could not be implicated because he stated in a very clear, absolute way that he was not involved.

(B) "contritely" (remorsefully) is a poor choice because the man wouldn't feel remorse if he were not involved in the crime.

(C) "elatedly" (joyfully) is inappropriate because the man wouldn't feel joyful if someone were trying to implicate him in a crime.

(D) "fallibly" (being deceived) and (E) "ignominiously" (disgracefully) make no sense in the context of this sentence.

• PROBLEM 1-87

The Civil War was the _____ of the inability of the North and South to _____ on an interpretation of the Constitution.

(A) epitome . . . concur

(D) chaos . . . harmonize

(B) climax . . . agree

(E) finalization . . . cooperate

(C) drama . . . unite

SOLUTION:

(B) In this sentence we must find words which fit into the cause-and-effect relationship. Some inability of the North and South caused the Civil War. Many wars are caused by disagreements, so it makes sense that this was caused by an inability to "agree." The first blank can be filled by logically assuming that the two parties had been struggling for some time to interpret the Constitution, but that the situation had gotten worse and worse. In such a case, war would come as a crucial moment or "climax."

Options (C) and (D) are not viable because it does not make sense to say the "drama of the inability" or "the chaos of the inability."

Choices (A) and (E) come closer to being appropriate, but they lack the connotation of the great impact of war that "climax" suggests.

• PROBLEM 1-88

If you are not a medical person, you may find it _____ to _____ a simple fracture from a sprain.

(A) necessary . . . ascertain

(D) difficult . . . distinguish

(B) easy . . . determine

(E) wont . . . figure

(C) illusory . . . analyze

SOLUTION:

(D) The second half of this sentence requires a word which describes the action of making a choice. The first half shows how the action of making this choice would affect someone who is not a doctor. The best answer is (D) because to "distinguish" (to perceive or show the difference) implies an ability to make a choice, and such an action would be "difficult" for someone without medical training.

(A) Although "ascertain" (to learn by inquiry) is possibly a good answer, "necessary" does not fit the context of the sentence because "if" you are not a medical person, you probably will NOT find it necessary to tell a fracture from a sprain.

(B) "easy" is inappropriate, because if you are not a medical person, it would not be easy to diagnose a medical situation.

(C) "illusory" (based on misconception, illusion) and (E) "wont" (custom, habit) are not the correct answers within the context of the sentence.

• PROBLEM 1-89

The spacecraft *Voyager,* which travelled to Jupiter, was _____ because it was the only space vehicle to _____ a recorded message from our planet to distant star systems.

(A) blasphemous ... meander

(B) egocentric ... trek

(C) profound ... provoke

(D) unique ... transport

(E) vital ... copy

SOLUTION:

(D)   The correct answer contains an adjective that supports the word "only" and a verb that shows how a "recorded message" goes to "distant star systems." "Unique" means "one of a kind" and is the best choice to describe "only space vehicle"; "transport" (to carry) is the best choice to describe how "a recorded message" is carried to "distant star systems."

(A) is not meaningful because "blasphemous" and "meander" cannot describe a spacecraft.

(B) "egocentric" (self-centered) describes a person, not an innate object such as a spacecraft.

(C) "profound" (knowledgeable) is also not a good way to describe a spacecraft, for while the message may have been profound, certainly a machine is not.

(E) "vital" (important) is a possibility, but not within the context of the sentence where we are looking for a word that means the spacecraft is the "only" one.

• PROBLEM 1-90

The spelling and pronunciation of some English words are _____ because they don't follow _____ rules.

(A) infamous ... prosaic

(B) erratic ... inevitable

(C) fallacious ... hypothetical

(D) hackneyed ... verbose

(E) incoherent ... prudent

SOLUTION:

(B)   The use of the word "because" in this relationship creates a cause-and-effect relationship. We are looking for one adjective for "rules" which has a specific effect on "words," demonstrated in this sentence by an adjective. However, the use of the negative "don't" in the second half of the sentence, turns the word around to its opposite. Therefore, the correct answer has two adjectives which are almost opposite in meaning. The best answer is (B) "erratic" (unpredictable, strange) and "inevitable" (sure to happen).

(A) is incorrect because words cannot be described as "infamous" (having a bad reputation).

(C) is not correct because although the words may be "fallacious" (misleading), the rules cannot be "hypothetical" (uncertain). These are not opposite in meaning.

(D) is wrong because although "hackneyed" (trite) may fit the first part of the sentence, "verbose" (wordy, talkative) does not fit into the second part. Rules may be "verbose," but that would not explain why the spelling and pronunciation of the English words are "hackneyed" (commonplace, trite).

(E) is a possibility, but not the best choice. Spelling and pronunciation may be "incoherent" (illogical) to some people, but not to all; "prudent" (wise) is not an acceptable way to describe spelling rules.

• PROBLEM 1-91

Before an inventor can receive a patent, the U.S. Patent and Trademark Office _____ the application to verify that a _____ invention doesn't exist.

(A) investigates ... distorted

(B) scrutinizes ... comparable

(C) expedites ... compatible

(D) questions ... probable

(E) analyzes ... contrasting

SOLUTION:

(B) "Scrutinizes ... comparable" is the correct answer because we are looking for a verb to describe the action of the Patent Office and an adjective to describe why an inventor wouldn't receive a patent. The inventor would receive the patent if a "comparable" (similar) type of invention "doesn't exist." All of the verbs except (C) could adequately fit into the sentence; therefore, it is the second word that makes the difference in the other choices: (A), (D), (E).

Choice (A) is wrong because if an inventor creates a "distorted" (to twist out of normal shape) invention, he would not necessarily receive a patent.

(C) "expedites" (to make easier) is incorrect because it does not imply that the Patent Office is created to look carefully at an application to "verify" (to confirm) that a similar one doesn't exist.

(D) is wrong because "probable" (possible) doesn't fit into the context of the sentence.

(E) "contrasting" (the opposite of) is incorrect because it would not matter if a contrasting invention exists.

• PROBLEM 1-92

George Burns, the poet, spent most of his youth as a farmer; as a result, some of his poems reflect his _____ background.

(A) trite

(D) ominous

(B) slavish

(E) urbane

(C) provincial

SOLUTION:

(C)   Choice (C) "provincial" is the best answer because we are looking for a word that is related to "farmer," and "provincial" means "regional or unsophisticated." "As a result" creates a cause-and-effect relationship which tells us that the subject of some of Burns' poetry is directly related to his upbringing.

(A) "trite" (commonplace, overused) is incorrect because it is not semantically related to the meaning of the sentence.

(B) "slavish" (obedient) and (D) "ominous" (threatening) are not appropriate words to describe a farmer.

(E) "urbane" (city-like) is the opposite of anything having to do with farming and is not a viable choice.

• PROBLEM 1-93

The salesperson's _____ voice was exceptionally annoying. Potential customers avoided going anywhere near her product.

(A) exorbitant

(D) strident

(B) uproarious

(E) egocentric

(C) docile

SOLUTION:

(D) "Strident" is the best answer because we are looking for a word to describe a voice that is a synonym to "exceptionally annoying." A "strident" (harsh-sounding) voice is annoying to hear and would keep people away.

(A) "exorbitant" (excessive), (B) "uproarious" (making a great tumult), (C) "docile" (easily taught, led, or managed), and (E) "egocentric" (self-centered) are all incorrect because not only are none of them synonymous with "annoying," but they are also all words better used to describe a person than a voice.

• PROBLEM 1-94

> Not all persons whose lives are _____ remain provincial; some have the intellectual and personal characteristics which enable them to develop a(n) _____ orientation to life.
>
> (A) confirmed . . . philanthropic   (D) restricted . . . cosmopolitan
>
> (B) limited . . . hedonistic   (E) restrained . . . fastidious
>
> (C) circumscribed . . . altruistic

SOLUTION:

(D) The best answer is (D) "restricted" (limited) . . . "cosmopolitan" (belonging to all the world). In the first part of the sentence, the correct word would be one which describes a "provincial" life. The best answer is "restricted." The second part of the sentence requires a word that relates to the following key sentence clues: "Not all." This means that the second word required will be an antonym of "restricted." The best choice is "cosmopolitan" (at home anywhere in the world).

(A) "confirmed" (ratified) and "philanthropic" (doing charitable acts or deeds) have no relation to the meaning of the sentence.

(B) "limited" is a good choice for the first part of the sentence; however, "hedonistic" (living for pleasure) is not appropriate for the second part of the sentence.

(C) "circumscribed" (limit narrowly a range of options) is also a possibility for the first part of the sentence, but "altruistic" (unselfish) is inappropriate for the second part.

(E) "restrained" (prevented from doing something) may be correctly inserted into the sentence, but "fastidious" (difficult to please) is not a correct word for the sentence.

• PROBLEM 1-95

The air around the overgrown boat dock reeked with the _____ odor of seaweed, damp, and dead fish.

(A) malodorous   (D) redolent

(B) rankling   (E) pungent

(C) flavorful

SOLUTION:

(A) We are looking for an adjective that describes the "odor of seaweed, damp, and dead fish." In addition, the verb "reeked" (to give off or become permeated with a strong, disagreeable odor) indicates that this will be a rather disgusting smell. (A) "malodorous" (having a bad odor) is the best choice.

(B) "rankling" (to fester, to cause anger) does not meet the conditions set forth in the previous sentences.

(C) "flavorful" is wrong because we are looking for a very disagreeable smell, and this word suggests the opposite. For the same reason, (D) "redolent" (fragrant, aromatic) is incorrect.

(E) "pungent" having a sharp taste or smell is not a correct substitute in this sentence because a pungent odor is not necessarily negative.

• PROBLEM 1-96

It is good advice to _____ any document that requires your signature.

(A) efface   (D) despoil

(B) mollify   (E) scrutinize

(C) broach

SOLUTION:

(E) If a document requires your signature, then it is a good idea to (E) "scrutinize" (examine closely, study) it. (E) is the best answer because it is logical and makes the most sense.

(A) is wrong, because it would not be a good idea or "good advice" to "efface" (wipe out, erase) your signature on a document.

"Mollify" (B) (to soothe in temper) and makes no sense in this sentence.

Choice (C) "broach" (introduce as a topic for a sentence or conversation) and choice (D) "despoil" (to strip of belongings) are meaningless in relation to the word "document."

• PROBLEM 1-97

The _____ mob _____ all semblance of law and order.

(A) ubiquitous . . . avoided   (D) impetuous . . . hindered

(B) tyrannical . . . thwarted   (E) indifferent . . . salvaged

(C) unruly . . . relinquished

SOLUTION:

(C)   In this question, we are looking for an adjective to describe a mob and a verb which relates the mob to "law and order." The best answer is (C). The "unruly" (not submitting to discipline, disobedient) mob "relinquished" (abandoned) all semblance (appearance) of law and order. A "mob" is usually described as "a large, disorderly group of people"; therefore, "unruly" is the best word to use as an adjective.

(A) "ubiquitous" (ever present in all places, universal) is not an appropriate adjective to use in describing a mob; and although "avoided" may be appropriate, this answer is wrong.

(B) "tyrannical" (having absolute power) is a possible way of describing a mob; however, it is not the best choice. In addition, "thwarted" (frustrate) is not appropriate with "semblance."

(D) "impetuous" (rash, impulsive) . . . "hindered" (blocked) and (E) "indifferent" (unbiased) . . . "salvaged" (rescued from loss) cannot be used in the sentence because they do not make any semantic sense.

• PROBLEM 1-98

The spectators were astounded by his _____ move. They had never seen anyone accomplish such a fearless maneuver.

(A) banal   (D) audacious

(B) truculent   (E) uncanny

(C) charismatic

SOLUTION:

(D) We are looking for an adjective that describes the kind of move that would relate to a "fearless maneuver" that would "astound" spectators. The best answer is (D) "audacious" (fearless, bold).

(A) "banal" (common, petty, ordinary) is incorrect because it is the opposite in meaning to the word we are looking for. A maneuver that is common or ordinary would not "astound" spectators.

(B) "truculent" (aggressive) is an adjective that describes a person, not an action.

(C) "charismatic" (appealing, magnetic personality) is an adjective that might relate, but it not the best choice, because, once again "charisma" is a word that often describes a personality, not an action.

(E) "uncanny" (of a strange nature, weird) does not fit with "fearless," and is not the correct choice.

• PROBLEM 1-99

Not wanting to face the dire consequences of her actions, she _____ for as long as she could before she appeared before the committee.

(A) tarried   (D) vacillated

(B) waned   (E) disparaged

(C) stagnated

SOLUTION:

(A) The sentence implies that she is reluctant to face "the dire consequences of her actions," and so we are looking for a word that would describe how she stretched the time "before she appeared before the committee." The best choice is (A) "tarried" (to go or move slowly, delay). (B) "waned" (grow gradually smaller) makes absolutely no sense when fitted into the sentence because a person cannot "wane."

(C) "stagnated" (motionless, dull, inactive) is a possibility, but is probably unlikely. People do not usually remain inactive when they know they have to do something.

(D) "vacillated" (fluctuated) makes some sense in the sentence but it is not as good a choice as "tarried," because it implies a choice between two options, which is not mentioned in the sentence.

(E) "disparaged" (belittled, undervalued) makes no sense when inserted into the sentence.

• PROBLEM 1-100

In the early 1900s the chinchilla became almost _____ because of the _____ demand for its fur.

(A) prosaic . . . redundant

(D) extinct . . . prodigious

(B) obsolete . . . incidental

(E) hypothetical . . . unique

(C) banal . . . inadvertent

SOLUTION:

(D) "Extinct" (no longer existing) and "prodigious" (exceptional, tremendous) are the best choices to complete this sentence. The word "because" makes us aware that we are looking for two words that relate logically to each other in a cause-and-effect relationship. Some quality of the chinchilla caused it to become a certain way. The chinchilla became almost "extinct" because of the "prodigious" demand for its fur; because so many people desired the chinchilla's fur, they almost wiped out the entire population of the animal.

(A) "prosaic" (tiresome, ordinary) is an inappropriate word to describe an animal.

(B) "obsolete" (no longer in use) is incorrect because "obsolete" refers to inanimate things, not people or animals.

(C) "banal" (common, petty, ordinary) is a word that is opposite in connotation to the meaning of the sentence.

(E) "hypothetical" (assumed, uncertain) is not meaningfully related to the context of the sentence.

Chapter 2
Analogies

CHAPTER 2

ANALOGIES

An analogy is simply a comparison between items that are basically different, but that also have some striking similarities. Because of these similarities, analogous terms may share a common bond or relationship that is the key to the analogy.

Actually, an analogy is the verbal equivalent of a proportion in mathematics. In math, recall that the colon between a pair of numbers shows that the numbers are a ratio, as, for example, "the odds are 4 : 1." The proportion then sets one ratio equal to a second ratio (for example, the relationship 4 : 1 is the same as the relationship 8 : 2). In a verbal comparison, a colon separates two words to be compared. We read "Word A is to Word B." In an SAT I analogy, a double colon between two such comparisons means that the relationship Word A to Word B is the same as the relationship Word C to Word D.

The SAT I will have 19 analogies for you to complete. They will be presented in one group of six items and one group of 13. The beginning items are usually simple, but later items become progressively more difficult. For each item, your task is to compare a given or sample pair of capitalized words with five other pairs, and then pick the pair that best matches the relationship between the words in the sample.

It is important that you do not feel discouraged if you cannot complete the first or second analogy on the test. The way to proceed on the Analogy section of the SAT I is to try to work each item in the order in which it is presented. If you are stumped by an item, mark it and leave it; then go on to the next one. At the very end of the section, return to any items you could not complete earlier. Often, you will find that you *can* complete analogies that stopped you earlier. This is because success breeds confidence, which breeds further success. If you have successfully solved several questions, you can sometimes reach back and find solutions that eluded you before.

The key to completing analogies is to identify the pattern, and to do so in a timely fashion. As you know, you are expected to spend a limited amount of time working each section of the SAT I. This is because one purpose of the test is to assess your ability to do college-level work. The test makers have already set the standards for accuracy and speed, and they have incorporated these standards into the SAT I items. In the Verbal section, you will have 80 minutes to answer 78 items. So, if you can complete each analogy in approximately one minute, you will be able to finish the Analogy section.

ABOUT THE DIRECTIONS

As with all sections of the SAT I, it is important that you know the directions before the day of the test. Therefore, you will not waste valuable time while taking the actual test.

The directions will appear similar to the following:

DIRECTIONS: Each question below consists of a related pair of words or phrases, followed by five lettered pairs of words or phrases. Select the lettered pair that best expresses a relationship similar to that expressed in the original pair.

Example:

SMILE : MOUTH ::

(A)   wink : eye

(B)   teeth : face

(C)   voice : speech

(D)   tan : skin

(E)   food : gums

ABOUT THE QUESTIONS

The following is an overview of the different types of questions you will encounter on the SAT I, along with strategies for solving them quickly and accurately.

Question Type 1: Part-to-Whole

One frequent pattern is a part of an item or concept to the whole idea or concept. Examples are:

SONG : REPERTORY   CHAPTER : BOOK

If we assume that a singer has a repertory of songs, we see that a "song" is a part of a whole "repertory." A "chapter" is also a part of a whole "book." So, the pattern is Part-to-Whole, and the option to look for will have the same pattern.

This pattern can also be reversed, as indicated below:

BANK : VAULT   ZOO : CAGE

Now the pattern is Whole-to-Part. For example, if we assume that a "bank" is the whole building or organization, then a "vault" is a smaller part of it. Also, a "zoo" is a whole organization and a "cage" is a part of this whole.

Question Type 2: Cause-and-Effect

Another frequent pattern is the relationship of the Cause to its Effect. Look at these examples:

BACTERIUM : DISEASE   SUN : HEAT

In the first example, "bacterium" is the cause of the result "disease." In the second example, "sun" is the cause of the result "heat." In each case so far, you will look for a pattern with nouns.

The reverse pattern is Result to Cause. Examples are:

FOOD : AGRICULTURE   LAUGHTER : JOKE

Here, "food" is the result of "agriculture," which causes it to be produced. And "laughter" is the result that follows (or *should* follow) a "joke."

Question Type 3: User-to-Tool

These are examples of a third pattern, the relationship of the User-to-Tool:

DENTIST : DRILL   GARDENER : RAKE

A "dentist" uses a "drill" as a tool, and a "gardener" uses a "rake" as a tool.

The reversal of this pattern is Tool-to-User. For example:

COMPUTER : PROGRAMMER   HAMMER : CARPENTER

The "computer" is the tool, and the "programmer" is the user. The "hammer" is the tool, and the "carpenter" is the user.

A variation of this pattern might be the Instrument-to-Application, or Tool-to-Application, and its reversal. For example:

COMPUTER : WRITING   TROWEL : GARDENING

Examples of the reverse are:

OVEN : BAKING   PIANO : CONCERT

In these examples, too, the words are nouns.

Question Type 4: Group-to-Member

A fourth common pattern is the Group-to-Member. Examples are:

PRIDE : LION   SENATE : SENATOR

A "pride" is the group to which a "lion" belongs. The "Senate" is the group to which a senator belongs.

The reversal then is Member-to-Group. For example:

WOLF : PACK   WITCH : COVEN

The "wolf" is a member of a group called a "pack"; and a "witch" is a member of a group called a "coven."

There are other variations of this basic pattern, such as Members-to-Group and the reverse.

Question Type 5: Trait-to-Example

Another pattern is a Trait or Characteristic to an Example of this Trait or Characteristic. For example:

DISHONESTY : LIE   BRILLIANCE : DIAMOND

Note that "dishonesty" is a character trait, and one example of this trait is a "lie." Also, "brilliance" is a physical trait and "diamond" is an example. Reversals of this pattern are common as well.

A variation of this pattern is a Greater Degree of a Characteristic to the Characteristic itself. For example:

INGENIOUS : INTELLIGENT   BRAZEN : EXTRAVERTED

In these examples, "ingenious" is a greater degree of the trait "intelligent," and "brazen" is a greater degree of the trait "extraverted." Note, too, that all four words here are adjectives.

One variation of the pattern is Lesser Degree of a Trait to the Trait itself. Another variation might be a Trait to an Opposite Trait, as here:

VALOR : COWARDICE   COURAGEOUS : PUSILLANIMOUS

The words in the first example are nouns; in the second example, they are adjectives.

At times, you may not know the exact meanings of all the words. In that case, you will have to make some educated guesses. For example, you probably know words that bear resemblance to "valor" and "cowardice," such as "valiant" and "coward." So, "valor" must be a trait resembling courage, whereas "cowardice" is the opposite trait. And don't give up on the second example because of "pusillanimous." You already know what "courageous" means. If you did not know what "pusillanimous" meant, you will know what it means from now on: it means "cowardly," or the trait opposite to "courageous." However, on a test, you will know that you are looking for an adjective either opposite in meaning to "courageous" or having the same meaning. That narrows your options considerably. If you should see the option "brave : fearful," you can be reasonably sure that it is the correct option.

Question Type 6: Object-to-Material

The pattern of Object-to-Material creates an analogy between an object and the material from which it is made. This type of question is quite common, as is its reversal. For example:

SKIRT : GABARDINE   or   COTTON : SHIRT

The "skirt" is the object made of the material "gabardine," and "cotton" is the material of which the object "shirt" is made.

Question Type 7: Word-to-Definition, Synonym, or Antonym

These patterns are heavily dependent on their dictionary meanings. Examples include:

Word-to-Definition	*Word-to-Synonym*	*Word-to-Antonym*
SEGREGATE : SEPARATE	VACUOUS : EMPTY	DESOLATE : JOYOUS

In the first example, the word "segregate" means "separate"—it is both a definition and a synonym. Next, a synonym and definition for the word "vacuous" is "empty." Finally, a word opposite in meaning to "desolate" is the word "joyous."

Question Type 8: Symbol-to-Institution

These are examples of the pattern Symbol-to-Institution:

FLAG : GOVERNMENT   CROWN : MONARCHY

In the first case, "flag" is a symbol of the institution "government"; "crown" is the symbol of a "monarchy."

These are the most commonly occurring patterns. However, many other types may appear including Plural-to-Singular, Creator-to-Creation, Male-to-Female, or Broad Category-to-Narrow Category (for example, FISH : SALMON).

ANSWERING ANALOGY QUESTIONS

The recommended strategy for completing an analogy is to examine the two sample words; then, from the meanings of these words, trace the pattern or relationship between them. It is also helpful to identify the grammatical form of the words. Once you can identify the pattern and form, you can forget the meanings and search the five options for the same pattern.

You will not be looking for a match of dictionary meanings, although you will certainly need to use the dictionary meanings as clues. The match you want is the option whose members resemble one another in the same way the words of the sample pair are related. For example, if the relationship between the same pair is "Part-to-Whole," you will look for the option showing "Part-to-Whole." If the link between the same pair is "Cause-to- Effect," then the matching option must also be "Cause-to-Effect."

There are four basic steps to answering any analogy question:

| STEP 1 | Identify the meanings of both words in the sample. |

| STEP 2 | From the meanings, identify the pattern of the sample. Also identify the part of speech and the number (singular or plural) of each word. |

| STEP 3 | Ignoring the meanings of the words in the sample, now look over the options. Use the meanings of the words in each option *only* to identify its pattern. Eliminate any options that do |

not match the pattern in every way, including the order of presentation and grammatical form.

STEP 4 | If one option remains, it is the exact match. If two options remain, examine them to see what is different about them. Compare these differences with the sample. Eliminate the option that does not match the sample perfectly.

For example, suppose the original pair is AUTOMOBILE : BRAKE. An "automobile" is a whole and the "brake" is a part. The options are:

(A) doer : thinker   (D) carburetor : choke

(B) man : conscience   (E) society : detergent

(C) horse : ride

We can eliminate (A), since the two words have opposite meanings, and also (C), since HORSE is the doer and RIDE is what is done. We can also eliminate (E), since SOCIETY is a whole, or producer, and DETERGENT is a soap—which is produced by society.

Two options remain: (B) and (D). In (D), a CARBURETOR is the part of an automobile that supplies the fuel, and CHOKE is a part that restricts the amount of fuel flowing to the engine. Since these are two separate parts, we can eliminate (D). What is left is (B), the perfect match, since CONSCIENCE is a part of the whole MAN. Besides, a conscience restrains a man just as the brake restrains an automobile.

Always look for options to eliminate. However, occasionally you can save a lot of time if you just happen to note the perfect match from the start. In that case, though, you might also quickly review the other options, just to be sure your hunch was correct. For example:

CLOCK : SECOND ::

(A) ruler : millimeter   (D) product : shelf life

(B) sundial : shadow   (E) quart : capacity

(C) arc : ellipse

Right from the start, option (A) looks right. The pattern seems to be an instrument and one of its measures, and option (A) fits nicely. A cursory look at the other options shows that no other option would be even tempting to choose.

Not all the analogies are so simple. In the previous example, suppose the original pair and all options except for option (B) remained the same. Then assume that option (B) is replaced by "scale : pounds." The pattern again is an instrument and one of its measures. Now we must choose between two options:

    (A)   ruler : millimeter   (B)   scale : pounds

What is different about them? A ruler is calibrated in centimeters first and then millimeters. A scale is calibrated in pounds and then ounces. There's the difference: a millimeter is the smaller measure, but a pound is the larger measure. How is a clock calibrated? By minutes and then seconds. Obviously, the matching option should show the smaller measure—option (A).

Let's try an example in which you may need to refine the pattern you first identify. For example, suppose the original pair is SHELL : WAL-NUT. The five options are:

    (A)   coating : candy   (D)   loaf : bread

    (B)   peel : banana   (E)   root : tree

    (C)   icing : cake

Our first assumption seems obvious here: Part-to-Whole. Looking more closely, we see this pattern won't work because it fits all the options except (D), loaf : bread. So, we need a more specific pattern. One possibility is Covering-to-What-is-Covered. A "shell" covers a "walnut." Now we can eliminate (E), since the ROOT doesn't cover the TREE, and also (C), since ICING doesn't cover the bottom of the CAKE. That leaves options (A) coating : candy and (B) peel : banana. So, what is different about a coating for a candy and the peel of a banana? The difference is that COATING on CANDY is edible, but PEEL on a BANANA is not. Since the shell of a walnut is not edible, we can eliminate (A). This means that (B) is the exact match.

Completing the following questions will help you learn to apply the information you have just studied.

> **DIRECTIONS**: Each question below consists of a related pair of words or phrases, followed by five lettered pairs of words or phrases. Select the lettered pair that best expresses a relationship similar to that expressed in the original pair.

• **PROBLEM 2-1**

MINISTER : BIBLE ::

(A) secretary : shoes

(B) Shakespeare : play

(C) comb : cosmetologist

(D) carpenter : hammer

(E) swimmer : dive

SOLUTION:

(D)   In this pair of words, the first word describes an occupation and the second is a tool without which someone working in this occupation cannot do his/her job. A MINISTER uses a BIBLE in his/her work as a CARPENTER uses a HAMMER in his/her work.

(A) is incorrect, because although a SECRETARY wears SHOES to work, they are not essential for his/her work. A COSMETOLOGIST also uses a COMB in his/her work (C), but these words are in the reverse order from the first pair. SHAKESPEARE did not use a PLAY (B); he wrote them. (E) Although a SWIMMER dives in the course of work, DIVE is a verb, and BIBLE is a noun.

• **PROBLEM 2-2**

WALK : SAUNTER ::

(A) desecrate : profane

(B) rise : risen

(C) banter : converse

(D) nullify : annul

(E) talk : whisper

SOLUTION:

(E)   The first word is a broad and general verb which is fairly neutral. The second word is a type of the first, which is more specific and has certain connotations. SAUNTER is a way to WALK, so the best answer is (E) because WHISPER is a way to TALK.

In choice (A) rather than one word being a type of the other, they are synonyms. (B) RISE and RISEN are simply two forms of the same verb. Choice (C) is similar to the original words, but the pair is presented in the opposite order, since BANTER, meaning talking playfully, is a specific kind of CONVERSING. (D) NULLIFY and ANNUL are synonymous.

• PROBLEM 2-3

PHILANTHROPIST : MONEY ::

(A) bigot : prejudice

(B) humanitarian : time

(C) doctor : medicine

(D) mother : cookies

(E) attorney : law

SOLUTION:

(B)   A PHILANTHROPIST is charitable with MONEY, while a HU-MANITARIAN is known for generously giving TIME to help others.

(A) While a BIGOT has PREJUDICE, it is not something given generously.

The people described in choices (C) and (E) are also known for dealing with the word described in the second item in each pair, but those are paid occupations whereas philanthropists and humanitarians are charitable and donate their money or time.

(D) A MOTHER's primary gift is not COOKIES, and not all mothers necessarily make cookies.

• PROBLEM 2-4

POACHER : GAME ::

(A) thief : property

(B) traitor : country

(C) dictator : law

(D) prisoner : jail

(E) referee : penalty

SOLUTION:

(A)   Poachers are defined by what they take illegally. A POACHER obtains GAME illegally. The same relationship exists for (A) THIEF : PROPERTY, since a thief obtains property illegally. This relationship is not present in the other alternatives. (B) A TRAITOR betrays a COUN-TRY rather than obtaining it. (C) DICTATOR : LAW has no necessary relationship. (D) A PRISONER is one who is in JAIL. (E) A REFEREE gives a PENALTY.

• PROBLEM 2-5

FRAGRANT : SMELL ::

(A) insipid : taste

(B) puzzling : memory

(C) oily : touch

(D) blurred : vision

(E) melodious : sound

SOLUTION:

(E) SMELL is a neutral word and FRAGRANT is an adjective which can be added to give it positive connotations. FRAGRANT is used to describe a pleasant SMELL. The same relationship exists for (E) MELODIOUS : SOUND, since melodious is used to describe a pleasant sound.

This relationship is not present in the other alternatives. In the remaining pairs of words, the first word is an adjective which adds specific connotations in the noun which is the second word, but in each case they are negative connotations.

• PROBLEM 2-6

DAY : MONTH ::

(A) time : year

(B) life : death

(C) word : grammar

(D) actor : script

(E) letter : alphabet

SOLUTION:

(E) A DAY is an individual component of a MONTH, and it has the same fixed number for each month every year. A DAY is one part of a MONTH. The same relationship exists for (E) LETTER : ALPHABET, since a letter is one part of the alphabet and each alphabet has a fixed number of letters.

(A) A YEAR is an individual component of TIME, but time is a much vaguer, broader word than MONTH, and there are not a fixed number of years in TIME. Furthermore, the pair appears in the opposite order.

(C) GRAMMAR is the study of WORD forms and arrangements, so word is directly related to grammar, but not as a component of a fixed number.

(D) A SCRIPT is a tool that an ACTOR uses.

• PROBLEM 2-7

ORIGAMI : PAPER ::

(A) ceramics : clay

(D) cathedral: stained glass

(B) sculpture : mold

(E) carving : wood

(C) recycling : aluminum

SOLUTION:

(A) ORIGAMI is the art of folding PAPER to make figures. Therefore, *paper* is the medium always associated with ORIGAMI. CERAMICS is the art of shaping CLAY to make figures, and clay is the medium always associated with ceramics, so (A) is the best choice.

(B) MOLD is a method rather than a medium used in the making of a SCULPTURE.

(C) RECYCLING may or may not involve ALUMINUM, and recycling is not an object or an art but a process.

(D) A CATHEDRAL might have STAINED GLASS in it, but it is not made necessarily or entirely of stained glass. Similarly, (E) CARVING may be done in WOOD, but this is not always the case. It is not a defining quality of it.

• PROBLEM 2-8

WRITER : DRAFT ::

(A) architect : building

(D) chef : souffle

(B) artist : sketch

(E) carpenter : awl

(C) minister : sermon

SOLUTION:

(B) A DRAFT is an unfinished product from a WRITER, just as a SKETCH is from an ARTIST. Choices (A), (C), and (D) also deal with the person and the product he produces, but all imply a finished product, not a stage in the process. Choice (E) also deals with a creative person, but an AWL is the tool a CARPENTER uses to finish his product.

• PROBLEM 2-9

TEACHER : CLASSROOM ::

(A) programmer : computer   (D) children : playground

(B) soldier : war   (E) judge : courtroom

(C) spouse : wife

SOLUTION:

(E) The first noun describes a professional person and the second noun describes a room most likely to be occupied by this person when engaged in this profession. A TEACHER works in a CLASSROOM as a JUDGE works in a COURTROOM. A COMPUTER is the tool a PROGRAMMER uses (A), WAR is the activity a SOLDIER is engaged in (B), and a WIFE is a SPOUSE (C). None of these options (A–C) contains a noun which is a place. CHILDREN play rather than work on a PLAYGROUND (D).

• PROBLEM 2-10

GAGGLE : GEESE ::

(A) players : team   (D) fish : school

(B) sheep : flock   (E) pack : wolves

(C) lions : pride

SOLUTION:

(E) A GAGGLE is the name of the social group of GEESE. The other choices also deal with social groups and members, but the individual members come first and the group name comes second in every choice except (E).

• PROBLEM 2-11

CHILE : CHILEAN ::

(A) Mongolia : Mongoloid   (D) Asia : Asian

(B) New York : New Yorker   (E) Canada : Canadian

(C) Peruvian : Peru

SOLUTION:

(E)   CHILEAN is the name given to a person who inhabits the country of CHILE. Choice (A) is a country, but its residents are called Mongolians. Choices (B) and (D) are also locations and the names given to their inhabitants, but one is a city and the other is a continent. Choice (C) is a country with the proper name given for its inhabitants, but it is presented in the reverse order from the initial pair.

• PROBLEM 2-12

CATERPILLAR : BUTTERFLY ::

(A) oyster : pearl   (D) raisin : grape

(B) tadpole : frog   (E) politician : lawyer

(C) clay : sculpture

SOLUTION:

(B)   A CATERPILLAR is the larval form of a BUTTERFLY. The same relationship exists for (B) TADPOLE : FROG. This relationship is not present in the other alternatives.

(A) An OYSTER is not a larval form of a PEARL. A pearl is a separate object that happens to grow inside of certain oysters.

(C) CLAY will not grow to be a SCULPTURE, and (E) a POLITICIAN will not grow to be a LAWYER. (D) A RAISIN is what a GRAPE starts out as when it is young, but what it may become if it is old and dried out.

• PROBLEM 2-13

GLUTTONY : STARVATION ::

(A) nutrition : health   (D) miser : wealth

(B) hunger : anorexia   (E) lavishness : luxury

(C) ignorant : knowledgeable

SOLUTION:

(C)   GLUTTONY means overeating, and STARVATION occurs when someone does not eat at all, so GLUTTONY is the opposite of STARVATION. The same relationship exists for (C) IGNORANT : KNOWLEDGEABLE since they, too, are antonyms.

    This relationship is not present in the other alternatives. (A) NUTRITION : HEALTH are similar, not opposites. (B) Someone who has ANOREXIA might not allow themselves to eat, but they still feel HUNGER; these words are not antonyms. (D) MISER is one who is stingy with WEALTH. (E) LAVISHNESS : LUXURY are synonyms, not antonyms.

• PROBLEM 2-14

CALORIE : HEAT ::

(A) sand : cement   (D) caliper : diameter

(B) succumb : yield   (E) retaliation : forgiveness

(C) metronome : music

SOLUTION:

(D)   A CALORIE measures HEAT, and a CALIPER measures DIAMETER (D). SAND is an ingredient of CEMENT (A); SUCCUMB and YIELD are synonyms (B); a METRONOME provides a consistent beat for MUSIC (C); and (E) RETALIATION is an opposite of FORGIVENESS.

• PROBLEM 2-15

CHEF : KITCHEN ::

(A) scientist : chemical

(B) physician : hospital

(C) guest : restaurant

(D) librarian : novel

(E) athlete : exercise

SOLUTION:

(B) Once again the first word is a noun describing a person in a certain profession, and the second noun is the place in which they work. A CHEF works in a KITCHEN as a (B) PHYSICIAN works in a HOSPITAL. Only one of the remaining options has a place for the second option (C) RESTAURANT. This option is incorrect because being a GUEST is not a profession, so a GUEST does not work in a RESTAURANT.

• PROBLEM 2-16

COMPULSORY : REQUIRED ::

(A) committed : promised

(B) normal : aberrant

(C) freedom : democracy

(D) voluntary : mandatory

(E) education : intelligence

SOLUTION:

(A) The words COMPULSORY and REQUIRED are synonyms. The only pair of words which shares this synonymous relationship are COMMITTED and PROMISED. Therefore, (A) is the correct choice. NORMAL and ABERRANT and VOLUNTARY and MANDATORY are antonyms. FREEDOM is hopefully a product of DEMOCRACY as INTELLIGENCE is of EDUCATION, but these pairs are not synonymous.

• PROBLEM 2-17

SUN : STARS ::

(A) piranha : fish

(B) plank : block

(C) ovicidal : chemical

(D) shrub : tree

(E) emotion : mood

SOLUTION:

(A)   STARS is a broad class of celestial body, and a SUN is a more specific member of that class. The same relationship exists in choice (A). A FISH is a broad class of creature that lives under water, and a PIRANHA is a more specific member of that class. SUN and STARS as well as PIRANHA and FISH are in a member-class relationship. PLANK and BLOCK possess a synonymous relationship as do EMOTION and MOOD. SHRUB and TREE are both members of a larger category. OVICIDAL and CHEMICAL are cause and effect.

• PROBLEM 2-18

OPPOSE : ADVOCATE ::

(A) attack : terrorist   (D) protest : student

(B) calculate : computer   (E) relax : child

(C) sleep : insomniac

SOLUTION:

(C)   An ADVOCATE is one who is in favor of something. Therefore, OPPOSE is an antonym of the verb to describe the action of an advocate. The same relationship exists for (C) SLEEP : INSOMNIAC since an insomniac is someone who does not sleep. This relationship is not present in the other alternatives. A TERRORIST does ATTACK. A COMPUTER does CALCULATE. A STUDENT may PROTEST. RELAX : CHILD does not have a necessary relationship.

• PROBLEM 2-19

ALLUDE : HINT ::

(A) shy : conspicuous   (D) self-conscious : assertive

(B) boisterous : obstreperous   (E) inference : deduction

(C) intelligent : sagacious

SOLUTION:

(E) The verbs ALLUDE and HINT are synonyms. There are no other verbs among the choices, but INFERENCE and DEDUCTION are synonymous nouns with similar meanings. SHY and CONSPICUOUS are not antonyms but they are contradictory. Shy suggests being easily frightened, disposed to avoid people, and conspicuous denotes the desire to attract attention. OBSTREPEROUS and BOISTEROUS are synonyms implying loud action. INTELLIGENT and SAGACIOUS are synonyms implying the ability to know. SELF-CONSCIOUS and ASSERTIVE are antonyms.

• PROBLEM 2-20

AFFABLE : FRIENDLY ::

(A) fun : smile

(B) amicable : congenial

(C) hilarious : delight

(D) speak : conversation

(E) outspoken : taciturn

SOLUTION:

(B) AFFABLE and FRIENDLY are synonymous adjectives. (B) is the correct answer because AMICABLE and CONGENIAL are synonymous adjectives as well. FUN and SMILE are related through a cause-and-effect relationship. Fun provides amusement or enjoyment producing the smile. HILARIOUS and DELIGHT are similarly related because hilarious is an exhilaration of the spirit which is expressed in an emotion called delight. SPEAK and CONVERSATION are not synonymous, one speaks during a conversation. TACITURN and OUTSPOKEN are antonyms, taciturn meaning inclined not to talk, while outspoken means inclined to speak.

• PROBLEM 2-21

QUILL : FOUNTAIN PEN ::

(A) rural : urban

(B) young : old

(C) truce : peace

(D) solo : quartet

(E) mangle : iron

SOLUTION:

(C) A QUILL is a precursor of a FOUNTAIN PEN. In the correct choice, (C), a TRUCE is a precursor of PEACE. The relationship in (A) RURAL : URBAN is one of opposites and in (B) YOUNG : OLD is one of progression. A young person, in time, progresses in age and becomes old. The relationship in (D) SOLO : QUARTET is a numerical one, specifically a one-to-four relationship. In choice (E), both a MANGLE and an IRON serve the same purpose, but a mangle is specifically designed to iron certain kind of items.

• PROBLEM 2–22

PEN : PIG ::

(A) sky : bird

(D) jungle : lion

(B) coop : chicken

(E) garage : dog

(C) hole : mouse

SOLUTION:

(C) A PEN is a confinement for a PIG. The same relationship exists for (C) COOP : CHICKEN, since a coop is a confinement for a chicken. This relationship is not present in the other choices. They each describe places where the animals may live, but not in which they are confined against their will.

• PROBLEM 2–23

FROWN : ANGER ::

(A) jest : joke

(D) tantrum : joy

(B) smile : picture

(E) nod : attention

(C) yawn : boredom

SOLUTION:

(C) The second word is an emotion, and the first is a facial expression caused by that emotion. A FROWN is an expression of ANGER. The same relationship exists for (C) YAWN : BOREDOM, since yawn is an expression of boredom. This relationship is not present in the other choices. (A) JEST and JOKE are synonyms. (B) A SMILE might be an expression in a PICTURE, but it is not an expression of a picture, and a picture is not an emotion.

• PROBLEM 2-24

DESIRE : WANT ::

(A) evade : dodge   (D) aspire : seek

(B) lampoon : ridicule   (E) avidity : greed

(C) disdain : inattention

SOLUTION:

(E) DESIRE is a longing or craving that is a more intense form of WANT, just as AVIDITY is a consuming GREED. Therefore, DESIRE and AVIDITY denote a maximum degree of WANT and GREED. (A) EVADE and DODGE are nearly synonymous, both meaning to avoid or escape. (B) LAMPOON and RIDICULE are also nearly synonymous, both meaning bitter satire or mocking. (C) DISDAIN suggests looking upon something with scorn. INATTENTION implies a lack of concentration. (D) ASPIRE and SEEK are synonymous, both implying the searching for and laboring to attain. In nine of the remaining synonymous pairs is one word to a greater degree than the other.

• PROBLEM 2-25

VARIABLE : EQUATION ::

(A) oxygen : water   (D) clay : sculpture

(B) paramecia : amoeba   (E) furnace : heat

(C) analysis : summary

SOLUTION:

(A) An EQUATION is something complex made up of simpler components. A VARIABLE is one of those simpler components. An equation contains variables. The analogy here is that of simple to complex. The correct choice is (A) OXYGEN : WATER. OXYGEN is a simpler element than WATER, which contains both hydrogen and oxygen. PARAMECIA and AMOEBA (B) are both simple one-celled life forms.

In choice (C) ANALYSIS : SUMMARY, the first term identifies a more complex process than the second term. Here the relationship is complex to simple. (D) CLAY : SCULPTURE presents an analogy of use: CLAY is used to make a SCULPTURE. (E) FURNACE : HEAT is an analogy of function; a FURNACE produces HEAT.

• PROBLEM 2–26

SAND : DUNE ::

(A) tree : forest

(B) rock : boulder

(C) shower : deluge

(D) clamor : tumult

(E) twig : log

SOLUTION:

(A)   The key relationship here is multiplicity. Many grains of SAND may form a DUNE. The answer is (A) because many TREES may form a FOREST. (B) is wrong because many ROCKS do not form a BOULDER, and (E) is wrong because many TWIGS do not form a LOG. CLAMOR and TUMULT (D) are interchangeable terms, and SHOWER : DELUGE (C) present a relationship of intensity. A light rain or shower, when intensified, becomes a deluge.

• PROBLEM 2–27

ARC : CIRCLE ::

(A) moon : earth

(B) hour : day

(C) cabin : mansion

(D) exercise : rest

(E) knowledge : wisdom

SOLUTION:

(B)   An ARC is one part, component, or segment of the CIRCLE. The correct choice is (B), an HOUR is one part of or segment of a DAY. MOON : EARTH (A) are both examples of celestial bodies. Their relationship is, as in choice (C), one of size. CABINS are small and MAN-

SIONS are large, but both are places to live; again, both are examples of the same entity—homes. (D) EXERCISE and REST are both components of a healthy lifestyle, rather than one being a component of the other. The relationship in choice (E) is one of like terms.

• PROBLEM 2-28

MINUTE : HOUR ::

(A) meter : kilometer   (D) student : class

(B) alto : choir   (E) boxcar : train

(C) state : federation

SOLUTION:

(A) This analogy is one of part to whole, but also includes the idea of progression. A certain number of MINUTES must elapse before an HOUR has passed. Likewise, in choice (A) METER : KILOMETER, a certain number of meters is required to be in place before a kilometer can be said to exist. Choice (B) CHOIR may have any number of ALTOS or even no altos and can still exist. Choice (C) FEDERATION may have any number of STATES, and choice (E) TRAIN may have any number of BOXCARS.

• PROBLEM 2-29

HARD-HEARTED : EMPATHY ::

(A) ambivalent : decisiveness   (D) creative : dogmatism

(B) assertive : independence   (E) avenge : friendship

(C) competitive : adversary

SOLUTION:

(A) HARD-HEARTED is an adjective to describe a person, and EM-PATHY is the character trait without which one will be hard-hearted. A person who is HARD-HEARTED lacks EMPATHY. The same relationship is evident in choice (A) AMBIVALENT : DECISIVENESS, as a person who is ambivalent lacks decisiveness. This relationship does not exist in the alternative pairs given. ASSERTIVE, COMPETITIVE, and CREATIVE are all adjectives to describe a person, but none of the words which follow are directly inversely related to them, as EMPATHY is to HARD-HEARTED. AVENGE is not an adjective.

• PROBLEM 2-30

COCOON : BUTTERFLY ::

(A) apple : pie

(B) blossom : fruit

(C) awareness : understanding

(D) adolescent : adult

(E) wood : house

SOLUTION:

(D) There are several stages of growth in the life of a butterfly. A COCOON is the penultimate one. A COCOON undergoes a metamorphosis which results in a changed form and appearance and produces a butterfly. This relationship also exists in choice (D) ADOLESCENT : ADULT, as adolescence is the stage a human goes through immediately prior to becoming an adult. (A) PIES can be made from APPLES and (E) HOUSES can be made from WOOD, but this happens only after the tree or fruit are dead, and is not a stage in their growth. In relation to choice (B) BLOSSOM : FRUIT, pollination is an external happening without which step the fruit does not appear. Choice (C) AWARENESS : UNDERSTANDING is incorrect because awareness does not always result in understanding.

• PROBLEM 2-31

NERVOUS : POISE ::

(A) angry : sensibility

(B) frightened : confidence

(C) empathetic : rationality

(D) energetic : enthusiasm

(E) calm : laziness

SOLUTION:

(B) To be NERVOUS is to lack POISE. This relationship also exists in choice (B) FRIGHTENED : CONFIDENCE. To be frightened is to lack confidence. Choice (A) ANGRY : SENSIBILITY is not right because sensibility (the capacity for physical sensation) can be present simultaneously with anger. Similarly, choice (C) EMPATHETIC : RATIONAL-ITY is incorrect because a person can be rational and also be emphathetic. (D) ENERGETIC : ENTHUSIASM is incorrect because an energetic person is defined as having enthusiasm rather than lacking it. (E) CALM : LAZINESS is incorrect because a calm person may or may not lack laziness, there is no necessary relation.

• PROBLEM 2-32

VULGAR : CRUDE ::

(A) attractive : personality

(B) tedious : charming

(C) bawdy : amusing

(D) biased : prejudiced

(E) intelligent : brain

SOLUTION:

(D)   The correct choice is (D) because VULGAR and CRUDE are synonyms, so we could express the relationship between the two words by saying that VULGAR means the same thing as CRUDE. The only choice that expresses the same relationship is (D). BIASED is a synonym of PREJUDICED.

(A) is incorrect because ATTRACTIVE is not a synonym of PERSONALITY.

(B) is the wrong choice because TEDIOUS does not mean the same thing as CHARMING. The words are not synonyms.

(C) is incorrect. If something is BAWDY it might be AMUSING; however, the two words are not synonyms of each other.

(E) is wrong because INTELLIGENT is related to BRAIN, but is not a synonym.

• PROBLEM 2-33

ACCOUNTANT : CALCULATOR ::

(A) actor : stage

(B) mechanic : screwdriver

(C) student : school

(D) senator : page

(E) waitress : restaurant

SOLUTION:

(B) The first word is a noun for a person engaged in a certain profession, and the second is a noun for an inanimate object which is a tool for someone working in that profession. An ACCOUNTANT uses a CALCULATOR, or an ACCOUNTANT works with a CALCULATOR. The best choice expresses the same kind of relationship: A MECHANIC uses (works with) a SCREWDRIVER.

Choice (A) is wrong because although an ACTOR uses a STAGE to work on, the STAGE is not a device used in the work.

Choice (C) is incorrect because a STUDENT works *in* a SCHOOL not *with* a school as a tool.

Choice (D) is wrong because a PAGE is a young person who works for the SENATOR so the senator may use the page, but not as an inanimate tool.

Choice (E) is wrong because a WAITRESS works in a RESTAURANT.

• PROBLEM 2–34

TINGE : COLOR ::

(A) anger : disapproval

(B) illusion : dream

(C) wave : hand

(D) whisper : voice

(E) power : motor

SOLUTION:

(D) A TINGE is a slight (faint) amount of COLOR. Choice (D) is the best choice because a WHISPER is a faint VOICE. (A) is incorrect because ANGER is not a faint form of DISAPPROVAL. Similarly, an ILLUSION (mistaken idea) is not a faint DREAM (B). Choice (C) is wrong because you use your HAND to WAVE. A wave is not a slight hand. Finally, POWER and MOTOR (E) are not related in the same way as the original pair, because the word power on its own has the opposite connotations of faintness.

• PROBLEM 2-35

BENEVOLENT : MALIGNANT ::

(A) cooperative : resistant   (D) prowess : skill

(B) opaque : dark   (E) valid : resilient

(C) elfish : dwarf

SOLUTION:

(A) This pair of adjectives are antonyms. The two original words, BE-NEVOLENT (good, generous) and MALIGNANT (bad, harmful) have opposite meanings. Choice (A) expresses the same kind of relationship. If something is COOPERATIVE, then it is not RESISTANT. Choice (B) OPAQUE and DARK are nearly synonymous, not opposites, as are ELF-ISH and DWARF (C). PROWESS and SKILL (D) are also related in a synonymous manner. Choice (E) VALID and RESILIENT are not related in any significant way.

• PROBLEM 2-36

CONCENTRATE : DISPERSE ::

(A) impeach : president   (D) release : fantasy

(B) disdain : scorn   (E) erode : expand

(C) inflict : trouble

SOLUTION:

(E) This is a pair of verbs which are antonyms. CONCENTRATE (verb—to gather together) is the opposite of DISPERSE (verb—break up). The best choice is (E) because ERODE (wear away) is the opposite of EXPAND (enlarge).

Choice (A) is wrong because IMPEACH is not the opposite of PRESIDENT. Choice (B) is incorrect because DISDAIN and SCORN are synonyms, not opposites. Choice (C) is incorrect because INFLICT is not the opposite of TROUBLE. You can INFLICT TROUBLE on someone, but the words are not opposites. Choice (D) is wrong because a FAN-TASY might serve as a RELEASE; these words are not antonyms.

• PROBLEM 2-37

EPILOGUE : SPEECH ::

(A) bibliography : actor   (D) dessert : dinner

(B) prototype : car   (E) year : month

(C) footnote : author

SOLUTION:

(D)   The relationship between the given words can be expressed as: An EPILOGUE is the end (conclusion) of a SPEECH. (D) is the best choice because a DESSERT is the end of a DINNER. Choice (A) is wrong because BIBLIOGRAPHY and ACTOR are not necessarily related. Choice (B) is wrong because a PROTOTYPE (original model) is not the end of a CAR. Just as in choice (C) a FOOTNOTE is not the end of an AUTHOR. Choice (E) a YEAR is made up of many MONTHS from beginning to end a month is not a terminal stage of a year.

• PROBLEM 2-38

ANTHOLOGY : POEMS ::

(A) word : mail   (D) forest : trees

(B) grass : concrete   (E) snow : ice

(C) cover : novels

SOLUTION:

(D)   The relationship between the given words can be expressed as: An ANTHOLOGY contains many POEMS. The best choice is (D), because a FOREST contains many TREES. Choice (A) is wrong because although MAIL might be made up of WORDS, this pair is in the reverse order to the original pair. Choice (B) is wrong because GRASS and CONCRETE are very different substances; one is not made of the other. Choice (C) is wrong because although a NOVEL probably has a COVER. it is not composed essentially of covers. Choice (E) is wrong, because SNOW and ICE may both be made of water, but they are not made of each other.

• PROBLEM 2-39

REQUEST : EXTORT ::

(A) respond : letter

(B) cheer : smile

(C) mute : speech

(D) defer : judgment

(E) entertain : regale

SOLUTION:

(E)   A REQUEST is a mild form of EXTORT. If you REQUEST some-
thing, you ask for it. If you EXTORT something, you get it by force.
Choice (E) is the answer because ENTERTAIN is a mild form of RE-
GALE (entertain lavishly). Choice (A) is incorrect, because RESPOND
and LETTER are not related in the same manner as REQUEST and EX-
TORT. (B) is wrong because CHEER is not a form of SMILE. MUTE is
not a mild form of SPEECH (C). A MUTE has no form of SPEECH.
DEFER and JUDGMENT (D) have no definite relationship.

• PROBLEM 2-40

EDIFICE : FACADE ::

(A) dorsal : ventral

(B) turtle : shell

(C) anachronism : chronologic

(D) body : skeleton

(E) counterfeit : fraudulent

SOLUTION:

(B)   This pair of words is related as a whole to one of its parts. An
EDIFICE is a building, and a FACADE is the front of a building. More
specifically it is the part that people are most likely to see. The same
relationship exists for (B). A TURTLE is the whole object, and the
SHELL is the part of the turtle which people are most likely to see.

(A) DORSAL (back) and VENTRAL (front) are both words for a
part of something, neither describes the whole object.

Since an ANACHRONISM (C) is something which is not in its
proper historical time, it cannot be a part of something CHRONOLOGIC
(arranged in the correct temporal order).

A SKELETON (D) is a part of the BODY, but it is the inner part, not
the part which people are likely to see.

(E) COUNTERFEIT and FRAUDULENT are synonyms.

• PROBLEM 2-41

CRUEL : ATROCIOUS ::

(A) stable : mercurial

(B) athletic : energetic

(C) tired : introverted

(D) interested : consumed

(E) accidental : intrinsic

SOLUTION:

(D) The definition of ATROCIOUS is "very cruel"; therefore, CRUEL is a synonym of lesser degree for ATROCIOUS. The same relationship exists for (D) INTERESTED : CONSUMED as someone consumed with something is very interested in it. This relationship is not present in the other alternatives. (A) STABLE is the opposite of MERCURIAL. Someone (B) ENERGETIC might not be ATHLETIC, so these are not two degrees of similar words. (C) TIRED : INTROVERTED has no necessary relationship. (E) ACCIDENTAL and INTRINSIC are contradictory ideas.

• PROBLEM 2-42

TWEETER : WOOFER ::

(A) grade : slope

(B) high : low

(C) replicate : duplicate

(D) tutelage : protection

(E) equivalent : equal

SOLUTION:

(B) A TWEETER is a small loudspeaker for reproducing high-frequency sounds, while a WOOFER is a large loudspeaker for reproducing low-frequency sounds. (B) HIGH : LOW identifies this relationship also. The other choices, (A), (C), (D), and (E), all express synonymous relationships.

• PROBLEM 2-43

GAUNTLET : HAND ::

(A) cannon : ball

(B) sword : hand

(C) body : shield

(D) lance : shield

(E) armor : body

SOLUTION:

(E)   A GAUNTLET is a protective device for the HAND. Just as AR-MOR is a protective suit for the BODY. CANONS and SWORDS are not defensive, or protective, they are offensive. A SHIELD does protect the BODY, but the words are in the opposite order. (C) is incorrect. A SHIELD is a protection *against* a LANCE not *for* a lance. (D) is incorrect.

• PROBLEM 2-44

ECOLOGIST : ENVIRONMENT ::

(A) psychologist : plants

(B) botanist : animals

(C) geologist : earth

(D) ventriloquist : dummy

(E) cartographer : people

SOLUTION:

(C)   ECOLOGIST is a noun to describe someone that specializes in a certain field of study, and ENVIRONMENT is the noun to describe that field of study. The pattern is that of an expert to a field of expertise. The correct answer is (C) because a GEOLOGIST studies the EARTH. (A), (B), and (E) are incorrect because the expert does not match his field of expertise. (D) is incorrect because a DUMMY is a prop used in the VENTRILOQUIST's act.

• PROBLEM 2-45

IMPROMPTU : MEMORIZED ::

(A) spontaneous : calculated   (D) unrehearsed : extemporaneous

(B) recited : read   (E) tacit : verbose

(C) glib : forced

SOLUTION:

(A)   The pattern for this pair of words is something unstudied opposed to something which must be learned and practiced. Something IM-PROMPTU cannot be studied beforehand, while it takes a lot of time and work to MEMORIZE something. The same relationship exists for (A). Something SPONTANEOUS is immediate and requires no preparation, whereas something CALCULATED is planned and worked on prior to its execution. (B) has a similar relationship, but the words are in the reverse order. The pair of words in (C) and in (E) are antonyms. In (D) the pair of words are synonyms.

• PROBLEM 2-46

VACILLATE : CHANGE ::

(A) vacate : rent   (D) fluctuate : move

(B) index : chart   (E) endure : stamina

(C) trend : graph

SOLUTION:

(D)   Both VACILLATE and CHANGE are verbs, with the first verb being similar to the second, but more specific. To VACILLATE is a way of CHANGING. A similar relationship exists for the verbs in (D), to FLUCTUATE is a way of MOVING. Choices (B), (C), and (E) are incorrect because the words are not verbs. Choice (A) is wrong because to VACATE and to RENT are contradictory rather than similar actions.

• PROBLEM 2-47

BEACH : LIFEGUARD ::

(A) fish : fisherman

(B) forest : ranger

(C) doctor : hospital

(D) mountain : climber

(E) restaurant : supplier

SOLUTION:

(B)   The correct response is (B). The relationship is that of a territory to its guardian. A RANGER guards a FOREST as a LIFEGUARD guards a BEACH. (A) is incorrect because FISH is not a territory. (C) is incorrect because the order is reversed, and because a DOCTOR works in a HOSPI-TAL, but does not guard it. (D) is wrong because a CLIMBER scales a MOUNTAIN for sport, it's not her or his job to guard it. (E) is incorrect because, although a SUPPLIER keeps a RESTAURANT open and running, it does not in any way guard or protect it.

• PROBLEM 2-48

BULB : TULIP ::

(A) pistil : stamen

(B) root : grass

(C) tree : leaf

(D) rose : thorn

(E) acorn : oak

SOLUTION:

(E)   A BULB is the seed planted in soil from which a TULIP will grow. The answer is (E) because the relationship is that of a seed, or a part that grows into the whole. A BULB grows into a TULIP as an ACORN grows into an OAK. (A) and (B) are incorrect because, although they are parts of a whole, they do not grow into, or form the basis of the product. (C) and (D) are incorrect because they depict the relationship between parts of the whole, but without causality. A THORN and LEAf are not seeds and they do not lie under the soil.

• PROBLEM 2-49

PROBLEM : SOLUTION ::

(A) crossword puzzle : design   (D) password : entry

(B) suitcase : handle   (E) door : key

(C) frame : window

SOLUTION:

(E) The correct response is (E). A KEY is used to unlock a DOOR just as a SOLUTION can unlock a PROBLEM. DESIGN and CROSSWORD PUZZLE (A) is not correct because the design of the crossword puzzle does not unlock it. A SUITCASE is carried by its HANDLE so (B) does not fit the pattern. (C) is incorrect because a FRAME holds a WINDOW and does not unlock or solve it. A PASSWORD may permit ENTRY (D), but this is not as good a response as (E), because the words appear in reverse order to the original pair.

• PROBLEM 2-50

GOSSIP : HAMLET ::

(A) village : reputation   (D) chapter : book

(B) truth : story   (E) rumor : newspaper

(C) press : nation

SOLUTION:

(C) The first word is a medium through which news is broadcast, and the second is the size of the place in which this occurs. The larger the place, the more sophistication necessary in order to spread information. Therefore, news is spread in a small town or HAMLET through GOSSIP, but to reach an entire NATION, a more complicated system of PRESS is necessary. (A) is incorrect because the place comes first, and because REPUTATION is not a means of spreading news. The remainder of the options are incorrect because none of them contain a word meaning a place.

• PROBLEM 2-51

LOOM : DISASTER ::

(A) impend : catastrophe   (D) question : puzzle

(B) howl : storm   (E) imminent : eminent

(C) hurt : penalty

SOLUTION:

(A) DISASTER is a noun meaning calamity, and LOOM is a verb describing the threat of the disaster before it actually occurs. A similar relationship exists in choice (A), IMPEND is a verb describing the threat of a CATASTROPHE. None of the remaining pairs of words share this relationship.

• PROBLEM 2-52

TALON : HAWK ::

(A) fang : snake   (D) tail : monkey

(B) horn : bull   (E) shell : tortoise

(C) claw : tiger

SOLUTION:

(C) A HAWK is a bird of prey, and a TALON is the claw, or hand-like appendage of the hawk. The same relationship exists in (C), because a CLAW is the hand-like appendage of the TIGER. The remaining options all describe animals and parts of animals, as the original pair does, but they are not correct because the part they describe is not that which corresponds to a hand.

• PROBLEM 2-53

REHEARSAL : PLAY ::

(A) draft : essay   (D) recital : concert

(B) manual : process   (E) journal : news

(C) applause : performance

SOLUTION:

(A) The correct response is (A) because the pattern fits that of a practice piece to the actual product. (B) is incorrect because a MANUAL describes a PROCESS; (C) is not correct because APPLAUSE shows appreciation for a PERFORMANCE; and in (D), both a RECITAL and a CONCERT are forms of performances. (E) is incorrect because a JOURNAL is a medium for the NEWS.

• PROBLEM 2-54

REFLEX : INVOLUNTARY ::

(A) apparition : real

(B) impulse : sudden

(C) kick : dangerous

(D) detail : general

(E) spasm : lengthy

SOLUTION:

(B) REFLEX is a noun, and INVOLUNTARY is an adjective to describe the nature of that noun. The same relationship exists for (B), because an IMPULSE is by definition SUDDEN. (A) and (D) are wrong because in each case the second word is an adjective which is antithetical to that which would describe the noun. (C) and (E) are wrong because the first word is a verb, not a noun, and the adjective is either inappropriate or antithetical.

• PROBLEM 2-55

ANARCHY : GOVERNMENT ::

(A) royalty : crown

(B) trivia : question

(C) vagrant : abode

(D) belief : superstition

(E) size : measurement

SOLUTION:

(C) ANARCHY is lack of GOVERNMENT. The same relationship exists for (C) VAGRANT : ABODE since a vagrant lacks an abode. This relationship is not present in the other choices. (A) A CROWN is a symbol of ROYALTY. (B) TRIVIA : QUESTION has no necessary relationship. (D) BELIEF : SUPERSTITION are synonyms. (E) SIZE is a type of MEASUREMENT.

• PROBLEM 2-56

CIRCULATORY : HEART ::

(A) excretory : sweat

(B) neurological : skeleton

(C) lungs : respiratory

(D) digestive : kidney

(E) reproductive : testes

SOLUTION:

(E) The HEART is a part of the CIRCULATORY system. The part comes before the whole in this analogy. Since the TESTES are a part of the male REPRODUCTIVE system, (E) is the answer. The EXCRETORY system of the body secretes SWEAT, but the analogy is not *whole to part* because sweat is not a part of the system. (A) is incorrect. The NEUROLOGICAL system involves the nervous system. The SKELETON is a part of the skeletal system, therefore, (B) is incorrect. The LUNGS are a part of the RESPIRATORY system, but the order is reversed, therefore, (C) is incorrect. A KIDNEY is not a part of the DIGESTIVE system, so (D) is not an appropriate answer.

• PROBLEM 2-57

REMOVAL : EXPURGATE ::

(A) consummation : initiate

(B) stimulation : kindle

(C) negligence : think

(D) ejection : possess

(E) lecture : mumble

SOLUTION:

(B) EXPURGATE means to cause the REMOVAL of something. The same relationship exists for (B) STIMULATION : KINDLE since kindle means to cause the stimulation of something. This relationship is not present in the other alternatives. (A) INITIATE is to cause the beginning, not CONSUMMATION of something. (C) NEGLIGENCE occurs when one does not THINK. (D) EJECTION : POSSESS and (E) LECTURE : MUMBLE have no necessary relationship.

• PROBLEM 2–58

ANXIOUS : NEUROTIC ::

(A) lackadaisical : animated
(B) contemporary : archaic
(C) weak : decrepit

(D) special : temporary
(E) vivacious : ironic

SOLUTION:

(C) NEUROTIC is a higher degree of being ANXIOUS. The same relationship exists for (C) WEAK : DECREPIT, since decrepit is a higher degree of being weak. This relationship is not present in the other alternatives. (A) LACKADAISICAL is the opposite of ANIMATED. (B) CONTEMPORARY is the opposite of ARCHAIC. (D) SPECIAL : TEMPORARY has no necessary relationship. (E) VIVACIOUS : IRONIC has no necessary relationship.

• PROBLEM 2–59

SUN : SOLAR SYSTEM ::

(A) moon : earth
(B) island : archipelago
(C) galaxy : star

(D) molecule : atom
(E) verses : poem

SOLUTION:

(B) The relationship is part to system. An ISLAND is a part of an ARCHIPELAGO, or group of islands, so (B) is the answer. The SUN is a part of the SOLAR SYSTEM, along with the group of celestial bodies which revolve around it.

The MOON revolves around the EARTH; the moon is not a part of the earth. Therefore, (A) is not the answer.

A GALAXY is formed from STARS, but the order is not the same as in the example, so (C) is not correct. Similarly, though a MOLECULE is made from ATOMS; the order MOLECULE : ATOMS is once again reversed. (D) is incorrect.

(E) is a possible answer, but not the best one for the following reasons. The SUN is one part of the SOLAR SYSTEM; together with other bodies it makes up the whole system. VERSES do make up a POEM; there may be only verse in a poem, however. VERSES is plural in contrast to SUN (singular).

• PROBLEM 2-60

OASIS : FERTILITY ::

(A) dungeon : confinement

(B) desert : refreshment

(C) restaurant : privacy

(D) dream : reality

(E) hospital : silence

SOLUTION:

(A)   In this pair of words the first is a place, and the second is the defining characteristic associated with that place. OASIS is a place of FERTILITY. The same relationship exists for (A) DUNGEON : CONFINEMENT, since a dungeon is a place of confinement. This relationship is not present in the other choices. (B) DESERT is not a place of REFRESHMENT. (C) RESTAURANT is a public place, not a place of PRIVACY. (D) DREAM is the opposite of REALITY. (E) HOSPITAL : SILENCE has no necessary relationship.

• PROBLEM 2-61

FLEDGLING : BIRD ::

(A) rooster : chicken

(B) ewe : lamb

(C) stallion : horse

(D) pack : wolf

(E) calf : bull

SOLUTION:

(E)   FLEDGLING is an infant BIRD. The same relationship exists for (E) CALF : BULL, since a calf is an infant bull. This relationship is not present in the other alternatives. (A) ROOSTER is a male CHICKEN. (B) EWE is a female LAMB. (C) STALLION is an adult, male HORSE. (D) A PACK is a group of WOLVES.

• PROBLEM 2-62

MERIDIAN : PARALLEL ::

(A) east : west

(B) deep : shallow

(C) longitude : latitude

(D) map : globe

(E) compass : direction

SOLUTION:

(C) LONGITUDE and LATITUDE compare well with MERIDIAN and PARALLEL. Through MERIDIANS one arrives at LONGITUDE; through PARALLELS one arrives at LATITUDE. Both LONGITUDE and LATITUDE are used in determining locations as are MERIDIANS and PARALLELS making (C) the best answer. The two are not just opposite terms; they must be used together for location, computation, etc.

(A) EAST and WEST are opposite directions. (B) is not the best choice since DEEP and SHALLOW are opposite terms. A MAP is a drawing representing the earth's surface; a GLOBE is a sphere with a map of the world on it. The two are not necessarily used together. They do not have the same relationship as do MERIDIAN : PARALLEL. (D) is not the best choice. (E) A COMPASS is used to find DIRECTION.

• PROBLEM 2-63

ENTHUSIASTIC : FANATIC ::

(A) painful : physician

(B) nutritious : athlete

(C) respectful : child

(D) knowledgeable : reader

(E) dishonest : liar

SOLUTION:

(E) The second word is a type of person, and the first is a defining characteristic of that person. A FANATIC is a person who is extremely ENTHUSIASTIC. The same relationship exists for (E) DISHONEST: LIAR, since a liar is very dishonest. This relationship is not present in the other choices. (A) PAINFUL : PHYSICIAN has no necessary relationship. (B) An ATHLETE is not considered NUTRITIOUS. (C) A CHILD may or may not be RESPECTFUL just as (D) a READER may or may not be extremely KNOWLEDGEABLE.

• PROBLEM 2-64

HOURGLASS : SAND ::

(A) thermometer : mercury   (D) barometer : tremor

(B) ruler : inch   (E) voltmeter : radiation

(C) scale : number

SOLUTION:

(A) The first word describes a measuring device, and the second is the physical medium used for measurement which is contained within the device. An HOURGLASS measures time using SAND. The same relationship exists for (A) THERMOMETER : MERCURY, since a thermometer measures temperature using mercury. This relationship is not present in the other choices.

(B) A RULER uses INCHES to measure length, but an inch is not a physical medium. (C) A SCALE is a system of NUMBERS. (D) A BAROMETER measures atmospheric pressure, not the intensity of a TREMOR. (E) VOLTMETER : RADIATION has no necessary relationship.

• PROBLEM 2-65

THERMOMETER : TEMPERATURE ::

(A) ruler : length   (D) instrument : sound

(B) recipe : dessert   (E) poll : questions

(C) vote : election

SOLUTION:

(A) THERMOMETER is a tool used to measure TEMPERATURE. The same relationship exists for (A) RULER : LENGTH, since a ruler is used to measure length. This relationship does not exist for the other choices. (B) RECIPE does not measure DESSERT. (C) An ELECTION is made up of VOTES. (D) An INSTRUMENT creates SOUND. (E) A POLL is made up of QUESTIONS.

• PROBLEM 2-66

COMPOSER : BALLAD ::

(A) painter : canvas

(B) teacher : pupil

(C) artist : sculpture

(D) waiter : restaurant

(E) poet : words

SOLUTION:

(C)   A BALLAD is a specific type of musical piece which is created by a COMPOSER. The same relationship exists for (C) ARTIST : SCULPTURE since sculptures are created by artists (called sculptors). This relationship is not present in the other choices. (A) A PAINTER uses, but does not make, CANVAS. (B) A TEACHER instructs a PUPIL. (D) A WAITER works at a RESTAURANT. (E) A POET uses, but does not ordinarily make, WORDS.

• PROBLEM 2-67

CRITIC : EVALUATION ::

(A) climax : portrait

(B) sponsor : promotion

(C) reporter : entertainment

(D) poem : representation

(E) artist : mood

SOLUTION:

(B)   A CRITIC provides an EVALUATION of something. The same relationship exists for (B) SPONSOR : PROMOTION since a sponsor provides a promotion for something. This relationship is not present in the other choices. (A) CLIMAX : PORTRAIT has no necessary relationship. (C) A REPORTER may or may not provide ENTERTAINMENT. (D) POEM : REPRESENTATION has no necessary relationship. (E) An ARTIST may or may not provide a MOOD.

• PROBLEM 2-68

IMPERIAL : POWER ::

(A) authoritative : admiration

(D) valorous : fear

(B) kindred : sympathy

(E) adamant : opinion

(C) feckless : spirit

SOLUTION:

(E)   To be IMPERIAL is to possess strong POWER. The same relationship exists for (E) ADAMANT : OPINION, since to be adamant is to possess a strong opinion. This relationship is not present in the other choices. (A) AUTHORITATIVE : ADMIRATION and (B) KINDRED : SYMPATHY have no necessary relationship. (C) FECKLESS is to be without SPIRIT. (D) VALOROUS is to be without FEAR.

• PROBLEM 2-69

HEIGHT : SKYSCRAPER ::

(A) age : monument

(D) width : bridge

(B) dryness : desert

(E) time : flower

(C) depth : stream

SOLUTION:

(B)   A SKYSCRAPER is defined as having extreme HEIGHT. The same relationship exists for (B) DRYNESS : DESERT, since a desert has extreme dryness. This relationship is not present in the other choices. (A) AGE : MONUMENT has no necessary relationship. (C) A STREAM does not have extreme DEPTH, in fact it is usually quite shallow. (D) A BRIDGE may or may not have extreme WIDTH. (E) TIME : FLOWER has no necessary relationship.

• PROBLEM 2-70

SPINY : THORNS ::

(A) dimpled : indentations

(D) tied : bows

(B) sharp : pins

(E) pricked : needles

(C) pruned : skin

SOLUTION:

(A) SPINY is a word used to describe an object with THORNS. The same relationship exists for (A) DIMPLED : INDENTATIONS, since dimpled is a word used to describe something with indentations. This relationship is not present in the other choices.

(B) Although some types of PINS might be described as SHARP, there are other types such as clothespins which are not sharp at all.

(C) SKIN may or may not be PRUNED.

(D) TIED is a verb explaining how BOWS are created, not an adjective describing them. NEEDLES can PRICK (also a verb), but cannot be described as "pricked."

• PROBLEM 2-71

FACADE : BUILDING ::

(A) grill : car

(D) picture : frames

(B) tongue : shoe

(E) head : body

(C) sheath : knife

SOLUTION:

(A) A FACADE is the frontmost part of a BUILDING. The corresponding analogy is (A) GRILL : CAR. A grill is the frontmost part of a car. None of the other choices describe this relationship, as a TONGUE is on the top of a SHOE, a SHEATH is around a KNIFE, a PICTURE is in a FRAME, and a HEAD is on top of the BODY.

• PROBLEM 2-72

GENEROSITY : PHILANTHROPIST ::

(A) convert : missionary

(B) dexterity : surgeon

(C) crops : farmer

(D) students : teacher

(E) schizophrenics : psychologist

SOLUTION:

(B)   A PHILANTHROPIST is a person whose concern for mankind leads him or her to help worthy causes through GENEROSITY. The relationship between these two terms is one of possession of a trait. The philanthropist must possess generosity in order to be a philanthropist. Likewise, a SURGEON must possess DEXTERITY to perform the duties of a surgeon.

With respect to choice (C), the first term is the result of the second. CROPS are the result of the FARMER's efforts.

In relation to choices (A), (D), and (E), the first term in each identifies those who benefit by the efforts of the second. CONVERTS are beneficiaries of MISSIONARIES' efforts, STUDENTS are taught by TEACHERS and SCHIZOPHRENICS are counseled by PSYCHOLOGISTS.

• PROBLEM 2-73

IGNORANT : KNOWLEDGE ::

(A) fast : hunger   (D) despair : hope

(B) old : antique   (E) good : moral

(C) syllable : word

SOLUTION:

(D)   To be IGNORANT is to lack KNOWLEDGE. This relationship is also present in choice (D) DESPAIR : HOPE. To despair is to lack hope. The relationship in choice (A) FAST : HUNGER is likely to be opposite, as someone fasting would feel, not lack, hunger. Choice (B) OLD : ANTIQUE is an analogy of degree. An item must be considered "very" old to be antique. Choice (C) SYLLABLE : WORD presents a part-to-whole analogy. Choice (E) GOOD : MORAL is once again opposite, to be considered good one must have morals, not lack them.

• PROBLEM 2-74

GAZPACHO : SOUP ::

(A) wine : dinner

(B) yeast : bread

(C) paella : fish

(D) bratwurst : sausage

(E) sauce : spaghetti

SOLUTION:

(D)   GAZPACHO is a kind of SOUP. The key relationship in this analogy is that the first term is one kind of the entity identified by the second term. The answer is (D). BRATWURST is one kind of SAUSAGE. The remaining options all mention a food and include a word which is somehow related to that food, but in none of them is that relationship that of a category to a specific kind.

• PROBLEM 2-75

DECODE : UNDERSTAND ::

(A) detonate : explode

(B) study : research

(C) destroy : build

(D) skill : practice

(E) sow : reap

SOLUTION:

(E)   This is an analogy of purpose. One DECODES in order to UNDERSTAND. The answer is (E), one SOWS in order to REAP, or harvest. Choice (A) is an analogy of likeness. DETONATE is synonymous with EXPLODE. Choice (B) is an analogy of general to specific, RESEARCH is a specific kind of STUDY. Choice (C) is wrong because the analogy here is that of opposition. To DESTROY is the opposite of to BUILD. Choice (D) is wrong because the order of the pair is reversed; one PRACTICES in order to have SKILL.

• PROBLEM 2-76

RIB : UMBRELLA ::

(A) leg : table

(D) hinge : door

(B) stud : wall

(E) knob : drawer

(C) shelf : closet

SOLUTION:

(B) This is an analogy of function. The metals RIBS of an UM-BRELLA give it its shape. The corresponding analogy is (B). The STUDS of a WALL form a frame which gives the wall its shape. Incorrect choices are (A), LEGS hold a TABLE up but do not give the table its shape; (C), a SHELF may be placed within a CLOSET; and (D) and (E), in which instances the HINGE and KNOB are extraneous to the DOOR and DRAWER, respectively.

• PROBLEM 2-77

SANGUINE : RUBICUND ::

(A) optimistic : pessimistic

(D) elated : despairing

(B) chagrin : confident

(E) pallid : colorless

(C) craven : spirited

SOLUTION:

(E) SANGUINE and RUBICUND are synonyms. The same relation-ship exists for (E) PALLID : COLORLESS since they are synonyms. This relationship is not present in the other choices. (A) OPTIMISTIC is the opposite of PESSIMISTIC. (B) CHAGRIN : CONFIDENT has no neces-sary relationship. (C) CRAVEN is the opposite of SPIRITED. (D) ELATED is the opposite of DESPAIRING.

• PROBLEM 2-78

DOOR : KEY ::

(A) gem : ring

(B) perfume : aroma

(C) enigma : clue

(D) effort : achievement

(E) mold : gelatin

SOLUTION:

(C)   A KEY can be used to unlock a DOOR. This relationship is also evidenced in choice (C) ENIGMA : CLUE. A clue may unlock an enigma (mystery). The relationship in (A) GEM : RING is that of use. A gem may be used in a ring. The relationship in (B) PERFUME : AROMA is that of entity and characteristic. Aroma is characteristic of perfume. Choice (D) EFFORT : ACHIEVEMENT presents the relationship of prerequisite : event. Effort is a prerequisite to achievement. In the final choice, a MOLD may be used to shape GELATIN (E).

• PROBLEM 2-79

TALENT : PRODIGY ::

(A) abode : vagabond

(B) youth : delinquent

(C) secretiveness : confidant

(D) seriousness : jester

(E) civilization : savage

SOLUTION:

(C)   The second noun is a type of person, and the first is the defining characteristic they must possess. A PRODIGY is a person who exhibits extreme TALENT. The same relationship exists for (C) SECRETIVE-NESS : CONFIDANT, since a confidant is one who exhibits extreme secrecy. This relationship is not present in the other choices. (A) A VAGABOND is a person without an ABODE. (B) A DELINQUENT is not necessarily a YOUTH. (D) A JESTER is a person who lacks SERI-OUSNESS. (E) A SAVAGE is a person who lacks CIVILIZATION.

• PROBLEM 2-80

IMPROMPTU : EXTEMPORANEOUS ::

(A) extraneous : irrelevant   (D) speechless : unpretentious

(B) rapacious : generous   (E) dilatory : conscientious

(C) romantic : exemplary

SOLUTION:

(A) IMPROMPTU is a synonym for EXTEMPORANEOUS. The same relationship exists for (A) EXTRANEOUS : IRRELEVANT, since they are synonyms. (B) RAPACIOUS is the opposite of GENEROUS. (C) ROMANTIC : EXEMPLARY, (D) SPEECHLESS : UNPRETENTIOUS, and (E) DILATORY : CONSCIENTIOUS have no necessary relationship.

• PROBLEM 2-81

DONNISH : PEDANT ::

(A) redolent : ammonia   (D) pedagogic : teacher

(B) jocund : pessimist   (E) esoteric : simpleton

(C) salacious : minister

SOLUTION:

(D) PEDAGOGIC is an adjective correctly describing a TEACHER, just as DONNISH is an adjective describing a PEDANT. The remaining selections contain adjectives which incorrectly describe the nouns following them.

• PROBLEM 2-82

TACITURN : TALKATIVE ::

(A) bewildered : informative   (D) poised : assured

(B) reserved : courageous   (E) tactful : ingenious

(C) mute : silent

SOLUTION:

(A) Someone who is TACITURN is not TALKATIVE; the terms are antithetical. The same relationship exists in option (A), as someone who is BEWILDERED would not be INFORMATIVE. This relationship is not present in the remaining choices. (B) and (E) have no necessary relationship at all, and (C) and (D) are closer to synonyms, and so are the opposite of antithetical.

• PROBLEM 2-83

TRIVIA : IMPORTANCE ::

(A) mansion : beauty   (D) soldier : allegiance

(B) magazine : model   (E) amateur : experience

(C) centipede : leg

SOLUTION:

(E) TRIVIA is defined as lacking IMPORTANCE. The same relationship exists for (E) AMATEUR : EXPERIENCE since an amateur lacks experience. This relationship is not present in the other choices. A MANSION does not necessarily lack BEAUTY. MAGAZINE : MODEL does not have a necessary relationship. A CENTIPEDE has many LEGS. A SOLDIER is not defined as lacking ALLEGIANCE.

• PROBLEM 2-84

BRAGGART : ARROGANT ::

(A) detective : ingenious   (D) klutz : ungraceful

(B) villain : honesty   (E) doctor : mad

(C) citizen : proud

SOLUTION:

(D) A BRAGGART is one who is extremely ARROGANT. The same relationship exists for (D) KLUTZ : UNGRACEFUL, since a klutz is extremely ungraceful. This relationship does not exist in the other choices. A DETECTIVE is not necessarily INGENIOUS. A VILLAIN is not

HONEST. A CITIZEN is not necessarily PROUD. A DOCTOR is not necessarily MAD.

• PROBLEM 2-85

AMPERE : ELECTRICITY ::

(A) heat : sun

(B) pound : weight

(C) bulb : light

(D) number : salary

(E) inch : ruler

SOLUTION:

(B) ELECTRICITY is measured by the AMPERE. The same relationship exists for (B) since WEIGHT is measured by the POUND. This relationship is not present in the other choices. (A) HEAT : SUN is incorrect because the sun is not measured by heat, it gives off heat. The same is true of (C) BULB : LIGHT as light is given off by a bulb. (D) NUMBER : SALARY has no necessary relationship. (E) INCH : RULER is incorrect because the order is reversed; a ruler measures by the inch, not the other way around.

• PROBLEM 2-86

SQUIRM : EMBARRASSMENT ::

(A) cower : fear

(B) wiggle : silliness

(C) squint : darkness

(D) sweat : perspiration

(E) journey : desire

SOLUTION:

(A) SQUIRM is a reaction to the feeling of EMBARRASSMENT. The same relationship exists for (A) COWER : FEAR, since cower is a reaction caused by the feeling of fear. This relationship is not present in the other choices. (B) WIGGLE : SILLINESS is incorrect, since wiggle is not a reaction caused by the feeling of silliness. (C) SQUINT : DARKNESS is incorrect, since it is brightness, not darkness, which causes the reaction of squinting. (D) SWEAT : PERSPIRATION is incorrect, since perspiration and sweat are synonyms. (E) JOURNEY : DESIRE has no necessary relationship.

• PROBLEM 2-87

RETINUE : FOLLOWER ::

(A) animal : menagerie

(B) state : federation

(C) word : vocabulary

(D) detritus : debris

(E) tune : medley

SOLUTION:

(D)   A RETINUE is a group of FOLLOWERS. The corresponding analogy is found in (D) DETRITUS : DEBRIS, since an accumulation of debris is referred to as detritus. The first term in the analogies refers to a collection of those things or items referred to by the second term. In each of the remaining choices, the reference to the whole follows instead of precedes reference to the part.

• PROBLEM 2-88

ANGER : RAGE ::

(A) stubborn : recalcitrant

(B) quarrelsome : pugnacious

(C) hot-tempered : irascible

(D) lucid : perspicuous

(E) failure : fiasco

SOLUTION:

(E)   RAGE is a heightened form of ANGER. The correct choice is (E) a FIASCO is a heightened form of FAILURE. A fiasco is a "complete, ridiculous failure." The other choices each present synonymous pairs of words. Although the second term in each pair may appear more serious in meaning, it is the same.

• PROBLEM 2-89

REQUEST : ULTIMATUM ::

(A) mar : ruin

(B) couplet : sonnet

(C) page : book

(D) branch : tree

(E) surfeit : gluttony

SOLUTION:

(A)   This is an analogy of intensity. An ULTIMATUM is an intensified REQUEST. This relationship also exists in choice (A) MAR : RUIN. To mar is to make imperfect. To ruin is to destroy something. A vase might be marred by a scratch, but would be ruined by dropping it on the floor and breaking it. Analogies of intensity have to do with quality. The foils used in the choices have to do with quantity.

In choice (B) COUPLET : SONNET, a couplet is made up of two lines while a sonnet is made up of 14 lines. This is an increase in quantity rather than an increase in quality. Increases in quantity are also apparent in choices (C) PAGE : BOOK and (D) BRANCH : TREE. Choice (E) SURFEIT : GLUTTONY is incorrect because both indicate an overindulgence, particularly of food or drink. There is no increase in intensity from one to the other.

• PROBLEM 2-90

RAIN : PRECIPITATION ::

(A) copper : metal

(B) ice : glacier

(C) oil : shale

(D) wind : abrasion

(E) heat : evaporation

SOLUTION:

(A)   RAIN is a form of PRECIPITATION. The analogy is one of example : class. The correct choice is (A) COPPER : METAL. Copper is a form of metal. The analogy in (B) ICE : GLACIER is wrong. A glacier is made of ice, but ice is not an example of a glacier. In relation to (C) OIL : SHALE, oil is found in shale but is not an example of shale. (D) WIND : ABRASION has the relationship of cause : effect. Wind is a cause of abrasion. This relationship also exists in (E) HEAT : EVAPORATION, as heat is a cause of evaporation.

• PROBLEM 2-91

OSMIUM : SILVER ::

(A) oak : pine

(B) wood : steel

(C) war : peace

(D) murky : cloudy

(E) artificial : genuine

SOLUTION:

(A) OSMIUM is a stronger metal than SILVER, just as OAK is a stronger type of wood than PINE. Choice (B) presents us with a similar relationship, but the second is stronger than the first (instead of vice versa). Choices (C) and (E) present us with simple antonyms, while choice (D) is merely a synonym.

• PROBLEM 2-92

CELESTIAL : INFERNAL ::

(A) heavenly : divine

(B) profane : sacrosanct

(C) lofty : nether

(D) truth : falsehood

(E) astronomical : biological

SOLUTION:

(C) CELESTIAL bears a relation to heaven, while INFERNAL bears a relation to hell, heaven's opposite. LOFTY (high) and NETHER (low or deep) adequately relate to these terms. Choice (A) presents synonyms, not antonyms. While choice (B) presents antonyms similar to celestial and infernal, it presents them in the wrong order. Choice (D) presents antonyms, but they are nouns, not adjectives. (E) ASTRONOMICAL and BIOLOGICAL refer to different branches of science, but are not opposites.

• PROBLEM 2-93

COLLABORATION : COLLUSION ::

(A) guile : illusion   (D) fame : notoriety

(B) clarity : brightness   (E) covert : overt

(C) hypocrite : deceiver

SOLUTION:

(D)   COLLABORATION is a neutral noun which means "working together," and COLLUSION is a noun which is similar in meaning but has
additional negative connotations, since it means working together for a
negative purpose. (D) FAME is a neutral word meaning "the state of being
well-known" and NOTORIETY is a similar word with negative connotations meaning the state of being well-known for negative accomplishments. Choices (A), (B), and (C) are all synonyms without distinction, and
choice (E) presents antonyms.

• PROBLEM 2-94

BANAL : TRITE ::

(A) grave : sad   (D) long : hard

(B) ephemeral : temporary   (E) novel : arduous

(C) murky : clear

SOLUTION:

(B)   BANAL and TRITE are synonyms meaning "commonplace."
EPHEMERAL and TEMPORARY are also synonyms meaning "short-
lived." Choice (A) presents related words but not synonyms. A GRAVE
person is serious, not necessarily SAD. Choice (C) presents antonyms.
Choice (E) shows no clear relationship, since NOVEL means new while
ARDUOUS is difficult.

• PROBLEM 2-95

OBVIOUS : APPARENT ::

(A) plaintiff : bailiff

(B) obtrusive : discernable

(C) manifest : evident

(D) dim : patent

(E) translucent : opaque

SOLUTION:

(C) Both MANIFEST and EVIDENT imply being apparent and are synonyms; therefore, (C) is correct. OBVIOUS and APPARENT are synonyms suggesting something evident to the beholder.

For (A), a PLAINTIFF brings charges against a defendant in court, and a BAILIFF is an officer, perhaps of the court. The two are not necessarily related so (A) should not be selected.

OBTRUSIVE (meddlesome) and DISCERNABLE (capable of being perceived or seen clearly) are not synonyms, so (B) should not be selected.

DIM means not bright, not clear. PATENT (as in Patent leather) can mean bright, glossy; the two, then, would be antonyms. (D) is wrong.

TRANSLUCENT means light-penetrable; an OPAQUE substance is unpenetrated by light. The two are antonyms; therefore, (E) is an incorrect choice.

• PROBLEM 2-96

SPELUNKER : CAVE ::

(A) conductor : maestro

(B) prestidigitator : magic

(C) purloiner : parish

(D) numismatist : books

(E) curator : coins

SOLUTION:

(B) A PRESTIDIGITATOR works with MAGIC. (B) is the answer. A SPELUNKER explores CAVES. The analogy is the worker (hobbyist) with the thing he/she is interested in. In (A), since a CONDUCTOR is a MAESTRO, the analogy is not the same as that in SPELUNKER : CAVE. (A) is not the correct choice. A PURLOINER (one who steals) is not directly related to PARISH. (C) is not the best choice. A NUMISMATIST collects coins—not BOOKS. (D) is incorrect. A CURATOR (an overseer, a keeper, a custodian) is not necessarily related to COINS. (E) should not be selected.

• PROBLEM 2-97

PERNICIOUS : DELETERIOUS ::

(A) perspicacious : obtuse

(B) lethargic : happy

(C) sagacious : unattractive

(D) prudent : foolish

(E) tumid : swollen

SOLUTION:

(E) PERNICIOUS and DELETERIOUS are synonyms meaning harmful. TUMID and SWOLLEN both mean inflated. Choices (A) and (D) are antonyms: PERSPICACIOUS means keen or shrewd, OBTUSE means dull or stupid; and PRUDENT means wise which is the opposite of FOOLISH. (C) SAGACIOUS means wise and (B) LETHARGIC means sluggish, so there is no clear relationship between either of these words and the other half of their pairs.

• PROBLEM 2-98

NOVICE : NEOPHYTE ::

(A) fugitive : road

(B) virtuoso : expert

(C) pacifist : war

(D) vagrant : street

(E) idealist : principle

SOLUTION:

(B) The answer is (B) because the relationship between the given words can be expressed as: A NOVICE (inexperienced, untrained) is a NEOPHYTE (novice, beginner), or NOVICE is a synonym of NEOPHYTE. Choice (B) expresses the same relationship: A VIRTUOSO is an EXPERT.

Choice (A) is incorrect because a FUGITIVE is not a ROAD.

Choice (C) is wrong because PACIFIST (someone who looks for calm, peace) is not a synonym for WAR. These words are semantically opposite, and not synonyms.

Choice (D) is incorrect because a VAGRANT (a person who wanders from place to place) is not a STREET.

Choice (E) is wrong because an IDEALIST has PRINCIPLES, but the words are not synonyms.

• PROBLEM 2-99

GRANDIOSE : EXTRAVAGANT ::

(A) shy : brash

(D) tumid : edematous

(B) tasteless : cultured

(E) prosaic : imaginative

(C) ample : healthy

SOLUTION:

(D) GRANDIOSE is a synonym for EXTRAVAGANT. The same relationship exists for (D) TUMID : EDEMATOUS, since they are synonymous words meaning swollen. This relationship is not present in the other choices. (A) SHY is the opposite of BRASH. (B) TASTELESS is the opposite of CULTURED. (C) AMPLE : HEALTHY has no necessary relationship. (E) PROSAIC is the opposite of IMAGINATIVE.

• PROBLEM 2-100

OPPROBRIOUS : HONOR ::

(A) significant : substance

(D) lecherous : confidence

(B) tranquil : agitation

(E) obtrusive : prominence

(C) transparent : truth

SOLUTION:

(A) OPPROBRIOUS describes something that lacks HONOR. The same relationship exists for (B) TRANQUIL : AGITATION, since tranquil describes something that lacks agitation. This relationship is not present in the other choices. (A) SIGNIFICANT describes something with SUBSTANCE. (C) TRANSPARENT : TRUTH has no necessary relationship. (D) LECHEROUS : CONFIDENCE has no necessary relationship. (E) OBTRUSIVE describes something that possesses PROMINENCE.

Chapter 3
Critical Reading

CHAPTER 3

CRITICAL READING

The Critical Reading sections of the SAT I are indeed critical, for they comprise 50 percent of the entire verbal section content and 75 percent of its allotted time. In all, you will encounter 40 Critical Reading questions. "Why," you must wonder, "would this much importance be attached to reading?" The reason is simple. Your ability to read at a strong pace, while grasping a solid understanding of the material, is a key factor in your high school performance and your potential college success. But "critical" can be taken in another sense, for the SAT I will ask you to be a reading critic. You'll need not only to be able to summarize the material, but analyze it, make judgments about it, and make educated guesses about what the writer implies and infers as well. Even your ability to understand vocabulary in context will come under scrutiny. "Can I," you ask yourself, "meet the challenge?" *Yes,* and preparation is the means!

CRITICAL READING PASSAGES AND QUESTIONS

Within the SAT I verbal section you will be given four Critical Reading passages: one of 400-550 words, one of 550-700 words, one of 700-850 words, and two reading selections of 700-850 words combined, which are referred to as a double passage. The double passage will be composed of two separate works which you will be asked to compare or contrast. The reading content of the passages will cover:

- the humanities (philosophy, the fine arts)

- the social sciences (psychology, archaeology, anthropology, economics, political science, sociology, history)

- the natural sciences (biology, geology, astronomy, chemistry, physics)

- narration (fiction, nonfiction)

Following each passage are about 5-13 questions, depending on the length of the passage. These questions are of four types:

1.   Synthesis/Analysis

2.   Evaluation

3.   Vocabulary-in-Context

4.   Interpretation

Through this review, you'll learn not only how to identify these types of questions, but how to attack each one successfully. Familiarity with the test format, combined with solid reading strategies, will prove invaluable in answering the questions quickly and accurately.

ABOUT THE DIRECTIONS

Make sure to study and learn the directions to save yourself time during the actual test. You should simply skim them when beginning the section. The directions will read similar to the following.

DIRECTIONS: Read each passage and answer the questions that follow. Each question will be based on the information stated or implied in the passage or its introduction.

A variation of these directions will be presented as follows for the double passage.

DIRECTIONS: Read the passages and answer the questions that follow. Each question will be based on the information stated or implied in the selections or their introductions, and may be based on the relationship between the passages.

ABOUT THE PASSAGES

You may encounter any number of passage types in the Critical Reading section of the SAT I. These passages may consist of straight text, dialogue and text, or narration. A passage may appear by itself or as part of a pair in a double passage. A brief introduction will be provided for each passage to set the scene for the text being presented.

To familiarize yourself with the types of passages you will encounter, review the examples which follow. Remember that one passage of the

SAT I will be 400-550 words, one will be 550-700 words, one will be 700-850 words, and that the two passages in the double passage will consist of 700-850 words combined. The content of the passages will include the humanities, social sciences, natural sciences, and also narrative text.

A **humanities passage** may discuss such topics as philosophy, the fine arts, and language. The following is an example of such a passage. It falls into the 550 to 700 word range.

> *Throughout his pursuit of knowledge and enlightenment, the philosopher Socrates made many enemies among the Greek citizens. The following passage is an account of the trial resulting from their accusations.*

1   The great philosopher Socrates was put on trial in Athens in 400 B.C. on charges of corrupting the youth and of impiety. As recorded in Plato's dialogue *The Apology,* Socrates began his defense by saying he was going to "speak plainly and honestly," unlike the eloquent sophists the Athenian
5 jury was accustomed to hearing. His appeal to unadorned language offended the jurors, who were expecting to be entertained.

    Socrates identified the two sets of accusers that he had to face: the past and the present. The former had filled the jurors' heads with lies about him when they were young and was considered by Socrates to be
10 the most dangerous. The accusers from the past could not be cross-examined; and they had already influenced the jurors when they were both naive and impressionable. This offended the jury because it called into question their ability to be objective and render a fair judgment.

    The philosopher addressed the charges himself, and dismissed them
15 as mere covers for the deeper attack on his philosophical activity. That activity, which involved questioning others until they revealed contradictions in their beliefs, had given rise to Socrates' motto, "The unexamined life is not worth living," and the "Socratic Method," which is still employed in many law schools today. This critical questioning of leading
20 Athenians had made Socrates very unpopular with those in power and was according to Socrates, what led to his trial. This challenge to the legitimacy of the legal system itself further alienated his judges.

    Socrates tried to explain that his philosophical life came about by accident. He had been content to be a humble stone mason until the day
25 that a friend informed him that the Oracle of Delphi had said that "Socrates is the wisest man in Greece." Socrates had been so surprised by this statement, and so sure of its inaccuracy, that he set about disproving it by talking to the reputed wise men of Athens and showing how much more knowledge they possessed. Unfortunately, as he told the jury, those

30 citizens reputed to be wise (politicians, businessmen, artists) turned out to be ignorant—either by knowing absolutely nothing or by having limited knowledge in their fields of expertise and assuming knowledge of everything else. Of these, Socrates had to admit, "I am wiser, because although all of us have little knowledge, I am aware of my ignorance, while they are
35 not." But this practice of revealing prominent citizens' ignorance and arrogance did not earn Socrates their affection, especially when the bright young men of Athens began following him around and delighting in the disgracing of their elders. Hence, in his view, the formal charges of "corrupting the youth" and "impiety" were a pretext to retaliate for the deeper
40 offense of challenging the pretensions of the establishment.

Although Socrates viewed the whole trial as a sham, he cleverly refuted the charges by using the same method of questioning that got him in trouble in the first place. Against the charges of corrupting the youth, Socrates asked his chief accuser, Meletus, if any wanted to harm himself,
45 to which Meletus answered, "no." Then, Socrates asked if one's associates had an effect on one: good people for good and evil people for evil, to which Meletus answered, "yes." Next, Socrates asked if corrupting one's companions makes them better or worse, to which Meletus responded, "worse." Finally, Socrates set the trap by asking Meletus if Socrates had
50 corrupted the youth intentionally or unintentionally. Meletus, wanting to make the charges as bad as possible, answered, "intentionally." Socrates showed the contradictory nature of the charge, since by intentionally corrupting his companions he made them worse, thereby bringing harm on himself. He also refuted the second charge of impiety in the same manner,
55 by showing that its two components (teaching about strange gods and atheism) were inconsistent.

Although Socrates had logically refuted the charges against him, the Athenian jury found him guilty, and Meletus proposed the death penalty. The defendant Socrates was allowed to propose an alternative penalty and
60 Socrates proposed a state pension, so he could continue his philosophical activity to the benefit of Athens. He stated that this is what he deserved. The Athenian jury, furious over his presumption, voted the death penalty and, thus, one of the great philosophers of the Western heritage was executed.

The **social sciences passage** may discuss such topics as psychology, archaeology, anthropology, economics, political science, sociology, and history. The following is an example of such a passage. It falls into the 400 to 550 word range.

Not only does music have the ability to entertain and enthrall, but it also has the capacity to heal. The following passage illustrates the recent indoctrination of music therapy.

1   Music's power to affect moods and stir emotions has been well-known for as long as music has existed. Stories about the music of ancient Greece tell of the healing powers of Greek music. Leopold Mozart, the father of Wolfgang, wrote that if the Greeks' music could heal the sick,
5   then our music should be able to bring the dead back to life. Unfortunately, today's music cannot do quite that much.

The healing power of music, taken for granted by ancient man and by many primitive societies, is only recently becoming accepted by medical professionals as a new way of healing the emotionally ill.

10   Using musical activities involving patients, the music therapist seeks to restore mental and physical health. Music therapists usually work with emotionally disturbed patients as part of a team of therapists and doctors. Music therapists work together with physicians, psychiatrists, psychologists, physical therapists, nurses, teachers, recreation leaders, and families
15 of patients.

The rehabilitation that a music therapist gives to patients can be in the form of listening, performing, teaching lessons on an instrument, or even composing. A therapist may help a patient regain lost coordination by teaching the patient how to play an instrument. Speech defects can some-
20 times be helped by singing activities. Some patients need the social awareness of group activities, but others may need individual attention to build self-confidence. The music therapist must learn what kinds of activities are best for each patient.

In addition to working with patients, the music therapist has to attend
25 meetings with other therapists and doctors who work with the same patients to discuss progress and plan new activities. Written reports to doctors about patients' responses to treatment are another facet of the music therapist's work.

Hospitals, schools, retirement homes, community agencies, and clin-
30 ics are some of the places in which music therapists work. Some music therapists work in private studies with patients who are sent to them by medical doctors, psychologists, and psychiatrists. Music therapy can be done in studios, recreation rooms, hospital wards, or classrooms, depending on the type of activity and needs of the patients.

35   Qualified music therapists have followed a four-year course, with a major emphasis in music, and have also taken courses in biology, anthropology, sociology, psychology, and music therapy. General studies in English, history, speech, and government complete the requirements for a Bachelor of Music Therapy. After college training, a music therapist must

40 participate in a six-month training internship under the guidance of a registered music therapist.

Students, who have completed college courses and have demonstrated their ability during the six-month internship, can become registered music therapists by applying to the National Association for Music
45 Therapy, Inc. New methods and techniques of music therapy are always being developed; so the trained therapist must continue to study new articles, books, and reports throughout his/her career.

The **natural sciences passage** may discuss such topics as biology, geology, astronomy, chemistry, and physics. The following is an example of such a passage. It falls into the 550 to 700 word range.

The following article was written by a physical chemist and recounts the conflict between volcanic matter in the atmosphere and airplane windows. It was published in a scientific periodical in 1989.

1   Several years ago the airlines discovered a new kind of problem—a window problem. The acrylic windows on some of their 747s were getting hazy and dirty-looking. Suspicious travelers thought the airlines might have stopped cleaning them, but the windows were not dirty; they were
5 inexplicably deteriorating within as little as 390 hours of flight time, even though they were supposed to last for five to ten years. Boeing looked into it.

At first the company thought the culprit might be one well known in modern technology, the component supplier who changes materials with-
10 out telling the customer. Boeing quickly learned this was not the case, so there followed an extensive investigation that eventually brought in the Air Transport Association, geologists, and specialists in upper-atmosphere chemistry, and the explanation turned out to be not nearly so mundane. Indeed, it began to look like a grand reenactment of an ancient Aztec
15 myth: the struggle between the eagle and the serpent, which is depicted on the Mexican flag.

The serpent in this case is an angry Mexican volcano, El Chichon. Like its reptilian counterpart, it knows how to spit venom at the eyes of its adversary. In March and April of 1982 the volcano, in an unusual eruption
20 pattern, ejected millions of tons of sulfur-rich material directly into the stratosphere. In less than a year, a stratospheric cloud had blanketed the entire Northern Hemisphere. Soon the photochemistry of the upper atmosphere converted much of the sulfur into tiny droplets of concentrated sulfuric acid.

25   The eagle in the story is the 747, poking into the lower part of the stratosphere in hundreds of passenger flights daily. Its two hundred windows are made from an acrylic polymer, which makes beautifully clear, strong windows but was never intended to withstand attack by strong acids.

30   The stratosphere is very different from our familiar troposphere environment. Down here the air is humid, with a lot of vertical convection to carry things up and down; the stratosphere is bone-dry, home to the continent-striding jet stream, with unceasing horizontal winds at an average of 120 miles per hour. A mist of acid droplets accumulated gradually near the
35   lower edge of the stratosphere, settling there at a thickness of about a mile a year, and was able to wait for planes to come along.

As for sulfuric acid, most people know only the relatively benign liquid in a car battery: 80 percent water and 20 percent acid. The stratosphere dehydrated the sulfuric acid into a persistent, corrosive mist 75
40   percent pure acid, an extremely aggressive liquid. Every time the 747 poked into the stratosphere—on almost every long flight—acid droplets struck the windows and began to react with their outer surface, causing it to swell. This built up stresses between the softened outer layer and the underlying material. Finally, parallel hairline cracks developed, creating
45   the hazy appearance. The hazing was sped up by the mechanical stresses always present in the windows of a pressurized cabin.

The airlines suffered through more than a year of window replacements before the acid cloud finally dissipated. Ultimately the drops reached the lower edge of the stratosphere, were carried away into the
50   lower atmosphere, and finally came down in the rain. In the meantime, more resistant window materials and coatings were developed. (As for the man-made sulfur dioxide that causes acid rain, it never gets concentrated enough to attack the window material. El Chichon was unusual in its ejection of sulfur directly into the stratosphere, and the 747 is unusual in
55   its frequent entrance into the stratosphere.)

As for the designers of those windows, it is hard to avoid the conclusion that a perfectly adequate engineering design was defeated by bad luck. After all, this was the only time since the invention of the airplane that there were acid droplets of this concentration in the upper atmosphere.
60   But reliability engineers, an eminently rational breed, are very uncomfortable when asked to talk about luck. In principle it should be possible to anticipate events, and the failure to do so somehow seems like a professional failure. The cosmos of the engineer has no room for poltergeists, demons, or other mystic elements. But might it accommodate the inexo-
65   rable scenario of an ancient Aztec myth?

A **narrative passage dealing with fictional material** may be in the form of dialogue between characters or one character speaking to the reader. The following is an example of the latter. It falls into the 700 to 850 word range.

In this passage, the narrator discovers that he has been transported to King Arthur's court in the year 528 A.D.

1   The moment I got a chance, I slipped aside privately and touched an ancient, common-looking man on the shoulder and said, in an insinuating, confidential way—

    "Friend, do me a kindness. Do you belong to the asylum, or are you
5 just here on a visit or something like that?"

    He looked me over stupidly, and said—

    "Marry, fair sir, me seemeth—"

    "That will do," I said; "I reckon you are a patient."

    I moved away, cogitating, and at the same time keeping an eye out
10 for any chance passenger in his right mind that might come along and give me some light. I judged I had found one, presently; so I drew him aside and said in his ear—

    "If I could see the head keeper a minute—only just a minute—"

    "Prithee do not let me."

15   "Let you *what?*"

    "*Hinder* me, then, if the word please thee better." Then he went on to say he was an under-cook and could not stop to gossip, though he would like it another time; for it would comfort his very liver to know where I got my clothes. As he started away, he pointed and said yonder was one
20 who was idle enough for my purpose, and was seeking me besides, no doubt. This was an airy slim boy in shrimp-colored tights that made him look like a forked carrot; the rest of his gear was blue silk and dainty laces and ruffles; and he had long yellow curls, and wore a plumed pink satin cap tilted complacently over his ear. By his look, he was good-natured; by
25 his gait, he was satisfied with himself. He was pretty enough to frame. He arrived, looked me over with a smiling and impudent curiosity, said he had come for me, and informed me that he was a page.

    "Go 'long," I said; "you ain't more than a paragraph."

    It was pretty severe, but I was nettled. However, it never phased him;
30 he didn't appear to know he was hurt. He began to talk and laugh, in happy, thoughtless, boyish fashion, as we walked along, and made himself old friends with me at once; asked me all sorts of questions about myself and about my clothes, but never waited for an answer—always chattered straight ahead, as if he didn't know he had asked a question and wasn't
35 expecting any reply, until at last he happened to mention that he was born

in the beginning of the year 513.

It made the cold chills creep over me! I stopped, and said, a little faintly:

"Maybe I didn't hear you just right. Say it again—and say it slow. 40 What year was it?"

"513."

"513! You don't look it! Come, my boy, I am a stranger and friend-less: be honest and honorable with me. Are you in your right mind?"

He said he was.

45   "Are these other people in their right minds?"

He said they were.

"And this isn't an asylum? I mean, it isn't a place where they cure crazy people?"

He said it wasn't.

50   "Well, then," I said, "either I am a lunatic, or something just as awful has happened. Now tell me, honest and true, where am I?"

"In King Arthur's Court."

I waited a minute, to let that idea shudder its way home, and then said:

55   "And according to your notions, what year is it now?"

"528—nineteenth of June."

I felt a mournful sinking at the heart, and muttered: "I shall never see my friends again—never, never again. They will not be born for more than thirteen hundred years yet."

60   I seemed to believe the boy, I didn't know why. *Something* in me seemed to believe him—my consciousness, as you may say; but my reason didn't. My reason straightaway began to clamor; that was natural. I didn't know how to go about satisfying it, because I knew that the testimony of men wouldn't serve—my reason would say they were lunatics, and throw 65 out their evidence. But all of a sudden I stumbled on the very thing, just by luck. I knew that the only total eclipse of the sun in the first half of the sixth century occurred on the 21st of June, A. D. 528, o. s., and began at 3 minutes after 12 noon. I also knew that no total eclipse of the sun was due in what to *me* was the present year—*i.e.,* 1879. So, if I could keep my 70 anxiety and curiosity from eating the heart out of me for forty-eight hours, I should then find out for certain whether this boy was telling me the truth or not.

A **narrative passage dealing with nonfiction material** may appear in the form of a speech or any such discourse in which one person speaks to a group of people or to the reader. The following two selections are examples of nonfiction narratives. Together, they are also an example of a double passage, in which the subject matter in the selections can be either compared or contrasted. As you will recall, the two selections will total 700 to 850 words.

The following passages are excerpts from two different presidential inaugural addresses. Passage 1 was given by President John F. Kennedy on January 20, 1961. Passage 2 comes from President Franklin D. Roosevelt's Inaugural Address, given on March 4, 1933.

Passage 1

1   Let every nation know, whether it wishes us well or ill, that we shall pay any price, bear any burden, meet any hardship, support any friend, oppose any foe to assure the survival and the success of liberty.

This much we pledge—and more.

5   To those old allies whose cultural and spiritual origins we share, we pledge the loyalty of faithful friends. United, there is little we cannot do in a host of co-operative ventures. Divided, there is little we can do, for we dare not meet a powerful challenge at odds and split asunder.

To those new states whom we welcome to the ranks of the free, we 10 pledge our word that one form of colonial control shall not have passed away merely to be replaced by a far more iron tyranny. We shall not always expect to find them supporting our view. But we shall always hope to find them strongly supporting their own freedom, and to remember that, in the past, those who foolishly sought power by riding the back of the 15 tiger ended up inside.

To those peoples in the huts and villages of half the globe struggling to break the bonds of mass misery, we pledge our best efforts to help them help themselves, for whatever period is required, not because the Communists may be doing it, not because we seek their votes, but because it is 20 right. If a free society cannot help the many who are poor, it cannot save the few who are rich.

Passage 2

This is pre-eminently the time to speak the truth, the whole truth, frankly and boldly. Nor need we shrink from honestly facing conditions in our country today. This great nation will endure as it has endured, will 25 revive, and will prosper.

So first of all let me assert my firm belief that the only thing we have to fear is fear itself—nameless, unreasoning, unjustified terror, which paralyzes needed efforts to convert retreat into advance.

In every dark hour of our national life a leadership of frankness and 30 vigor has met with that understanding and support of the people themselves which is essential to victory. I am convinced that you will again give that support to leadership in these critical days.

In such a spirit on my part and yours we face our common difficulties. They concern, thank God, only material things. Values have shrunken
35 to fantastic levels; taxes have risen; our ability to pay has fallen; government of all kinds is faced by serious curtailment of income; the means of exchange are frozen in the currents of trade; the withered leaves of industrial enterprise lie on every side; farmers find no markets for their produce; the savings of many years in thousands of families are gone.

40 More important, a host of unemployed citizens face the grim problem of existence, and an equally great number toil with little return. Only a foolish optimist can deny the dark realities of the moment.

Yet our distress comes from no failure of substance. We are stricken by no plague of locusts. Compared with the perils which our forefathers
45 conquered because they believed and were not afraid, we have still much to be thankful for. Nature still offers her bounty, and human efforts have multiplied it. Plenty is at our doorstep, but a generous use of it languishes in the very sight of the supply.

Primarily, this is because the rulers of the exchange of mankind's
50 goods have failed through their own stubbornness and their own incompetence, have admitted their failure and abdicated. Practices of the unscrupulous money-changers stand indicted in the court of public opinion, rejected by the hearts and minds of men.

ABOUT THE QUESTIONS

As previously mentioned, there are four major question types which appear in the Critical Reading section of the SAT I. The following explains what these questions will cover.

Question Type 1: Synthesis/Analysis

Synthesis/analysis questions deal with the structure of the passage and how one part relates to another part or to the text as a whole. These questions may ask you to look at passage details and from them, point out general themes or concepts. They might ask you to trace problems, causes, effects, and solutions or to understand the points of an argument or persuasive passage. They might ask you to compare or contrast different aspects of the passage. Synthesis/analysis questions may also involve inferences, asking you to decide what the details of the passage imply about the author's general tone or attitude. Key terms in synthesis/analysis questions are example, difference, general, compare, contrast, cause, effect, and result.

Question Type 2: Evaluation

Evaluation questions involve judgments about the worth of the essay as a whole. You may be asked to consider concepts the author assumes rather than factually proves and to judge whether or not the author presents a logically consistent case. Does he/she prove the points through generalization, citing an authority, use of example, implication, personal experience, or factual data? You'll need to be able to distinguish the supportive bases for the argumentative theme. Almost as a book reviewer, you'll also be asked to pinpoint the author's writing techniques. What is the style, the tone? Who is the intended audience? How might the author's points relate to information outside the essay itself? Key terms you'll often see in evaluation questions and answer choices are generalization, implication, and support.

Question Type 3: Vocabulary-in-Context

Vocabulary-in-context questions occur in several formats. You'll be given easy words with challenging choices or the reverse. You'll need to know multiple meanings of words. You'll encounter difficult words and difficult choices. In some cases, your knowledge of prefixes-roots-suffixes will gain you clear advantage. In addition, connotations will be the means of deciding, in some cases, which answer is the best. Of course, how the term works in the textual context is the key to the issue.

Question Type 4: Interpretation

Interpretation questions ask you to decide on a valid explanation or clarification of the author's points. Based on the text, you'll be asked to distinguish probable motivations and effects or actions not stated outright in the essay. Furthermore, you'll need to be familiar with clichés, euphemisms, catch phrases, colloquialisms, metaphors, and similes and to explain them in straightforward language. Interpretation question stems usually have a word or phrase enclosed in quotation marks.

Keep in mind that being able to categorize accurately is not of prime importance. What is important, however, is that you are familiar with all the types of information you will be asked and that you have a set of basic strategies to use when answering questions. The remainder of this review will give you these skills.

ANSWERING CRITICAL READING QUESTIONS

You should follow these steps as you begin each critical reading passage. They will act as a guide when answering the questions.

| STEP 1 | Before you address the critical reading, answer all analogies and sentence completions within the given verbal section. You can answer more questions per minute in these short sections than in the reading; and since all answers are credited equally, you'll get the most for your time here.

Now, find the Critical Reading passage(s). If more than one passage appears, give each a brief overview. Attack the easiest and most interesting passages first. Critical Reading passages are not automatically presented in the order of least-to-most difficult. The difficulty or ease of a reading selection is an individual matter, determined by the reader's own specific interests and past experience; so what you might consider easy, someone else might consider hard, and *vice-versa*. Again, time is an issue; so you need to begin with something you can quickly understand in order to get to the questions, where the pay-off lies.

| STEP 2 | First, read the question stems following the passage, making sure to block out the answer choices with your free hand. (You don't want to be misled by incorrect choices.) |

In question stems, underline key words, phrases, and dates. For example:

1. In line 27, "<u>stand</u>" means:

2. From <u>1776</u> to <u>1812,</u> King <u>George</u> did:

3. <u>Lincoln</u> was <u>similar</u> to <u>Pericles</u> in that:

The act of underlining takes little time and will force you to focus first on the main ideas in the questions, then in the essays.

You will notice that questions often note a line number for reference. Place a small mark by the appropriate lines in the essay itself to remind yourself to read those parts very carefully. You'll still have to refer to these lines upon answering the questions, but you'll be able to find them quickly.

| STEP 3 | If the passage is not divided into paragraphs, read the first 10 lines. If the passage is divided into manageable paragraphs, read the first paragraph. Make sure to read at a moderate pace, as fast skimming will not be sufficient for comprehension, while slow, forced reading will take too much time and yield too little understanding of the overall passage. |

In the margin of your test booklet, using two or three words, note the main point of the paragraph/section. Don't labor long over the exact wording. Underline key terms, phrases, or ideas when you notice them. If a sentence is particularly difficult, don't spend too much time trying to figure it out. Bracket it, though, for easy reference in the remote instance that it might serve as the basis for a question.

You should proceed through each paragraph/section in a similar manner. Don't read the whole passage with the intention of going back and filling in the main points. Read carefully and consistently, annotating and underlining to keep your mind on the context.

Upon finishing the entire passage, quickly review your notes in the margin. They should give you main ideas and passage structure (chronological, cause and effect, process, comparison-contrast). Ask yourself what the author's attitude is toward his/her subject. What might you infer from the selection? What might the author say next? Some of these questions may appear, and you'll be prepared to answer immediately.

STEP 4 | Start with the first question and work through to the last question. The order in which the questions are presented follows the order of the passage; so going for the "easy" questions first, rather than answering the questions consecutively; will cost you valuable time in searching and backtracking.

Be sure to block the answer choices for each question before you read the question itself. Again, you don't want to be misled.

If a line number is mentioned, quickly re-read that section. In addition, circle your own answer to the question *before* viewing the choices. Then, carefully examine each answer choice, eliminating those which are obviously incorrect. If you find a close match to your own answer, don't assume that it is the best answer, as an even better one may be among the last choices. Remember, in the SAT I, only one answer is correct, and it is the *best* one, not simply one that will work.

Once you've proceeded through all the choices, eliminating incorrect answers as you go, choose from among those remaining. If the choice is not clear, re-read the question stem and the referenced passage lines to seek tone or content you might have missed. If the answer is not readily obvious now and you have reduced your choices by eliminating at least one, then simply choose one of the remaining and proceed to the next question. Place a small mark in your test booklet to remind you, should you have time at the end of this test section, to review the question and seek a more accurate answer.

Now, let's go back to our natural sciences passage. Read the passage, and then answer the questions which follow using the skills gained through this review.

The following article was written by a physical chemist and recounts the conflict between volcanic matter in the atmosphere and airplane windows. It was published in a scientific periodical in 1989.

1   Several years ago the airlines discovered a new kind of problem—a window problem. The acrylic windows on some of their 747s were getting hazy and dirty-looking. Suspicious travelers thought the airlines might have stopped cleaning them, but the windows were not dirty; they were
5   inexplicably deteriorating within as little as 390 hours of flight time, even though they were supposed to last for five to ten years. Boeing looked into it.

At first the company thought the culprit might be one well known in

10 modern technology, the component supplier who changes materials without telling the customer. Boeing quickly learned this was not the case, so there followed an extensive investigation that eventually brought in the Air Transport Association, geologists, and specialists in upper-atmosphere chemistry, and the explanation turned out to be not nearly so mundane. Indeed, it began to look like a grand reenactment of an ancient Aztec
15 myth: the struggle between the eagle and the serpent, which is depicted on the Mexican flag.

The serpent in this case is an angry Mexican volcano, El Chichon. Like its reptilian counterpart, it knows how to spit venom at the eyes of its adversary. In March and April of 1982 the volcano, in an unusual eruption
20 pattern, ejected millions of tons of sulfur-rich material directly into the stratosphere. In less than a year, a stratospheric cloud had blanketed the entire Northern Hemisphere. Soon the photochemistry of the upper atmosphere converted much of the sulfur into tiny droplets of concentrated sulfuric acid.

25 The eagle in the story is the 747, poking into the lower part of the stratosphere in hundreds of passenger flights daily. Its two hundred windows are made from an acrylic polymer, which makes beautifully clear, strong windows but was never intended to withstand attack by strong acids.

30 The stratosphere is very different from our familiar troposphere environment. Down here the air is humid, with a lot of vertical convection to carry things up and down; the stratosphere is bone-dry, home to the continent-striding jet stream, with unceasing horizontal winds at an average of 120 miles per hour. A mist of acid droplets accumulated gradually near the
35 lower edge of the stratosphere, settling there at a thickness of about a mile a year, and was able to wait for planes to come along.

As for sulfuric acid, most people know only the relatively benign liquid in a car battery: 80 percent water and 20 percent acid. The stratosphere dehydrated the sulfuric acid into a persistent, corrosive mist 75
40 percent pure acid, an extremely aggressive liquid. Every time the 747 poked into the stratosphere—on almost every long flight—acid droplets struck the windows and began to react with their outer surface, causing it to swell. This built up stresses between the softened outer layer and the underlying material. Finally, parallel hairline cracks developed, creating
45 the hazy appearance. The hazing was sped up by the mechanical stresses always present in the windows of a pressurized cabin.

The airlines suffered through more than a year of window replacements before the acid cloud finally dissipated. Ultimately the drops reached the lower edge of the stratosphere, were carried away into the
50 lower atmosphere, and finally came down in the rain. In the meantime,

more resistant window materials and coatings were developed. (As for the
man-made sulfur dioxide that causes acid rain, it never gets concentrated
enough to attack the window material. El Chichon was unusual in its
ejection of sulfur directly into the stratosphere, and the 747 is unusual in
55 its frequent entrance into the stratosphere.)

As for the designers of those windows, it is hard to avoid the conclusion that a perfectly adequate engineering design was defeated by bad
luck. After all, this was the only time since the invention of the airplane
that there were acid droplets of this concentration in the upper atmosphere.
60 But reliability engineers, an eminently rational breed, are very uncomfortable when asked to talk about luck. In principle it should be possible to
anticipate events, and the failure to do so somehow seems like a professional failure. The cosmos of the engineer has no room for poltergeists,
demons, or other mystic elements. But might it accommodate the inexo-
65 rable scenario of an ancient Aztec myth?

1.   Initially, the company thought the hazy windows were a result of

(A) small particles of volcanic glass abrading their surfaces.

(B) substandard window material substituted by the parts supplier.

(C) ineffectual cleaning products used by the maintenance crew.

(D) a build-up of the man-made sulfur dioxide that also causes acid
     rain.

(E) the humidity.

2.   When first seeking a reason for the abraded windows, both the pas-
     sengers and Boeing management exhibited attitudes of

(A) disbelief.   (D) pacifism.

(B) optimism.   (E) disregard.

(C) cynicism.

3.   In line 13, "mundane" means

(A) simple.   (D) ordinary.

(B) complicated.   (E) important.

(C) far-reaching.

4. In what ways is El Chichon like the serpent on the Mexican flag, knowing how to "spit venom at the eyes of its adversary" (lines 18-19)?

    (A) It seeks to poison its adversary with its bite.

    (B) It carefully plans its attack on an awaited intruder.

    (C) It ejects tons of destructive sulfuric acid to damage jet windows.

    (D) It angrily blankets the Northern Hemisphere with sulfuric acid.

    (E) It protects itself with the acid rain it produces.

5. The term "photochemistry" in line 22 refers to a chemical change caused by

    (A) the proximity of the sun.

    (B) the drop in temperature at stratospheric altitudes.

    (C) the jet stream's "unceasing horizontal winds."

    (D) the vertical convection of the troposphere.

    (E) the amount of sulfur present in the atmosphere.

6. Unlike the troposphere, the stratosphere

    (A) is extremely humid because it is home to the jet stream.

    (B) contains primarily vertical convections, which cause air particles to rise and fall rapidly.

    (C) is approximately one mile thick.

    (D) contains powerful horizontal winds resulting in an excessively dry atmosphere.

    (E) contains very little wind activity.

7. In line 40, "aggressive" means

    (A) exasperating.   (D) assertive.

    (B) enterprising.   (E) surprising.

    (C) prone to attack.

8. As the eagle triumphed over the serpent in the Mexican flag,

    (A) El Chichon triumphed over the plane as the 747s had to change their flight altitudes.

    (B) the newly designed window material deflected the damaging acid droplets.

    (C) the 747 was able to fly unchallenged by acid droplets a year later as they drifted away to the lower atmosphere.

    (D) the reliability engineers are now prepared for any run of "bad luck" which may approach their aircraft.

    (E) the component supplier of the windows changed materials without telling the customers.

9. The reliability engineers are typified as people who

    (A) are uncomfortable considering natural disasters.

    (B) believe that all events are predictable through scientific methodology.

    (C) accept luck as an inevitable and unpredictable part of life.

    (D) easily accept their failure to predict and protect against nature's surprises.

    (E) are extremely irrational and are comfortable speaking about luck.

The questions following the passage which you just read are typical of those in the Critical Reading section. After carefully reading the passage, you can begin to answer these questions. Let's look again at the questions.

1. Initially, the company thought the hazy windows were a result of

    (A) small particles of volcanic glass abrading their surfaces.

    (B) substandard window material substituted by the parts supplier.

    (C) ineffectual cleaning products used by the maintenance crew.

    (D) a build-up of the man-made sulfur dioxide that also causes acid rain.

    (E) the humidity.

As you read the question stem, blocking the answer choices, you'll note the key term "result," which should alert you to the question category, *synthesis/analysis*. Argument structure is the focus here. Ask yourself what part of the argument is being questioned: cause, problem, result, or solution. Careful reading of the stem and perhaps mental rewording to "_____ caused hazy windows" reveals cause is the issue. Once you're clear on the stem, proceed to the choices.

The word "initially" clues you in to the fact that the correct answer should be the first cause considered. Answer choice (B) is the correct response, as "substandard window material" was the *company's* first (initial) culprit, as explained in the first sentence of the second paragraph. They had no hint of (A) a volcanic eruption's ability to cause such damage. In addition, they were not concerned, as were the *passengers,* that (C) the windows were not properly cleaned. Answer (D) is not correct since scientists had yet to consider testing the atmosphere. Along the same lines, answer choice (E) is incorrect.

2. When first seeking a reason for the abraded windows, both the passengers and Boeing management exhibited attitudes of

    (A) disbelief.   (D) pacifism.

    (B) optimism.   (E) disregard.

    (C) cynicism.

As you read the stem before viewing the choices, you'll know you're being asked to judge or *evaluate* the tone of a passage. The tone is not stated outright; so you'll need to rely on your perception as you re-read that section, if necessary. Remember, questions follow the order of the passage, so you know to look after the initial company reaction to the windows, but not far after, as many more questions are to follow. Now, formulate your own word for the attitude of the passengers and employees. "Skepticism" or "criticism" works well.

If you can't come up with a term, at least note if the tone is negative or positive. In this case, negative is clearly indicated since the passengers are distrustful of the maintenance crew and the company mistrusts the window supplier. Proceed to each choice, seeking the closest match to your term and/or eliminating words with positive connotations.

Choice (C) is correct because "cynicism" best describes the skepticism and distrust with which the passengers view the cleaning company and the company views the parts suppliers.

Choice (A) is not correct because both Boeing and the passengers believed the windows were hazy; they just didn't know why.

Choice (B) is not correct because people were somewhat agitated that the windows were hazy—certainly not "optimistic."

Choice (D), "pacifism," has a rather positive connotation, which the tone of the section does not.

Choice (E) is incorrect because the people involved took notice of the situation and did not disregard it. In addition to the ability to discern tone, of course, your vocabulary knowledge is being tested. "Cynicism," should you be unsure of the term, can be viewed by its root, "cynic," which may trigger you to remember that it is negative and, therefore, appropriate in tone.

3. In line 13, "mundane" means

   (A) simple.   (D) ordinary.

   (B) complicated.   (E) important.

   (C) far-reaching.

This question obviously tests *vocabulary-in-context.* Your strategy here should be to view line 13 quickly to confirm usage, to block answer choices while devising your own synonym for "mundane"—perhaps "common"—and then to view each choice separately, looking for the closest match. Although you might not be familiar with "mundane," the choices are all relatively simple terms. Look for contextual clues in the passage if you can't define the term outright. While the "component supplies" explanation is "mundane," the Aztec myth is not. Perhaps, you could then look for an opposite of mythical: "real" or "down-to-earth" comes to mind.

Choice (D), "ordinary," fits best as it is clearly the opposite of the extraordinary Aztec myth of the serpent and the eagle, which is not as common as a supplier switching materials.

Choice (A), "simple," works contextually, but not as an accurate synonym for the word "mundane;" it does not deal with "mundane's" "down-to-earth" definition.

Choice (B), "complicated," is inaccurate because the parts switch is anything but complicated.

Choice (C), "far-reaching," is not better as it would apply to the myth rather than the common, everyday action of switching parts.

Choice (E), "important," does not work either, because the explanation was an integral part of solving the problem.

Had you eliminated (B), (C), and (E) due to contextual inappropriateness, you were left with "ordinary" and "simple." A quick re-reading of the section, then, should clarify the better choice. But, if the re-reading did not clarify the better choice, your strategy would be to choose one answer, place a small mark in the booklet, and proceed to the next question. If time is left at the end of the test, you can then review your answer choice.

4. In what ways is El Chichon like the serpent on the Mexican flag, knowing how to "spit venom at the eyes of its adversary" (lines 18-19)?

(A) It seeks to poison its adversary with its bite.

(B) It carefully plans its attack on an awaited intruder.

(C) It ejects tons of destructive sulfuric acid to damage jet windows.

(D) It angrily blankets the Northern Hemisphere with sulfuric acid.

(E) It protects itself with the acid rain it produces.

As you view the question, note the word "like" indicates a comparison is being made. The quoted simile forms the comparative basis of the question, and you must *interpret* that phrase with respect to the actual process. You must carefully seek to duplicate the tenor of the terms, coming close to the spitting action in which a harmful substance is expelled in the direction of an object similar to the eyes of an opponent. Look for key words when comparing images. "Spit," "venom," "eyes," and "adversary" are these keys.

In choice (C), the verb that is most similar to the serpent's "spitting" venom is the sulfuric acid "ejected" from the Mexican volcano, El Chichon. Also, the jet windows most closely resemble the "eyes of the adversary" that are struck by El Chichon. Being a volcano, El Chichon is certainly incapable of injecting poison into an adversary, as in choice (A), or planning an attack on an intruder, as in choice (B).

In choice (D), although the volcano does indeed "blanket the Northern Hemisphere" with sulfuric acid, this image does not coincide with the "spitting" image of the serpent.

Finally, in choice (E), although a volcano can indirectly cause acid rain, it cannot produce acid rain on its own and then spew it out into the atmosphere.

5. The term "photochemistry" in line 22 refers to a chemical change caused by

   (A) the proximity of the sun.

   (B) the drop in temperature at stratospheric altitudes.

   (C) the jet stream's "unceasing horizontal winds."

   (D) the vertical convection of the troposphere.

   (E) the amount of sulfur present in the atmosphere.

   Even if you are unfamiliar with the term "photochemistry," you probably know its root or its prefix. Clearly, this question fits in the *vocabulary-in-context* mode. Your first step may be a quick reference to line 22. If you don't know the term, context may provide you a clue. The conversion of sulfur-rich *upper* atmosphere into droplets may help. If context does not yield information, look at the term "photochemistry," itself. "Photo" has to do with light or sun, as in photosynthesis. Chemistry deals with substance composition and change. Knowing these two parts can take you a long way toward a correct answer.

   Answer choice (A) is the correct response, as the light of the sun closely compares with the prefix "photo." Although choice (B), "the drop in temperature," might lead you to associate the droplet formation with condensation, light is not a factor here; nor is it in choice (C), "the jet stream's winds"; choice (D), "the vertical convection"; or choice (E), "the amount of sulfur present."

6. Unlike the troposphere, the stratosphere

   (A) is extremely humid because it is home to the jet stream.

   (B) contains primarily vertical convections, which cause air particles to rise and fall rapidly.

   (C) is approximately one mile thick.

   (D) contains powerful horizontal winds resulting in an excessively dry atmosphere.

   (E) contains very little wind activity.

   "Unlike" should immediately alert you to a *synthesis/analysis* question, asking you to contrast specific parts of the text. Your margin notes should take you right to the section contrasting the atmospheres. Quickly scan it before considering the answers. Usually you won't remember this broad type of comparison from your first passage reading. Don't spend much time, though, on the scan before beginning to answer, as time is still a factor.

This question is tricky because all the answer choices contain key elements/ phrases in the passage, but again, a quick, careful scan will yield results. Answer (D) proves best as the "horizontal winds" dry the air of the stratosphere.

Choices (A), (B), (C), and (E) are all characteristic of the troposphere, while only the acid droplets accumulate at the rate of one mile per year within the much larger stratosphere. As you answer such questions, remember to eliminate incorrect choices as you go; don't be misled by what seems familiar, yet isn't accurate—read all the answer choices.

7. In line 40, "aggressive" means

    (A) exasperating.   (D) assertive.

    (B) enterprising.   (E) surprising.

    (C) prone to attack.

Another *vocabulary-in-context* surfaces here; yet, this time, the word is probably familiar to you. Again, before forming a synonym, quickly refer to the line number, aware that perhaps a secondary meaning is appropriate as the term already is a familiar one. Upon reading the line, you'll note "persistent" and "corrosive"—both strong terms, the latter being quite negative in its destruction. Now, form an appropriate synonym for aggressive—one that has a negative connotation. "Hostile" might come to mind. At this point you are ready to view all choices for a match.

Using your vocabulary knowledge, you can answer this question. "Hostile" most closely resembles choice (C), "prone to attack," and is therefore the correct response. Choice (A), "exasperating," or irritating, is too weak a term, while choice (B), "enterprising," and (D), "assertive," are too positive. Choice (E), "surprising," is not a synonym for "aggressive."

8. As the eagle triumphed over the serpent in the Mexican flag,

    (A) El Chichon triumphed over the plane because the 747s had to change their flight altitudes.

    (B) the newly designed window material deflected the damaging acid droplets.

    (C) the 747 was able to fly unchallenged by acid droplets a year later because they drifted away to the lower atmosphere.

(D) the reliability engineers are now prepared for any run of "bad luck" which may approach their aircraft.

(E) the component supplier of the windows changed materials without telling the customer.

This question asks you to compare the eagle's triumph over the serpent to another part of the text. "As" often signals comparative relationships; so you are forewarned of the *synthesis/analysis* question. You are also dealing again with a simile; so, of course, the question can also be categorized as *interpretation*. The eagle-serpent issue is a major theme in the text. As you will soon discover in the answer choices, you are being asked what this general theme is. Look at the stem keys: eagle, triumphed, and serpent. Ask yourself to what each corresponds. You'll arrive at the eagle and the 747, some sort of victory, and the volcano or its sulfur. Now that you've formed that corresponding image in your own mind, you're ready to view the choices.

Choice (C) is the correct choice because we know the statement "the 747 was able to fly unchallenged . . . " to be true. Not only do the remaining choices fail to reflect the eagle-triumphs-over-serpent image, but choice (A) is inaccurate because the 747 did not "change its flight altitudes."

In choice (B), the windows did not deflect "the damaging acid droplets."

Furthermore, in choice (D), "the reliability engineers" cannot be correct because they cannot possibly predict the future and, therefore, cannot anticipate what could go wrong in the future.

Finally, we know that in (E) the window materials were never changed.

9. The reliability engineers are typified as people who

   (A) are uncomfortable considering natural disasters.

   (B) believe that all events are predictable through scientific methodology.

   (C) accept luck as an inevitable and unpredictable part of life.

   (D) easily accept their failure to predict and protect against nature's surprises.

   (E) are extremely irrational and are comfortable speaking about luck.

When the question involves such terms as type, kind, example, or typified, be aware of possible *synthesis/analysis* or *interpretation* issues. Here the question deals with implications: what the author means but doesn't state outright. Types can also lead you to situations which ask you to make an unstated generalization based on specifically stated details. In fact, this question could even be categorized as *evaluation* because specific detail to generalization is a type of argument/essay structure. In any case, before viewing the answer choices, ask yourself what general traits the reliability engineers portray. You may need to check back in the text for typical characteristics. You'll find the engineers to be rational unbelievers in luck. These key characteristics will help you to make a step toward a correct answer.

Choice (B) is the correct answer because the passage specifically states that the reliability engineers "are very uncomfortable when asked to talk about luck" and believe "it should be possible to anticipate events" scientifically. The engineers might be uncomfortable, as in choice (A), but this is not a main concern in the passage.

Choice (C) is obviously incorrect, because the engineers do not believe in luck at all, and choice (D) is not correct because "professional failure" is certainly unacceptable to these scientists.

There is no indication in the passage that (E) the scientists are "irrational and are comfortable speaking about luck."

Now, use what you have learned to anser the follwoing questions.

DIRECTIONS: Read each passage and answer the questions that follow. Each question will be based on the information stated or implied in the passage or its introduction.

A variation of these directions will be presented as follows for the double passage.

DIRECTIONS: Read the passages and answer the questions that follow. Each question will be based on the information stated or implied in the selections or their introductions, and may be based on the relationship between the passages.

Questions 1–13 are based on the following passages.

Both of the following selections discuss the authors' early education at home. Passage 1 was written by Arthur Rubinstein; Passage 2 was written by Vladimir Nabokov.

Passage 1

1   My new life started right away. Heinrich Barth, the senior piano professor of the Imperial and Royal Academy, accepted me, on Joachim's recommendation. Moreover, he agreed to teach me without any remuneration, and to take charge of all money matters on my behalf—such as
5   gathering the contributions of the other four subscribers and paying from the fund all my living expenses, other lessons, and so on. Things looked pretty good at that moment, and my near future seemed assured and in excellent hands.

    The question of my schooling was a very important one, and
10 Joachim, Barth and my mother had many discussions about it. Finally, they agreed not to send me to a *Realgymnasium,* deciding instead that it would be better for me to be tutored at home. It was not easy to find the right person for such a task, which entailed preparing me for yearly examinations at the *Gymnasium* and following the school's full curriculum.

15   Eventually they found a Dr. Theodor Altmann, a man who would assume the great responsibility for my education all by himself, and I was taken by Professor Barth to my first lesson at nine o'clock one morning, The lessons were to be for two hours every day.

    So this was the unforgettable day when I met Theodor Altmann! He
20 appeared to me to be tall (I was still small, of course), a heavy-set, rather fat man around forty, with a huge, round face, his nose ridden by a steel-rimmed pince-nez held by a black ribbon. His hair was cropped in the German fashion; but a warm and intelligent twinkle in his eye made me love him right away.

25   At this point I must express my heart's gratitude to this wonderful man. My dear, dear Theodor Altmann—you began by giving me lessons like any other normal teacher. We would start with German history, geography, Latin, and oh, the dreaded and hated mathematics. You were brilliant at introducing all these different subjects to me, and I was eager to
30 absorb every word you said. You used precise, clear terms to express your thought, and it was delightful and exciting to listen to you.

As to mathematics—my lack of interest in it was a real calamity! You used to get angry, even going to complain to Professor Barth—but to no
35 avail. The great Pythagoras and Euclid and the sublime science of algebra were a deadly bore to me! "Why do you make me verify their great theories?" I would protest in despair. "I give them full credit!" After a few stormy lessons, though, I saw through an unmistakable twinkle in your eye
40 a sympathy and a secret understanding of my ordeal. You knew well that my ignorance of higher mathematics was not going to paralyze the real course of my future. From that point on, thanks to you, life became a constant joy in learning. You revealed to me the philosophers of all time— Plato and Socrates, Aristotle, and later Kant and Schopenhauer. We read
45 Nietzsche's *Also Sprach Zarathustra* together, and I was impressed by the beauty of his prose—less by the trend of his thought, although his first book, *The Birth of Tragedy,* where he points so clearly to the distinction between music and the other fine arts, found me completely in accord. When it came to history, you abandoned very soon the dryness of the
35 showing me the results of frailty upon our own time, and the greed for power, the wickedness of men.

The next moment, you would open my eyes to the beauty of living in all its incessant variety, to the infinite possibilities of life, and at the same time foster my encourage for facing it.

The books you gave me to read became my best friends forever;
55 thanks to you I made the acquaintance of Goethe, Heine, Kleist, Balzac, Maupassant, Dostoevsky, Gogol, and Tolstoy. At the age of eleven I was deeply stirred by them. Yes, you treated me like a grownup, and you listened with indulgence and apparent interest to my interjections or opinions—tolerating even my sharply expressed criticisms.
60   Thank you for all this, my dear Theodor Altmann, from the bottom of my heart.

Passage 2

The close of Russia's disastrous campaign in the Far East was accompanied by furious internal disorders. Undaunted by them, my mother, with her three children, returned to St. Petersburg after almost a year of
65 foreign resorts. This was in the beginning of 1905. State matters required the presence of my father in the capital; the Constitutional Democratic Party, of which he was one of the founders, was to win a majority of seats in the First Parliament the following year. During one of his short stays with us in the country that summer, he ascertained, with patriotic dismay,

70 that my brother and I could read and write English but not Russian (except
KAKAO and MAMA). It was decided that the village schoolmaster
should come every afternoon to give us lessons and take us for walks.

   With a sharp and merry blast from the whistle that was part of my
first sailor suit, my childhood calls me back into that distant past to have
75 me shake hands with my delightful teacher. Vasily Martinovich
Zhernosekov had a fuzzy brown beard, a balding head, and china-blue
eyes, one of which bore a fascinating excrescence on the upper lid. The
first day he came he brought a boxful of tremendously appetizing blocks
with a different letter painted on each side; these cubes he would manipu-
80 late as if they were infinitely precious things, which for that matter, they
were (besides forming splendid tunnels for my trains). He revered my
father who had recently rebuilt and modernized the village school. In old-
fashioned token of free thought, he sported a flowing black tie carelessly
knotted in a bowlike arrangement. When addressing me, a small boy, he
85 used the plural of the second person—not in the stiff way servants did, and
not as my mother would do in moments of intense tenderness, when my
temperature had gone up or I had lost a tiny train-passenger (as if the
singular were too thin to bear the load of her love), but with the polite
plainness of one man speaking to another whom he does not know well
90 enough to use "thou." A fiery revolutionary, he would gesture vehemently
on our country rambles and speak of humanity and freedom and the badness of warfare and the sad (but interesting, I thought) necessity of blow-
ing up tyrants, and sometimes he would produce the then popular pacifist
book *Doloy Oruzhie!* (a translation of Bertha von Suttner's *Die Waffen*
95 *Nieder!*), and treat me, a child of six, to tedious quotations; I tried to refute
them: at that tender and bellicose age I spoke up for bloodshed in angry
defense of my world of toy pistols and Arthurian knights. Under Lenin's
regime, when all non-Communist radicals were ruthlessly persecuted,
Zhernosekov was sent to a hard-labor camp but managed to escape abroad,
100 and died in Narva in 1939.

• PROBLEM 3-1

We can infer from the *second* narrator's penchant for "bloodshed" and "toy pistols" (lines 96–97) that

(A) Zhernosekov's recommended book was a hawkish demand for arms.

(B) Zhernosekov exploited the narrator's sympathy for Communism.

(C) he was listening to quotes from a book on disarmament.

(D) his teacher was trying to persuade him to support Lenin.

(E) his teacher found him too immature for intelligent debate.

SOLUTION:

(C)   According to Nabokov, a six-year-old boy is inclined to be "belli-cose," or warlike. He raises the subject when describing how, at that age, he was inclined to refute passages which his teacher read to him from a contemporarily popular pacifist book. Therefore, (C) is the best answer.

We can assume that if the teacher, Zhernosekov, was reading from a pacifist book, he was not "hawkish," so (A) is incorrect.

Since he was sent to a hard-labor camp for non-Communist radicals, (B) is incorrect; and since this imprisonment occurred during Lenin's regime, (D) is incorrect as well. The very fact that the teacher engaged young Nabokov in debate testifies to the assumption of equality, not immaturity.

• PROBLEM 3-2

Both narrative passages portray teachers who

(A) come from the "old-school" notion of cold authoritarianism.

(B) treat their charges as intellectual equals.

(C) limit their instruction to particular technical skills.

(D) constantly refer controversial issues back to the students' parents.

(E) ultimately had to bow before the superior intellect of the pupil.

SOLUTION:

(B)   Both passages contain glowing remembrances of teachers who treated their pupils as intellectual equals, despite their difference in age; so (B) is the correct response.

(A) is incorrect as neither teacher assumes an authoritative role, nor does either report back to the parents (D) for justification. Equality of intellect seems mutual in both instances, not inverse superiority (E). Both teachers display a range of skills, mostly in humanistic studies; so (C) is incorrect.

• PROBLEM 3-3

Rubinstein's reference to "the sublime science of algebra" (line 34)

(A) is employed ironically, since his talents lay elsewhere.

(B) is indicative of the universal respect he had for learning.

(C) demonstrates his native mathematical leanings.

(D) is only said to pacify his teacher, who insisted he study it.

(E) is paradoxical, given his preference for other aspects of mathematics.

SOLUTION:

(A)   Although Rubinstein displayed a great intellectual interest in a broad variety of fields of knowledge, mathematics was not one of these. He goes so far as to describe his lack of interest in it as a real calamity. Following this statement, the phrase "the sublime science of algebra" can only be ironic; so (A) is the correct answer.

Since he did not enjoy studying mathematics, (C) and (E) are obviously incorrect. Although he did have many interests, his distaste for math proved that his respect for learning was not quite "universal" (B). Rubinstein made his dislike of math quite clear to his teacher, and did not try to hide it; so (D) is incorrect.

• PROBLEM 3-4

Rubinstein responded to the philosopher Nietzsche because

(A) of the mathematical precision of Nietzsche's arguments.

(B) of their mutual interest in the arts, especially music.

(C) Theodor Altmann had demonstrated Nietzsche's correctness.

(D) of his attraction to the formal study of logic.

(E) *Thus Spake Zarathustra* made a case for the arts.

SOLUTION:

(B)   Nietzsche's *Birth of Tragedy* touched the chord of music in Rubinstein. It is not cited as formally "logical" (D) nor "mathematical" (A), which would only have repelled Rubinstein. Nietzsche's *Zarathustra* only appealed to Rubinstein because of its style, not its content (E). Altmann's sympathies (C) for Nietzsche are not discussed.

• PROBLEM 3-5

Nabokov claims that his teacher admired his father

(A) for having the good sense to choose him in the first place.

(B) as a fellow revolutionary committed to overthrowing tyranny.

(C) as a political leader no less concerned about education.

(D) because of the father's involvement in the Eastern campaign.

(E) for the latter's pro-Leninist tracts and pamphlets.

SOLUTION:

(C)   Nabokov's teacher respected the father as a diplomat and cultured man. Nabokov's father is nowhere cited as a revolutionary (B) or as a Leninist (E), which certainly would have displeased the teacher. Nabokov does not describe his teacher as a monster of ego (A), which this choice would imply. (D) is a distractor not based on the text.

• PROBLEM 3-6

The education of the respective narrators

(A) is virtually identical, given their mutually exact levels of maturity.

(B) tends to be more scientifically-oriented in Rubinstein's narrative.

(C) differs insofar as the political orientation in Rubinstein's narrative supports a conservative point of view.

(D) demonstrates the extreme care with which handicapped children were tutored.

(E) acknowledges a liberty with which gifted children received private instruction.

SOLUTION:

(E)   Both narrators speak with gratitude of the special education they received. Both were gifted as children, and this caused their parents to seek a unique education for them, which would allow them to take full advantage of their talents and interests. They both had private instruction in which they worked individually with one teacher rather than attending school. Therefore, (E) is correct.

Both narrators are gifted, not handicapped (D); and each received a liberal tutor's instruction, although at different age levels and maturity, causing (A) to be wrong. Rubinstein preferred humanities to science (B), and his education was liberal, not conservative (C).

• PROBLEM 3-7

The manner in which the respective narrators addressed unpopular or unpleasant topics

(A) reveals a degree of outspoken freedom on each of their parts.

(B) demonstrates the utter subservience of students to their teachers.

(C) shows a defiance on the part of Rubinstein, but timidity on the part of Nabokov.

(D) suggests that the political climate in each case was repressive.

(E) reveals timidity on the part of Rubinstein, but defiance on the part of Nabokov.

SOLUTION:

(A) Both Rubinstein and Nabokov expressed their youthful opinions openly with their teachers; there was no timid subservience (B) or repression (D). Nabokov was forthright in defense of his toy guns, making (C) incorrect. Rubinstein attacked mathematics with a certain candor, and so (E) is incorrect as well.

• PROBLEM 3–8

Nabokov's simultaneously "tender and bellicose" (line 96) age

(A) reflects his mature reaction to his teacher's pacifist views.

(B) tries to convey the complexity of the youth's mind.

(C) captures the father's strong influence on his son's opinions.

(D) expresses the warlike instincts of young children.

(E) indicates the degree to which his mother had nurtured him.

SOLUTION:

(D) When Nabokov describes a six-year-old boy as "tender and bellicose," he is speaking with a fond memory of childish innocence. We know this partially because his symbols of war are Arthurian knights and toy pistols—two aspects of childish fantasy. Therefore, (D) is correct.

He specifically speaks of his reaction to his teacher's pacifist views as childish; so (A) is incorrect. He represents his views as tender and innocent, not "complex." There is no mention that his father is warlike (C), and there is no mention of his mother at all (E).

• PROBLEM 3–9

Through his guided studies in history and literature, Rubinstein came to see

(A) that humanity is beneficent and kindly in nature.

(B) the value of a practical, businesslike approach to everyday life.

(C) that mathematics would play a relatively unimportant role in his life.

(D) men's lives as blending good and evil, baseness and beauty.

(E) only the inherent evil in man, the dark side of human nature.

SOLUTION:

(D) Rubinstein came to see the totality of life (lines 47–53) through Altmann's lessons, not merely its extremes of good (A) and evil (E). There is no mention of any business instinct (B) in him. Rubinstein had always known that mathematics would not play an important role in his life.

• PROBLEM 3-10

Rubinstein's use of the phrase "dryness of the textbook" (lines 47–48)

(A) betrays his intrinsic hatred of all academic discipline.

(B) suggests that his real problem lay in respecting any form of authority.

(C) stands in opposition to the method of his beloved teacher.

(D) stresses the basic difference in teaching strategies between Altmann and Zhernosekov (in Nabokov's narrative).

(E) merely reminds us how little he cared for reading.

SOLUTION:

(C) Altmann enriched education beyond the textbook; so (C) is the correct answer. Altmann was an authority figure and an enforcer of academic discipline who was beloved by Rubinstein, denying (B) and (A). A youthful and passionate reader, Rubinstein negates (E) by the testimony of his list of authors (lines 55–56). Both teachers used similar strategies with their charges; so (D) is wrong.

• PROBLEM 3-11

The word "rambles" in Nabokov's narrative (line 91) is used

(A) to suggest the illogical nature of Zhernosekov's instruction.

(B) as a metaphor for the tangents on which their debates would wander.

(C) to imply that "forbidden" topics often entered into discussions.

(D) to indicate that teacher and pupil did not confine their interactions to a fixed classroom.

(E) to suggest the politically opposite viewpoints teacher and pupil maintained.

SOLUTION:

(D) Nabokov uses the word "rambles" literally to state that he and his teacher went on walks in the country as they were engaged in lessons. Therefore, (D) is correct. There is no mention that the instruction was illogical (A). There seemed to be no fixed plan to Nabokov's education: everything was important enough to be discussed and learned; so nothing could be considered tangential (B) and nothing was taboo (C). Although teacher and pupil may have had disagreements, and they did discuss volatile subjects (E), this could not be described as "rambling."

• PROBLEM 3-12

Both authors describe their tutors with

(A) disdain.

(B) admiration.

(C) apathy.

(D) anger.

(E) reverence.

SOLUTION:

(E) Reverence is the correct response because this is the sense one gets after reading both passages. Both authors have fond and respectful feelings about their teachers. So (A) and (D) are not correct. From their descriptions, we sense that the narrators revere these men; admiration (B) could be used to describe the author's tone, but it does not fully describe the emotion as vehemently as it is expressed. (C) is also incorrect because it suggests that there was no feeling behind the descriptions and this is just not the case.

• PROBLEM 3-13

It can be inferred from the passages that both authors felt

(A) privileged to have received such an extensive education.

(B) resentful for having had to endure a horrible childhood.

(C) different because of their unique circumstances.

(D) that there was nothing exceptional about their youth.

(E) their education provided them with nothing but trivial knowledge.

SOLUTION:

(A) Both authors seem to be thankful that they received the education they did from the tutors they had. Resentful (B) does not describe the attitude of the authors. Although it is possible that their unique education made them feel "different," they make no specific mention of this. Through their expression of feeling privileged, they also seem to be saying that their youth was exceptional; so (D) is incorrect. The authors were very positive in the passages and did not express triviality about their education (E).

The following selections are excerpts from two presidential inaugural speeches. Passage 1 is from John F. Kennedy; Passage 2 was delivered by Franklin D. Roosevelt.

Passage 1

1   Let every nation know, whether it wishes us well or ill, that we shall pay any price, bear any burden, meet any hardship, support any friend, oppose any foe to assure the survival and the success of liberty.

    This much we pledge—and more.

5   To those old allies whose cultural and spiritual origins we share, we pledge the loyalty of faithful friends. United, there is little we cannot do in a host of co-operative ventures. Divided, there is little we can do, for we dare not meet a powerful challenge at odds and split asunder.

    To those new states whom we welcome to the ranks of the free, we 10 pledge our word that one form of colonial control shall not have passed away merely to be replaced by a far more iron tyranny. We shall not always expect to find them supporting our view. But we shall always hope to find them strongly supporting their own freedom, and to remember that, in the past, those who foolishly sought power by riding the back of the 15 tiger ended up inside.

    To those people in the huts and villages of half the globe struggling to break the bonds of mass misery, we pledge our best efforts to help them help themselves, for whatever period is required, not because the Communists may be doing it, not because we seek their votes, but because it is 20 right. If a free society cannot help the many who are poor, it cannot save the few who are rich.

Passage 2

    This is pre-eminently the time to speak the truth, the whole truth, frankly and boldly. Nor need we shrink from honestly facing conditions in

our country today. This great nation will endure as it has endured, will
25 revive, and will prosper.

So first of all let me assert my firm belief that the only thing we have
to fear is fear itself—nameless, unreasoning, unjustified terror, which
paralyzes needed efforts to convert retreat into advance.

In every dark hour of our national life a leadership of frankness and
30 vigor has met with that understanding and support of the people themselves which is essential to victory. I am convinced that you will again
give that support to leadership in these critical days.

In such a spirit on my part and yours we face our common difficulties. They concern, thank God, only material things. Values have shrunken
35 to fantastic levels; taxes have risen; our ability to pay has fallen; government of all kinds is faced by serious curtailment of income; the means of
exchange are frozen in the currents of trade; the withered leaves of industrial enterprise lie on every side; farmers find no markets for their produce;
the savings of many years in thousands of families are gone.

40   More important, a host of unemployed citizens face the grim problem
of existence, and an equally great number toil with little return. Only a
foolish optimist can deny the dark realities of the moment.

Yet our distress comes from no failure of substance. We are stricken
by no plague of locusts. Compared with the perils which our forefathers
45 conquered because they believed and were not afraid, we have still much
to be thankful for. Nature still offers her bounty, and human efforts have
multiplied it. Plenty is at our doorstep, but a generous use of it languishes
in the very sight of the supply.

Primarily, this is because the rulers of the exchange of mankind's
50 goods have failed through their own stubbornness and their own incompetence, have admitted their failure and abdicated. Practices of the unscrupulous money-changers stand indicted in the court of public opinion, rejected
by the hearts and minds of men.

• PROBLEM 3–14

In line 3, "liberty" most nearly means

(A) privilege.   (D) freedom.

(B) familiarity.   (E) cooperation.

(C) emancipation.

SOLUTION:

(D)   In the broad sense in which it is employed here, liberty most nearly means freedom, the absence for necessity or constraint in thought or action. (A) and (B) are also synonyms for liberty, but make little sense in this context. (C) implies the removal of bondage, which is an added connotation not mentioned by the author. (E) Cooperation is not a definition for liberty.

• PROBLEM 3-15

In lines 12–13, the use of "supporting" in two ways emphasizes the

(A) idea that liberty itself is more important than the form it takes.

(B) struggle between freedom and tyranny.

(C) power that countries can wield in alliance with one another.

(D) desire of the speaker to influence the politics of weaker countries.

(E) importance the speaker places on individual freedom.

SOLUTION:

(A)   The double use of the word is meant to imply that the author will not be selfish in defending only the liberty of Americans. He suggests that even if they don't agree with our ideals, he hopes that they will be active in defending their own. This supports answer (A), as it implies a non-selfish, non-judgmental love for liberty.

(B) and (C) are both discussed by the author, but do not relate to this portion of the passage. In this sentence the author is not talking about influencing the politics of other countries; he hopes, instead, that they are defending their own interests.

(E) is wrong since the author does not speak of liberty as it relates to individuals.

• PROBLEM 3-16

In lines 14–15, the phrase "in the past . . . ended up inside" is a reference to

(A) nations of the past who built great empires through cooperative efforts.

(B) the importance of remembering all those who have lost their lives defending liberty.

(C) the importance of remembering the struggles and hardships that the first free societies fought in order to preserve liberty.

(D) the importance of remembering that those who tried to gain by following despotic governments in the past eventually lost their freedom.

(E) the valor of nations that declared their independence against overwhelming odds.

SOLUTION:

(D)   The metaphor clearly states that following something inherently bloodthirsty, such as a despot or a tiger, will lead to being consumed by the stronger power. With this understanding of the metaphor, (A), (B), and (C) are seen to be incorrect. While (E) may express an idea similar to the one implied by the metaphor, the word "valor" makes it incorrect because the author describes such nations as "foolish."

• PROBLEM 3-17

The statement "If a free society . . . save the few who are rich" (lines 20–21) suggests that the author believes that

(A) supporting the poor is the function of government in a free society.

(B) protecting liberty abroad is a necessary component of a free society.

(C) suppressing communism is the goal of a free society.

(D) democracy is synonymous with a free society.

(E) defending liberty is not a valid reason to go to war.

SOLUTION:

(B) This summation restates the author's main idea: is the duty of a strong nation to support liberty the world over. (A) could be taken to be literally correct; however, the author speaks not of supporting the poor, but of helping them to help themselves.

(C) and (E) are both in direct opposition to other sections of the passage, the author states that neither imitating nor suppressing the Communists is the reason for helping other nations and he states that no burden is too great to ensure liberty. (D) is incorrect since the author never mentions democracy.

• PROBLEM 3–18

In line 24, the word "endure" most nearly means

(A) exist.

(D) confirm.

(B) linger.

(E) flourish.

(C) withstand.

SOLUTION:

(C) Throughout this passage, it becomes obvious that the author is speaking to a nation facing huge problems and dangers. Therefore, "withstand" is correct because it means to oppose with firm determination and to resist successfully. If this resistance were possible, it would lead to the nation reviving and prospering—enduring. Both (A) and (B) are synonyms but they mean to continue and do not imply opposition or resistance. (D) and (E) are incorrect because they bear no relation to the word "endure."

• PROBLEM 3-19

The author of Passage 2 uses the phrase "the only thing we have to fear is fear itself" (lines 26–27) to suggest that

(A) the problems of which he speaks are illusory and inconsequential.

(B) the dire problems of which he speaks can be overcome if a strong effort is put forth.

(C) once the unscrupulous people in power are exposed that the economy will improve.

(D) the nation will eventually prosper despite the grim present outlook.

(E) speaking the truth will lead to greater prosperity.

SOLUTION:

(B) The author is eloquently saying that no circumstances warrant fear if they are directly confronted. (A) makes no sense because the author describes the problems in detail and they are very concrete. (C), (D), and (E) are all points made by the author elsewhere in the speech, but have little to do with this particular phrase.

• PROBLEM 3-20

In lines 33–39 the author most likely describes "our common difficulties" in order to

(A) illustrate the near impossibility of conquering these problems.

(B) back up his earlier statement about the importance of speaking the whole truth.

(C) portray the powers of observation that a leader must possess.

(D) show that farmers are the hardest hit by economic difficulties.

(E) point out that these difficulties are merely transitory in nature.

SOLUTION:

(B) The author is directly stating the grim reality of which he speaks. (A) and (E) stand in direct opposition to the author's ideas. (C) may be true, but is of only slight—if any—relevance here. (D) is incorrect since the author states that many, besides farmers, are experiencing hard times.

• PROBLEM 3-21

The author of Passage 2 most likely mentions "the perils which our forefathers conquered" (lines 44–45) in order to

(A) escape from present misery by drawing on the past.

(B) put current hardships in an historical context to show that no problem is insurmountable.

(C) illustrate that despite hardship, conditions could be much worse than they are.

(D) draw strength from the fact that our forefathers were able to overcome adversity.

(E) remind his audience that perils have existed in every age and will continue to exist.

SOLUTION:

(C) The complete sentence this quote is taken from reads, "Compared with the perils which our forefathers conquered because they believed and were not afraid, we have still much to be thankful for." The fact that he mentions that they have much to be thankful for shows that he is using the comparison to prove that their forefathers were much worse off; so by projection, their own troubles could be much worse than they were.

The author never suggests that they escape from their problems (A), but that they try to solve them. The author is showing how different the problems were from their forefathers,' not trying to put them in the same context (B). Although (D) and (E) state part of the author's purpose, they both leave out the sense of comparison that is implicit in the quote.

• PROBLEM 3-22

The overall tone of Passage 2 can be said to be one of

(A) hopeless fatalism.   (D) cautious optimism.

(B) desperate fear.   (E) frank honesty.

(C) grim acceptance.

SOLUTION:

(D) The author believes that hardship will be overcome by facing the grim conditions that exist. (A) and (B) ignore the hope displayed by the author. (C) is closer; however, the narrator does not encourage his listeners to accept the grim situation, but to take steps to change it. The author speaks of the importance of honesty (E), but as a means of combating the dire circumstances. This is just one characteristic of the overall tone.

• PROBLEM 3-23

The authors of both passages are concerned with

(A) the ability of their nation to thrive despite any adversarial conditions.

(B) the ability of their nation to overcome economic hardship.

(C) what it means to be free.

(D) the role of the president in a democratic society.

(E) the role of their nation on a global scale.

SOLUTION:

(A) In both passages the authors describe problems that a nation may have to face, either from within or without, but they also speak of the strength and courage available to face these problems. Both authors state that their nation can endure any hardship. (B) is a concern only in the second passage. (C) Passage 1 discusses the importance of freedom, but not its meaning, and passage 2 does not mention it at all. (D) is not addressed in either passage; and (E) is a concern only in the first passage.

• PROBLEM 3-24

Which statement best describes the contrast between the intended audience for the two passages?

(A) Passage 1 addresses the whole free world, while Passage 2 addresses only one nation.

(B) Both passages address only one nation.

(C) Both passages address the free world.

(D) It is impossible to generalize about the intended audiences from the information given.

(E) Passage 1 addresses a much smaller audience than Passage 2.

SOLUTION:

(A) Both passages are concerned mainly with their own nation; but the first passage, in relating one nation to the rest of the world, addresses "every nation." The first passage addresses the whole world, while in Passage 2 the author is speaking directly to the citizens of his "great nation," therefore making (B), (C), and (E) incorrect. There is ample evidence to infer the intended audience of both passages, so (D) is incorrect.

• PROBLEM 3-25

Lines 20–21 of Passage 1 echoes what theme from Passage 2?

(A) A strong nation has to have the capacity to help those who are struggling to survive.

(B) A thriving nation must protect the rich.

(C) A free society must completely support the poor.

(D) A clearly defined class structure is necessary if a nation is to survive.

(E) A nation must be prosperous if it is to influence world events.

SOLUTION:

(A) Both passages speak of helping those less well-off. The first speaks of those in developing countries, and the second speaks of those hard hit by a faltering economy in their own country. (B) and (C) are blindly literal interpretations that pay no attention to the context in which they are framed. (D) has no basis in either passage. (E) could be inferred to be true, but it is not a theme of Passage 2.

• PROBLEM 3–26

Both passages mention which of the following as being important to the success of a nation as they describe it?

(A) Unity among peoples or countries

(B) Powerful leadership

(C) A strong foreign policy

(D) A willingness to protect liberty at all costs

(E) The ability to overcome material difficulties

SOLUTION:

(A)   Both authors speak of the importance of understanding and support that is gained through unity. Passage 2 says that leadership must be frank and vigorous, but no mention is made of being powerful; so (B) is incorrect. (C) and (D) are preoccupations of only Passage 1, while (E) is only a concern in Passage 2.

In this passage, John Donne discusses the philosophical similarities between Earth and Man.

1   It is too little to call man a little world; except God, man is diminutive to nothing. Man consists of more pieces, more parts, than the world; than the world doth, nay, than the world is. And if these pieces were extended and stretched out in man as they are in the world, man would be
5   the giant and the world the dwarf; the world but the map, and the man the world. If all the veins in our bodies were extended to rivers, and all the sinews to veins of mines, and all the muscles that lie upon one another to hills, and all the bones to quarries of stones, and all the other pieces to the proportion of those which correspond to them in the world, the air would
10   be too little for this orb of man to move in, the firmament would be but enough for this star. For as the whole world hath nothing to which something in man doth not answer, so hath man many pieces of which the whole world hath no representation. Enlarge this meditation upon this

great world, man, so far as to consider the immensity of the creatures this
15 world produces. Our creatures are our thoughts, creatures that are born
giants, that reach from east to west, from earth to heaven, that do not only
bestride all the sea and land, but span the sun and firmament at once: my
thoughts reach all, comprehend all.

Inexplicable mystery! I their creator am in a close prison, in a sick
20 bed, anywhere, and any one of my creatures, my thoughts, is with the sun,
and beyond the sun, overtakes the sun, and overgoes the sun in one pace,
one step, everywhere. And then as the other world produces serpents and
vipers, malignant and venomous creatures, and worms and caterpillars,
that endeavor to devour that world which produces them, and monsters
25 compiled and complicated of divers parents and kinds, so this world, our
selves, produces all these in us, producing diseases and sicknesses of all
those sorts; venomous and infectious diseases, feeding and consuming
diseases, and manifold and entangles diseases made up of many several
ones. And can the other world name so many venomous, so many consum-
30 ing, so many monstrous creatures, as we can diseases, of all these kinds?
O miserable abundance, O beggarly riches! How much do we lack of
having remedies for every disease when as yet we have not names for
them?

But we have a Hercules against these giants, these monsters: that is
35 the physician. He musters up all the resources of the other world to succor
this, all nature to relieve man. We have the physician but we are not the
physician. Here we shrink in our proportion, sink in our dignity in respect
of very mean creatures who are physicians to themselves. The hart that is
pursued and wounded, they say, knows an herb which, being eaten, throws
40 off the arrow: a strange kind of vomit. The dog that pursues it, though he
is subject to sickness, even proverbially knows his grass that recovers him.
And it may be true that the drugger is as near to man as to other creatures;
it may be that obvious and present simples, easy to be had, would cure
him; but the apothecary is not so near him, nor the physician so near him,
45 as they too are to other creatures. Man hath not that innate instinct to apply
these nature medicines to his present danger, as those inferior creatures
have. He is not his own apothecary, his own physician, as they are. Call
back therefore thy meditation again, and bring it down. What's become of
man's great extent and proportion, when himself shrinks himself and con-
50 sumes himself to a handful of dust? What's become of his soaring
thoughts, his compassing thoughts, when himself brings himself to the
ignorance, to the thoughtlessness of the grave? His diseases are his own,
but the physician is not, he hath them at home, but he must send for the
physician.

• PROBLEM 3-27

Donne finds an ironic contrast

(A) among the venomous creatures of this world.

(B) between Hercules and the physician.

(C) between the hart and the dog.

(D) between man's confinements and man's thoughts.

(E) between apothecaries and physicians.

SOLUTION:

(D) Lines 19–22 describe how a confined man may still enjoy imaginative freedom and dominance of the universe. Apothecaries and physicians (line 47) are not contrasted; they are both admired as benefactors of man, denying (E) and by extension (B), since physicians are directly compared to the Greek hero (lines 34–35). He describes the venomous creatures (A) as a cohesive group, and he draws a comparison between the hart and the dog (C).

• PROBLEM 3-28

The word "simples" (line 43) means

(A) uncomplicated possessions.

(B) foolish people.

(C) direct procedures.

(D) remedies.

(E) mathematical formulas.

SOLUTION:

(D) Donne speaks of "simples" as easy to be had and sure to cure an illness; so, in context, "simples" are remedies, prescriptions from a druggist. The rest of the options are possible meanings for "simple," but none of them bear any relation to this passage.

•PROBLEM 3-29

In his opening discussion, Donne inverts

(A) microscopic organisms with cosmic giants.

(B) the relation between maps and geographic locations.

(C) the magnitude of men with that of Earth.

(D) the proportions of sinews and muscles.

(E) the relationship of hills to stones.

SOLUTION:

(C)   The breadth of men and Earth are given inverse proportions in Donne's conceit (lines 2–3); (A) is a strong distractor only if the reader superimposes "microcosmic" onto the image of man which Donne has not. World and map are inverted (line 5), not geography and map, and only in contrast to man as the world, choice (B). Both (D) and (E) are incorrect based on misreading analogies; Donne speaks of sinews, muscles, hills, and stones, but only in order to support his original inversion of the size of man and the size of the Earth.

• PROBLEM 3-30

Phrases like "O miserable abundance, O beggarly riches!" (line 31) reveal

(A) Donne's contradictory style.

(B) Donne's inability to see the positive aspects of life.

(C) the effects of venom on the human constitution.

(D) the poet's use of oxymoron in describing a union of opposites.

(E) how much happier beasts are than men.

SOLUTION:

(D)   An "oxymoron" is a figure of speech in which opposite or contradictory ideas are combined. This is what Donne does when he combines the antonyms, "miserable" and "abundance," and "beggarly" and "riches." (A) is insufficient to explain the reversals Donne posits throughout the passage as an explanation of his mystical humanism. The contradictions are not important to the style but to the content of Donne's work. All of paragraph one is grandly positive and assertive, denying choices (B) and (C). The disposition of beasts (E) does not arise until the final paragraph (lines 38–41).

• PROBLEM 3-31

Donne employs the word "answer" (line 12) to mean

(A) correspond.

(B) verbally reply.

(C) justify itself.

(D) intuitively respond.

(E) anticipate.

SOLUTION:

(A) The entire passage is an elaborate comparison and contrast of man and the Earth. In this particular sentence, he states that the Earth has nothing which doesn't have some correspondence in man. Donne's metaphysical style searches for analogies and correspondences in nature; it is based on comparisons. The remainder of the words might be appropriate meanings of the word "answer" in other contexts, but they bear no relation to this passage.

• PROBLEM 3-32

Donne's reference to "the other world" (line 35) signifies

(A) the world of supernatural beings.

(B) the physician relies on his imagination.

(C) the world of books.

(D) the religious order.

(E) remedies made from natural sources.

SOLUTION:

(E) In this particular section of the passage, Donne is speaking of physicians and of the source of their remedies. Physicians rely on nature, not the supernatural (A), pure imagination (B), or religion (D). "Books" (C) in fact never appear in the text.

• PROBLEM 3-33

The nature of the "very mean creatures" (line 38)

(A) tends to raise man's estimate of himself.

(B) provides the proper study for science.

(C) prohibits their adapting to change or struggle.

(D) shows man to be comparatively inept at healing himself.

(E) raises the dignity of the physician's skill.

SOLUTION:

(D)   Ironically, the "mean creatures" prove more able to heal themselves than man; so we "shrink in proportion," negating (A) and (E), as well as contradicting (C) (see lines 45–46). (B) is never discussed.

• PROBLEM 3-34

For Donne, the ultimate negation of the power of thought is

(A) sleep.

(B) unscientific speculation.

(C) death.

(D) simple nature.

(E) imaginary concern with "monsters."

SOLUTION:

(C)   Death is explicit in the phrase "the thoughtlessness of the grave" (line 52). (D) is incorrect since nature provokes thought (lines 37–48). (E) The ability to create imaginary "monsters" is a tribute to the power of thought. (A) and (B) are never addressed as subjects.

• PROBLEM 3–35

When Donne says that "he hath them at home" (line 53), the "them" refers to

(A) man's imaginings.

(B) man's illnesses.

(C) the physicians.

(D) creatures.

(E) medicines.

SOLUTION:

(B)   The complete sentence from which this is taken states, "His diseases are his own ... he hath them at home." So, taken in context, (B) is obviously correct. Man nurtures his diseases, his own destruction, at home. Grammatical (and logical) scrutiny should dismiss (C) and (E) quickly; (A) and (D) are almost synonymous—and wrong.

• PROBLEM 3–36

The "diseases and sicknesses" (line 26) of men

(A) are sent as a punishment for human pride.

(B) are produced by men themselves.

(C) are no worse than the venomous beasts in nature.

(D) baffle the physicians who try to cure them.

(E) are merely metaphors for Donne's troubled times.

SOLUTION:

(B)   In lines 25–26, Donne explicitly states that " ... ourselves, produces all these in us, producing diseases and sicknesses of all those sorts ... " So (B) is the correct answer. Donne does not dwell on "pride" (A) or on his "troubled times" (E).

Donne speaks of the physicians as curing the diseases, not being baffled by them (D). Donne does draw similarities between diseases and beasts of nature (C), but not to say one is "worse" than another.

• PROBLEM 3-37

When Donne says, "my thoughts reach all, comprehend all" (lines 17–18), he confirms

(A) his earlier estimation of the power of poetry.

(B) his prior comparison of man with God.

(C) the pride and conceit that he says lead to downfall.

(D) his contrasting ideas on the creatures of this world.

(E) his claim that the world is literally populated by giants.

SOLUTION:

(B)   Among the defining qualities of God are omniscience and omnipresence. Donne's metaphysics elevate man to godlike proportions. Only later does he qualify his mediation and find man inferior to the simple beasts, (D). "If these pieces were extended" (line 3) is a concession to metaphor, not a literal belief in giants, choice (E). (C) might be inferred by the Biblical or literary reader of Donne; it is not stated. (A) is not addressed in the passage.

• PROBLEM 3-38

Donne's command to "bring it down" (line 48)

(A) means he wishes to simplify the language.

(B) forces us to reassess the position of man in the universe.

(C) symbolizes the lack of morals and compassion in the world.

(D) suggests that the sphere of heaven be made available on Earth.

(E) warns us that we are too materialistic in our values.

SOLUTION:

(B)   The first part of Donne's meditation glorifies mankind, making it seem larger than the Earth. When he admonishes us to "bring it down," he is showing us how disease and death can quickly make man seem much smaller and "forcing us to reassess the position of man in the universe" (B). He does not simplify his language (A). He never addresses our morals

(C) or our "materialistic . . . values" (E). Nor does he mention the sphere of heaven (D).

In this excerpt from Jules Vernes's Twenty Thousand Leagues Under the Sea, *we are presented with a danger on board the* Nautilus, *Captain Nemo's legendary submarine.*

1   The next day, the 22nd of March, at six in the morning, preparations for departure were begun. The last gleams of twilight were melting into night. The cold was great, the constellations shone with wonderful intensity. In the zenith glittered that wondrous Southern Cross—the polar bear
5 of Antarctic regions. The thermometer showed 12° below zero, and when the wind freshened it was most biting. Flakes of ice increased on the open water. The sea seemed everywhere alike. Numerous blackish patches spread on the surface, showing the formation of fresh ice. Evidently the southern basin, frozen during the six winter months, was absolutely inac-
10 cessible. What became of the whales in that time? Doubtless they went beneath the icebergs, seeking more practicable seas. As to the seals and morses, accustomed to life in a hard climate, they remained on these icy shores. The creatures have the instinct to break holes in the ice-fields and to keep them open. To these holes they come for breath; when the birds,
15 driven away by the cold, have emigrated to the north, these sea mammals remain sole masters of the polar continent. But the reservoirs were filling with water, and the *Nautilus* was slowly descending. At 1,000 feet deep it stopped; its screw beat the waves, and it advanced straight towards the north at a speed of fifteen miles an hour. Towards night it was already
20 floating under the immense body of the iceberg. At three in the morning I was awakened by a violent shock. I sat up in my bed and listened in the darkness, when I was thrown into the middle of the room. The *Nautilus*, after having struck, had rebounded violently. I groped along the partition, and by the staircase to the saloon, which was lit by the luminous ceiling.
25 The future was upset. Fortunately the windows were firmly set, and had held fast. The pictures on the starboard side, from being no longer vertical, were clinging to the paper, whilst those of the port side were hanging at least a foot from the wall. The *Nautilus* was lying on its starboard side perfectly motionless. I heard footsteps, and a confusion of voices; but Captain
30 Nemo did not appear. As I was leaving the saloon, Ned Land and Conseil entered. . . .

    We left the saloon. There was no one in the library. At the centre staircase, by the berths of the ship's crew, there was no one. I thought that Captain Nemo must be in the pilot's cage. It was best to wait. We all

35 returned to the saloon. For twenty minutes we remained thus, trying to
hear the slightest noise which might be made on board the *Nautilus*, when
Captain Nemo entered. He seemed not to see us; his face, generally so
impassive, showed signs of uneasiness. He watched the compass silently,
then the manometer; and, going to the planisphere, placed his finger on a
40 spot representing the southern seas. I would not interrupt him; but, some
minutes later, when he turned towards me, I said, using one of his own
expressions in the Torres Straits:

"An incident, Captain?"

"No, sir; an accident this time."

45 "Serious?"

"Perhaps."

"Is the danger immediate?"

"No."

"The *Nautilus* has stranded?"

50 "Yes."

"And this has happened—how?"

"From a caprice of nature, not from the ignorance of man. Not a
mistake has been made in the working. But we cannot prevent equilibrium
from producing its effects. We may brave human laws, but we cannot
55 resist natural ones."

Captain Nemo had chosen a strange moment for uttering this philosophical reflection. On the whole, his answer helped me little.

• PROBLEM 3-39

Why do the birds fly to the north in lines 14–16?

(A) The only type of cold that they can endure is in the North Pole.

(B) Extreme cold allows them to hibernate until the summer
months.

(C) The seals and morses, seeking supremacy in the land, drive the
birds away.

(D) The birds flee to the warmer climates of the north.

(E) The cold drives the birds into a panic, and they fly in the wrong
direction.

SOLUTION:

(D)   The passage states that the *Nautilus* was in the "Antarctic regions,"
and that the birds who flew to the north were "driven away by the cold." It

becomes clear from this that the birds fly north from the freezing South Pole to reach warmer climates.

The scene takes place on the opposite end of the world from the North Pole (A); so going north will not bring the birds to a place of extreme cold in order to "hibernate" (B). Although the seals and morses remain behind, they do not seek to drive the birds away (C). The passage does not imply that the birds were flying about in a blind panic (E).

• PROBLEM 3-40

What is meant when the narrator informs us that the *Nautilus* has "stopped" in line 18?

(A) The *Nautilus* has completely ceased to move.

(B) The *Nautilus* has paused only briefly before descending further.

(C) The *Nautilus* no longer descends, but continues to move.

(D) The *Nautilus* halts only long enough to fill its reservoirs with much-needed water.

(E) The *Nautilus* never ended its descent completely; it only slowed down its continuing descent.

SOLUTION:

(C)   The passage states that "the reservoirs were filling with water, and the *Nautilus* was slowly descending. At 1,000 feet deep it stopped; its screw beat the waves, and it advanced straight towards the north at a speed of fifteen miles an hour." Therefore, even though the *Nautilus* stopped descending, it continued to run straight towards the north. Because of this, it did not completely cease to move (A); nor did it descend any further (B). Its reservoirs were filled to allow the *Nautilus* to descend; there was no reason for them to be filled after the vessel had finished its descent (D). We have already shown that the *Nautilus* did indeed halt its descent (E).

• PROBLEM 3-41

In line 24, "luminous" most nearly means

(A) extravagant.   (D) artificial.

(B) glowing.   (E) damaged.

(C) enormous.

SOLUTION:

(B) "Luminous" means brilliant, shining, or glowing. This is exemplified by the fact that the saloon "was lit by the luminous ceiling." While the other selections may or may not have applied to the saloon's ceiling, these qualities were not included in the use of the word "luminous."

• PROBLEM 3-42

What is the message of Nemo's "philosophical reflection" in lines 52–55?

(A) Nature despises the artificial creations of mankind.

(B) Were it not for man's fallibility, anything would be possible.

(C) Despite man's perfection of the sciences, he may still succumb to the whims of Nature.

(D) Human beings are unable to complete a great project without including some terrible, fatal flaw.

(E) Man is ignorant only because Nature makes him so.

SOLUTION:

(C) The key word here is the "caprice," or whim, of Nature, to which all of Nemo's excellent planning falls victim. Nemo does not mention that Nature has any particular vendetta against man's accomplishments; it is a mere whim that the tides have turned against them (A). Nemo is sure to note that it is not the "ignorance of man" or a "mistake" that has endangered them; therefore, human fallibility of any sort [(B) and (D)] is not an issue here. Once again, Nemo does not feel that man's ignorance is important here; nor does he suggest that Nature would cause a state of ignorance (E).

• PROBLEM 3-43

What is the narrator's overall attitude toward Captain Nemo?

(A) Contempt   (D) Confusion

(B) Respect   (E) Condescension

(C) Anger

SOLUTION:

(B)   It is clear from several factors that the narrator has a great deal of respect for Captain Nemo. Not only did he wait anxiously for Nemo's arrival to fix matters, but when the captain did arrive, the narrator "would not interrupt him," but held his tongue until Nemo turned specifically to him. The narrator never considers Nemo in a tone of contempt (A), anger (C), or condescension (E). Although the narrator is sometimes unsure of Nemo's motives, he does not express a state of overall confusion when regarding the captain (D).

• PROBLEM 3-44

Why does Nemo feel the need to qualify the narrator's suggestion that the *Nautilus*'s situation be considered an "incident" (lines 43–44)?

(A) Nemo always corrects the narrator, no matter what the latter suggests.

(B) Nemo believes their current situation is of a significantly different character from what they experienced in the Torres Straits.

(C) Nemo considers "accidents" to be far more important than "incidents."

(D) Nemo fears that they will never survive their current situation and therefore changes the narrator's choice of definition.

(E) Nemo blames himself for his folly in bringing them into dangerous, uncharted territory.

SOLUTION:

(B)   The narrator uses the word "incident" in his conversation with Nemo to refer directly back to Nemo's own use of the word to describe an occurrence in the Torres Straits. Nemo's need to correct the narrator shows that he feels the narrator is incorrect in his assumption that the current situation is similar to whatever occurred in the Torres Straits.

There is no indication in the passage that Nemo constantly corrects the narrator (A), nor that "accidents" are normally of a graver nature than "incidents," although such may coincidentally be the case (C). Nemo never suggests that an "accident" is irreparable (D); nor does he reprimand himself for their current crisis (E).

• PROBLEM 3–45

The narrator notes that Nemo's face is normally "so impassive" (lines 37–38) in order to

(A) show how Nemo's current visage emphasizes the gravity of their situation.

(B) stress Nemo's arrogance to others whom he feels are beneath his station.

(C) explain why Nemo's expression is so uneasy.

(D) show why others are never able to approach Nemo intimately.

(E) reiterate Nemo's inability to deal with a crisis situation.

SOLUTION:

(A) The narrator is concerned that Nemo's apparent uneasiness bodes a serious problem merely because Nemo's countenance does not normally reflect his internal emotions. The narrator does not imply that this is a measure of Nemo's arrogance (B), nor that the captain is unable to communicate with others intimately (D). Nemo's normally stoic expression does not in itself explain his present uneasiness (C). There is no indication in the passage that Nemo is unable to deal with a crisis situation (E).

• PROBLEM 3–46

What is the most likely reason that the narrator seeks Captain Nemo after he leaves the saloon?

(A) He is angry and wishes to chastise Nemo for his ineptitude.

(B) He wants to do a favor for Ned Land and Conseil, who were looking for Nemo.

(C) He wants Nemo to repair the furniture in the saloon.

(D) He knows that Nemo is the only person capable of rectifying the situation.

(E) He is afraid that Nemo may have been injured in the collision.

SOLUTION:

(D) It is apparent from his later questioning of Nemo that the narrator has absolutely no idea what has happened to the *Nautilus,* much less any idea how to go about rectifying the situation; he clearly believes Nemo has the ability to right the matter.

There is no indication in the passage that the narrator is angry at Nemo (A), nor that he has any interest at the present in repairing the saloon furniture (C). The narrator was curious about Nemo's locale before he met Ned Land and Conseil; he is obviously seeking the captain for his own reasons (B). The fact that the narrator decided to wait for Nemo's arrival in the saloon indicates that he probably did not imagine that the captain was injured (E).

• PROBLEM 3-47

Why is the furniture "upset" in line 25?

(A) The furniture is inundated with flooding water and is therefore completely ruined.

(B) The furniture was broken to pieces during the shock of collision.

(C) The furniture's expensive luster has faded over the years.

(D) The furniture is in disarray after a shady gathering took place in the saloon.

(E) The furniture now rests on the walls, instead of the floor.

SOLUTION:

(E)   The passage states that "the *Nautilus* was lying on its starboard side perfectly motionless." The narrator describes how the pictures were either hanging or clinging to the walls, depending upon which walls they were hung (starboard or port). The furniture would have had nowhere to go but the starboard wall, which, in effect, had become the new floor.

There is no indication in the passage that there was flooding aboard the *Nautilus*; the narrator himself notes that the "windows were firmly set" (A). Nor is there any indication that the furniture was splintered by the collision (B). There is no mention at all about the furniture's luster (C); nor is there any indication that some form of secret gathering took place in the saloon prior to the collision (D).

*The following passage describes the development and use
of the submarine as an offensive weapon of war.*

1   A submarine was first used as an offensive weapon during the American Revolutionary War. The Turtle, a one-man submersible designed by
an American inventor named David Bushnell and hand-operated by a
screw propeller, attempted to sink a British man-of-war in New York
5 Harbor. The plan was to attach a charge of gunpowder to the ship's bottom
with screws and explode it with a time fuse. After repeated failures to
force the screws through the copper sheathing of the hull of the *H.M.S.
Eagle,* the submarine gave up and withdrew, exploding its powder a short
distance from the *Eagle.* Although the attack was unsuccessful, it caused
10 the British to move their blockading ships from the harbor to the outer
bay.

      On 17 February 1864, a Confederate craft, a hand-propelled submers-
ible, carrying a crew of eight men, sank a federal corvette that was blockading Charleston Harbor. The hit was accomplished by a torpedo sus-
15 pended ahead of the Confederate Hunley, as she rammed the Union frigate
Housatonic, and is the first recorded instance of a submarine sinking a
warship.

      The submarine first became a major component in naval warfare
during World War I, when Germany demonstrated its full potential.
20 Wholesale sinking of Allied shipping by the German U-boats almost
swung the war in favor of the Central Powers. Then, as now, the
submarine's greatest advantage was that it could operate beneath the ocean
surface where detection was difficult. Sinking a submarine was comparatively easy, once it was found—but finding it before it could attack was
25 another matter.

      During the closing months of World War I, the Allied Submarine
Devices Investigation Committee was formed to obtain from science and
technology more effective underwater detection equipment. The committee developed a reasonably accurate device for locating a submerged sub-
30 marine. This device was a trainable hydrophone, which was attached to
the bottom of the ASW ship, and used to detect screw noises and other
sounds that came from a submarine. Although the committee disbanded
after World War I, the British made improvements on the locating device,
during the interval between then and World War II, and named it ASDIC
35 after the committee.

      American scientists further improved on the device, calling it SO-
NAR, a name derived from the underlined initials of the words <u>so</u>und
<u>na</u>vigation and <u>ra</u>nging.

      At the end of World War II, the United States improved the snorkel
40 (a device for bringing air to the crew and engines when operating sub-

merged on diesels) and developed the Guppy (short for greater underwater propulsion power), a conversion of the fleet-type submarine of World War II fame. The superstructure was changed by reducing the surface area, streamlining every protruding object, and enclosing the periscope shears in
45 a streamlined metal fairing. Performance increased greatly with improved electronic equipment, additional battery capacity, and the addition of the snorkel.

• PROBLEM 3-48

The thematic emphasis of the passage lies in

(A) the Americans' improvements in the design of the submarine.

(B) the discussion of the submarine in nonmilitary contexts.

(C) the technical explanation of the snorkel as a device.

(D) the history of submarine development as an effective weapon.

(E) submarine advancements specific to the Second World War.

SOLUTION:

(D)   This passage is an extensive description of the development and use of the submarine by several different countries, dating from the Revolutionary War to sometime after WW II. The passage traces the history of the submarine "as an offensive weapon" (line 1). The dates from 1864 negate the specific reference to WW II in (E). Both German and English advances discussed in lines 17–35 negate (A). The opening sentence specifies military contexts, negating (B). Innovations discussed extend beyond the snorkel (C).

• PROBLEM 3-49

World War I has particular import for the submarine because

(A) of the antidetection devices that were developed.

(B) German use of the submarine exploited its offensive power.

(C) the sinking of the vessel became comparatively simple.

(D) the obsolescence of land-craft was made increasingly obvious.

(E) increasing government subsidies of science and technology aided the War Department.

SOLUTION:

(B)   Lines 17–18 state, "The submarine first became a major component in naval warfare during World War I, when Germany demonstrated its full potential." Germany exploited the full resources of the submarine. While (A) is a strong distractor, detection devices did not become refined until after WW I. (C) is ambiguous as to whether "the vessel" means the sub or its target—it is untrue in any case. (E) No mention is made of the war department. (D) is not discussed.

• PROBLEM 3–50

We can infer from the British removal of their ships from New York Harbor

(A)   that the British interests lay in the outer bay.

(B)   that the British were confident their men-of-war could withstand assault.

(C)   that submarine warfare had proved of some tactical advantage.

(D)   that they indicated their need to overhaul the *H.M.S. Eagle*.

(E)   that they insured that the importation of American gunpowder would be limited.

SOLUTION:

(C)   The passage states that during the Revolutionary War the Americans attempted to sink a British man-of-war using a submarine. Although it proved a failure, the very attempt to sink a British man-of-war proved intimidating. (B) is the wrong conclusion judging from the fact that the British moved their ships. (A) may be a rationalization of the British, but it is not mentioned in the text. (E) merely correlates to that misreading. (D) is a distractor.

• PROBLEM 3–51

The word "trainable" (line 29) means

(A) having domestic, not military use.

(B) relating to transportation.

(C) capable of being adapted to various sea transports.

(D) capable of being focused on a specific target.

(E) easily dismantled and reassembled onboard ship.

SOLUTION:

(D)   The hydrophone could be "aimed" at a specific target. (B) is the only "reasonable" distractor.

• PROBLEM 3–52

The function of the final paragraph is

(A) to review the contributions the submarine had made to warfare until World War II.

(B) to develop the operational use of SONAR.

(C) to discuss the function of the snorkel.

(D) to telescope several developments in the design of submarine offensive capability.

(E) to compare SONAR with the use of the Guppy.

SOLUTION:

(D)   The last paragraph of this passage describes important features of the submarine developed since WW II. It covers quite a lot of time and information in a short space. So (D) is the correct choice.

While (A) is a reasonable choice, the last paragraph, exceeds the chronology of WW II. (B) and (E) list specific technologies incidental to submarine history mentioned in the final paragraph, but not the sole function of the final paragraph. (C) also deals with a specific element, which is mentioned in the course of a list of technological innovations.

•PROBLEM 3–53

Lines 31–34 attribute improvements in submarine technology to

(A) the British exclusively, who worked on the location device.

(B) the Allied Submarine Devices Investigation Committee.

(C) the desire to end the World War as quickly as possible.

(D) a desire to develop antidetection devices to protect the submarine crew.

(E) the British, who advanced work already performed by ASDIC.

SOLUTION:

(E)   In lines 31–34, the passage explicitly states that although the AS-DIC committee disbanded, the British "made improvements." So (E) is correct. (A) is incorrect because the British didn't create anything, they "improved" work already done by the committee. (B) is wrong because the work was done after the committee had been disbanded; and (C) is wrong because this occurred after the war was over. (D) suggests that they were developing "antidetection" devices while, in reality, they were working on a "locating" device.

In the following passage Martin Luther King
presents his vision of racial unity.

1   We cannot walk alone, and as we walk, we must make the pledge that we shall always march ahead. We cannot turn back. There are those who are asking the devotees of civil rights: "When will you be satisfied?" We can never be satisfied as long as the Negro is the victim of unspeakable
5 horrors of police brutality. We can never be satisfied as long as our bodies, heavy with the fatigue of travel, cannot gain lodging in the motels of the highways and the hotels of the cities. We can never be satisfied as long as the Negro's basic mobility is from a smaller ghetto to a larger one. We can never be satisfied as long as our children are stripped of their selfhood and
10 robbed of their dignity by signs stating "For Whites Only."

       We cannot be satisfied so long as the Negro in Mississippi cannot vote and the Negro in New York believes he has nothing for which to vote. No, no, we will not be satisfied until justice rolls down like water and righteousness like a mighty stream.

15   I am not unmindful that some of you have come here out of great trials and tribulations. Some of you have come from narrow jail cells. Some of you have come from areas where your quest for freedom left you battered by the storms of persecution and staggered by the winds of police brutality. You have been the veterans of creative suffering. Continue to
20 work with the faith that unearned suffering is redemptive.

     Go back to Mississippi. Go back to Alabama; go back to South Carolina; go back to Georgia; go back to Louisiana; go back to the slums and ghettoes of our northern cities knowing that somehow this situation can and will be changed. Let us not wallow in the valley of despair.

25   I say to you today, my friends, even though we face the difficulties of today and tomorrow, I still have a dream. It is a dream deeply rooted in the American dream. I have a dream that one day this Nation will rise up and live out the true meaning of its creeds—"we hold these truths to be self-evident that all men are created equal."

30   I have a dream that one day on the red hills of Georgia the sons of slaves and the sons of former slaveowners will be able to sit down together at the table of brotherhood. I have a dream that one day even the state of Mississippi, sweltering with the heat of injustice, sweltering with the heat of oppression, will be transformed into an oasis of freedom and
35 justice.

     I have a dream that my four little children will one day live in a Nation where they will not be judged by the color of their skins, but by the content of their character.

     I have a dream that one day in Alabama, with this vicious racist, its
40 Governor, having his lips dripping the words of interposition and nullification—one day right there in Alabama, little black boys and black girls will be able to join hands with little white boys and little white girls as brothers and sisters.

     I have a dream that one day every valley shall be exalted: every hill
45 and mountain shall be made low, the rough places will be made plane, the crooked places will be made straight and the glory of the Lord shall be revealed and all flesh shall see it together.

     This is our hope. This is the faith that I go back to the South with. With this faith, we will be able to hew out of the mountains of despair a
50 stone of hope. With this faith, we will be able to transform the jangling discord of our Nation into a beautiful symphony of brotherhood. With this faith, we will be able to work together; to play together; to struggle together; to go to jail together; to stand up for freedom together knowing that we will be free one day. . . .

• PROBLEM 3–54

In line 40, the word "interposition" most nearly means

(A) a mixing, a conglomeration.

(B) a lofty height or position.

(C) a coming together, a union.

(D) a uniting.

(E) an intervention.

SOLUTION:

(E)   The word "interposition" means an intervention or a mediation. Answer (E) most nearly satisfies that definition.

A conglomeration is not an intervention or a coming between, but a mixing; (A) would not be the best choice. One who intervenes does not necessarily have to be in a lofty position; (B) is not, therefore, the best answer; perhaps the person who chose this answer selected it merely because both the word being considered and the answer contained the letters "position."

After an intervention, there may be a coming together (C) or a uniting (D), but interposition does not necessarily ensure this result; (C) and (D) are not, therefore, the best answers.

• PROBLEM 3–55

In lines 13–14, the words "justice rolls down like water and righteousness like a mighty stream" can best be described as

(A) onomatopoeic words.

(B) an alliterative expression.

(C) an understatement.

(D) an analogy.

(E) a fantasy.

SOLUTION:

(D)   In lines 13–14, the words "justice rolls down like water and righteousness like a mighty stream" can best be described as a comparison, or an analogy (D).

Since an onomatopoeic word is formed by making an imitation of the sound associated with the object or action and these words don't sound like water or a stream, onomatopoeic (A) is not the best answer.

An alliterative expression repeats the same sound at the beginning of each word; this has not been done in the phrase, "justice rolls down like water and righteousness like a mighty stream." It is not alliterative, so (B) is incorrect. Using terms like "mighty stream" and "righteousness" are not understatements; (C) should not be selected. The words in question do not describe a fantasy, but a vision capable of being fulfilled. (D) should not be selected since it expresses this quotation as being a fantasy.

• PROBLEM 3–56

The Southern states, the slums, and the ghettos in the fourth paragraph were listed

(A) in order to show that though the United States is large, racial inequality is limited to two main areas.

(B) in order to name the areas from which most of the audience came.

(C) in order to single out areas where political leaders were most biased.

(D) to warn those areas of the violence planned.

(E) to remind people in those areas that even though times may be rough, they should not give up.

SOLUTION:

(E) The Southern states, the slums, and the ghettos in the fourth paragraph were listed to inspire hope; even if those areas were desolate at this time, King had faith that in the future things would change. (E) is the best answer.

Unfortunately, racial bias and inequality are not just evident in two areas; (A), then, was an inadequate answer.

The audience did not necessarily come only from the areas listed above; (B) is not the best answer.

Biased political leaders are not restricted to slums, ghettos, and Southern states; (C) is not the best choice. King did not plan violence; so answer (D) is not appropriate.

• PROBLEM 3–57

King reminded the audience that "unearned suffering is redemptive" in line 20. The best explanation for this statement is that

(A) some suffering is earned; it is deserved.

(B) some suffering is justified; it is purifying, as such.

(C) unearned suffering is cruel and unforgivable.

(D) unearned suffering is desirable.

(E) some undeserved suffering is freeing and releasing.

SOLUTION:

(E) King reminded the audience that "unearned suffering is redemptive" in line 20. He said this to give them hope and to make their suffering a little easier to bear. The best explanation for this statement is that King was suggesting that some undeserved suffering may actually be freeing and releasing. (E) is the best choice.

King makes no reference to the fact that some of the suffering endured was earned or deserved. (A) is not the best choice. King does not see suffering as being justified; so (B) is incorrect. King does not advocate unforgiveness; (C) is incorrect. King does not advocate followers seeking to suffer for no reason; he does not see unearned suffering as something to be sought or desired; (D) is incorrect.

• PROBLEM 3–58

King compares his audience to those who had fought in great battles by calling them

(A) veterans.   (D) flesh.

(B) battered.   (E) devotees.

(C) staggered.

SOLUTION:

(A) In line 19, King uses the phrase " . . . the veterans of creative suffering." King best compared his audience to those who had fought in great battles by calling them (A) veterans. It is true that the audience may have been (B) battered, but that does not necessarily go along with war alone;

victims of other situations may be battered; (B) should not be chosen. The audience may be oppressed and may stagger, but this does not necessarily relate to war; staggered (C) is not a good choice. Flesh (D) does not describe people; so (D) should not be selected. A devotee (E) may or may not relate to war; (E) should not be chosen.

• PROBLEM 3-59

The "old saying" which best fits lines 36–38 is

(A) "A soft answer turneth away wrath."

(B) "You can't judge a book by its cover."

(C) "Birds of a feather flock together."

(D) "Let sleeping dogs lie."

(E) "A good name is rather to be chosen than great riches."

SOLUTION:

(B) The "old saying" which best fits lines 36–38 is (B), "You can't judge a book by its cover." King is looking forward to the day when people are judged by their character and not by their skin color; (B) is the answer to be chosen.

Although (A) is an oft-repeated statement and even though it does fit some of King's speeches, it does not fit in this context; (A) should not be chosen.

Judging little children by their skin color does not relate to "birds of a feather flock(ing) together;" (C) should not be chosen.

Not disturbing the situation, or "let(ting) sleeping dogs lie," does not relate to the color of the children's skin; (D) does not fit. "A good name is rather to be chosen than great riches" has nothing to do with judging children by their skin color; (E) is not the best answer.

• PROBLEM 3-60

King used the analogy of winds for police brutality because winds

(A) rise up and then die.

(B) turn first one way and then another.

(C) are easy to protect oneself against.

(D) can be harnessed and used, as by a windmill.

(E) can be a damaging and a fearful obstacle, when strong.

SOLUTION:

(E)   The word "brutality" implies dangerous and destructive forces. King used the analogy of winds for police brutality because winds when strong can be damaging and a fearful obstacle; (E) is the best choice.

Winds do rise up and then die, but that analogy is not the best here; it does not seem to relate to the police; and therefore, (A) is not the best answer.

King does not describe the police as turning first one way and then another; (B) is not the best answer.

Since winds are not always easy to protect oneself against, (C) is not the best choice.

A wind, which can be harnessed and used as a windmill, does not seem to be a good analogy here; one does not usually think of harnessing police; thus, (D) is not the best answer.

• PROBLEM 3-61

The main theme of this writing is

(A) dissatisfaction.   (D) struggle and defeat.

(B) despair.   (E) faith and hope.

(C) judgment.

SOLUTION:

(E)   Although King is describing great difficulties, the main theme of this writing is faith and hope; (E) is the best answer. King is trying to inspire as he speaks.

There is an element of dissatisfaction (A) with current conditions, but this is not the overriding theme; (A) should not be chosen.

King is not urging his audience to feel despair (B); rather, he is encouraging them with a dream of better times to come.

King is not seeking judgment (C) for those who oppress; (C) should not be chosen. King's speech is one of optimism, faith, and hope—not struggle and defeat (D); therefore, (D) is not the best answer.

• PROBLEM 3-62

The writer's main feeling toward the Constitution and the Declaration of Independence was

(A) disgust.

(B) disappointment.

(C) amusement.

(D) faith.

(E) curiosity.

SOLUTION:

(D) The writer's main feeling toward the Constitution and the Declaration of Independence was a feeling of confidence and faith (D); (D) is the correct answer. King never expressed disgust (A) toward the Constitution and Declaration of Independence—only with the way they had been interpreted; (A) is not the right answer. King did not express disappointment (B) with the documents themselves—only with those who used them; thus, (B) is not the correct answer. Nothing in King's speech suggests amusement (C); (C) should not be selected. Nothing in King's speech indicates curiosity (E) about these two documents; therefore (E) should not be selected.

In this passage, the author highlights events from the Watergate crisis, which occurred during the Nixon administration.

1 What became known as the Watergate crisis began during the 1972 presidential campaign. Early on the morning of June 17, James McCord, a security officer for the Committee to Re-elect the President (CREEP), and four other men broke into Democratic headquarters at the Watergate apart-
5 ment complex in Washington, D.C., and were caught while going through files and installing electronic eavesdropping devices. On June 22, Nixon announced that the administration was in no way involved in the burglary attempt.

The trial of the burglars began in early 1973, with all but McCord,
10 who was convicted, pleading guilty. Before sentencing, McCord wrote a
letter to Judge John J. Sirica arguing that high Republican officials had
known in advance about the burglary and that perjury had been committed
at the trial.

Soon Jeb Stuart Magruder, head of CREEP, and John W. Dean,
15 Nixon's attorney, stated that they had been involved. Dean testified before
a Senate Watergate investigating committee that Nixon had been involved
in covering up the incident. Over the next several months, extensive involvement of the administration, including payment of "silence" money to
the burglars, destruction of FBI records, forgery of documents, and wire-
20 tapping, was revealed. Dean was fired and H. R. Haldeman and John
Ehrlichman, who headed the White House Staff, and Attorney General
Richard Kleindienst resigned. Nixon claimed that he had not personally
been involved in the cover-up but refused, on the grounds of executive
privilege, to allow investigation of White House documents.

25 Under considerable pressure, Nixon agreed to the appointment of a
special prosecutor, Archibald Cox of Harvard Law School. When Cox
obtained a subpoena for tape recordings of White House conversations
(whose existence had been revealed during the Senate hearings)—and the
administration lost an appeal in the appellate court—Nixon ordered Elliot
30 Richardson, now the attorney general, to fire Cox. Both Richardson and
his subordinate, William Ruckelshaus, resigned, leaving Robert Bork, the
solicitor general, to carry out the order. This "Saturday Night Massacre,"
which took place on October 20, 1973, aroused a storm of controversy.
The House Judiciary Committee, headed by Peter Rodino of New Jersey,
35 began looking into the possibilities of impeachment. Nixon agreed to turn
the tapes over to Judge Sirica and named Leon Jaworski as the new special
prosecutor. But it soon became known that some of the tapes were missing
and that a portion of another had been erased.

In March 1974, a grand jury indicted Haldeman, Ehrlichman, former
40 Attorney General John Mitchell, and four other White House aides and
named Nixon an unindicted co-conspirator.

In April, Nixon released edited transcripts of the White House tapes,
the contents of which led to further calls for his resignation. Jaworski
subpoenaed 64 additional tapes, which Nixon refused to turn over, and the
45 case went to the Supreme Court.

Meanwhile, the House Judiciary Committee televised its debate over
impeachment, adopting three articles of impeachment. It charged the
President with obstructing justice, misusing presidential power, and failing
to obey the committee's subpoenas.

50   Before the House began to debate impeachment, the Supreme Court ordered the President to release the subpoenaed tapes to the special prosecutor. On August 5, Nixon, under pressure from his advisors, released the tape of June 23, 1972, to the public. This tape, recorded less than a week after the break-in, revealed that Nixon had used the CIA to keep the FBI
55 from investigating the case. Nixon announced his resignation on August 8, 1973, to take effect at noon the following day. Gerald Ford then became president.

• PROBLEM 3–63

The idea of impeaching President Nixon arose

(A) out of CREEP, an organization whose acronym proved ironic.

(B) when Archibald Cox subpoenaed White House tapes.

(C) right after John Ehrlichman and Richard Kleindienst resigned.

(D) from a suggestion made by solicitor general Robert Bork.

(E) from the House Judiciary Committee led by Peter Rodino.

SOLUTION:

(E)   Lines 34-35 overtly broach the subject of impeachment with the sentence, "The House Judiciary Committee, headed by Peter Rodino of New Jersey, began...." (A) is a clear distractor, since CREEP supported President Nixon. (B) is a distractor, because Cox's subpoena led to further doubts concerning the President. (C) and (D) are incorrect, especially as Bork supported Nixon, and the two resignees defended the office of the President.

• PROBLEM 3-64

The so-called "Saturday Night Massacre" (line 32)

(A) was a media attempt to smear President Nixon as an Al Capone-like gangster.

(B) was a domino effect caused by Nixon's fear of what could be revealed on the White House tapes.

(C) was a label provided by the Democrats to Nixon's appointment of Archibald Cox.

(D) was President Nixon's just policy of firing anyone connected with the Watergate break-in.

(E) revealed the panic in several Presidential appointees who had to carry out unpopular orders.

SOLUTION:

(B) President Nixon's attempt to fire Archibald Cox created antagonistic repercussions about a cover-up, during which several officials resigned (see line 33). While the media likely labeled the firings, (A) is a distractor related to the St. Valentine's Day Massacre. (D) is a clear reversal of history's judgment. (E) is partly true, psychologically, but the actions were not due to fear so much as the desire to maintain integrity. (C) is unjustified by the text.

• PROBLEM 3-65

The final paragraph suggests that President Nixon

(A) suffered deep regrets over the Watergate scandal.

(B) used one government agency against another in order to maintain power.

(C) enjoyed a certain prestige with and immunity from the Supreme Court.

(D) remained indifferent to the advisors that he himself selected.

(E) managed to extend his policies in the administration of Gerald Ford.

SOLUTION:

(B) The final paragraph states that " . . . Nixon had used the CIA to keep the FBI from investigating the case." President Nixon abused his power in order to destroy opposition (see lines 53–55). The Watergate scandal disabused (C), since the President was not above the law. (A) may be true in retrospect, but the text does not discuss regret per se. President Nixon's relation to his advisors (D) is undiscussed. Gerald Ford's administration (E) is likewise undiscussed.

• PROBLEM 3-66

President Nixon's first line of defense against his being investigated was

(A) his disassociation from Jeb Stuart Magruder and John W. Dean.

(B) his confirmation that James McCord had masterminded the Watergate operation.

(C) his naming of Leon Jaworski as special prosecutor.

(D) his permitting the hearings to be televised.

(E) his claim of executive privileges.

SOLUTION:

(E) Lines 22–24 explicitly state "Nixon . . . refused, on grounds of executive privilege, to allow investigation. . . . " The claim of executive privilege (line 23) was supposed to insulate President Nixon from investigation, negating (A) and (B), since the President did not have to answer for his underlings. Both (C) and (D) ironically aggravated the President's situation (see lines 36–37).

• PROBLEM 3-67

The payment of "silence" money (line 18)

(A) was part of a major conspiracy to cover up White House involvement.

(B) meant that the media would not mention President Nixon's involvement.

(C) managed to satisfy the Democrats that little damage had been done to their campaign.

(D) reduced the original charges to simply burglary and bribery.

(E) created a major financial drain on CREEP.

SOLUTION:

(A) Lines 17–19 list a host of cover-up activities used to mask administration involvement. Both (B) and (E) are clear misreadings, because (B) the media was never silenced and (E) a financial drain is not mentioned. (C) is never addressed. (D) is possibly implied, but it represents a false conclusion.

• PROBLEM 3-68

The ramifications of James McCord's testimony

(A) centered around his claim that perjury had occurred.

(B) were nullified because of the use of illegal wire-tapping.

(C) immediately implicated H. R. Haldeman.

(D) led him to destroy FBI records.

(E) vindicated the Republican party of further blame.

SOLUTION:

(A) McCord's letter is described in lines 10–14, which say that "... high Republican officials had known ... about the burglary and that perjury had been committed at the trial." McCord's letter implicated higher-ups in the GOP. (B), (D), and (E) are clear misreadings, because none of these things happened. (C) is an indirect—rather than a direct—result of his letter to Judge Sirica.

• PROBLEM 3-69

The actual process of "impeachment" (line 35) means

(A) that the President is immediately dismissed from office.

(B) that the Senate assumes the executive leadership of government.

(C) that executive power is diverted to the Supreme Court.

(D) that the President is formally accused of wrongdoing.

(E) that the House of Representatives replaces the Cabinet.

SOLUTION:

(D)   "Impeachment" merely means accusation, not (A), dismissal. (B), (C), and (E) exploit the misuse of the term.

• PROBLEM 3-70

The House Judiciary Committee felt that

(A) its subpoenas had no power to compel a President to act.

(B) the White House tapes should be protected in the interest of national security.

(C) media publicity would prove detrimental to the office of the President.

(D) no executive privilege put a President above the law.

(E) a definition of "misuse of power" could not be achieved.

SOLUTION:

(D)   Lines 46–49 state that the House Judiciary Committee adopted three articles of impeachment, which clearly proves that they believed that (D) "no executive privilege put a President above the law." Therefore, they believed that their subpoenas did have power over the President (A). Since they did act, they must not have been paralyzed by a fear for "national security" or of "media publicity;" (B) and (C) are, therefore, incorrect. Since one of the charges was "misusing presidential power," they must have reached a definition of this phrase (E).

Communicable illness and disease were often rampant in the ancient
world, incapacitating and killing hundreds on a daily basis. The following
passage describes the effects of the Athenian plague on history.

(From *Rats, Lice, and History* by Hans Zinsser. Copyright © 1934, 1935, 1963 by Hans
Zinsser. By permission of Little, Brown and Company.)

1   The oldest recorded epidemic, often regarded as an outbreak of ty-
phus, is the Athenian plague of the Peloponnesian Wars, which is described in the Second Book of the *History* of Thucydides.
    In trying to make the diagnosis of epidemics from ancient descrip-
5 tions, when the differentiation of simultaneously occurring diseases was
impossible, it is important to remember that in any great outbreak, while
the large majority of cases may represent a single type of infection, there
is usually a coincident increase of other forms of contagious diseases; for
the circumstances which favor the spread of one infectious agent often
10 create opportunities for the transmission of others. Very rarely is there a
pure transmission of a single malady. It is not unlikely that the description
of Thucydides is confused by the fact that a number of diseases were
epidemic in Athens at the time of the great plague. The conditions were
ripe for it. Early in the summer of 430 B.C. large armies were camped in
15 Attica. The country population swarmed into Athens, which became very
much overcrowded. The disease seems to have started in Ethiopia . . .
thence traveled through Egypt and Libya, and at length reached the seaport
of Piraeus. It spread rapidly. Patients were seized suddenly, out of a clear
sky. The first symptoms were severe headache and redness of the eyes.
20 These were followed by inflammation of the tongue and pharynx, accompanied by sneezing, hoarseness, and cough. Soon after this, there was
acute intestinal involvement, with vomiting, diarrhea, and excessive thirst.
Delirium was common. The patients that perished usually died between
the seventh and ninth days. Many of those who survived the acute stage
25 suffered from extreme weakness and a continued diarrhea that yielded to
no treatment. At the height of the fever, the body became covered with
reddish spots . . . some of which ulcerated. When one of the severe cases
recovered, convalescence was often accompanied by necrosis of the fingers and the toes. Some lost their eyesight. In many there was complete
30 loss of memory. Those who recovered were immune, so that they could
nurse the sick without further danger. None of those who, not thoroughly
immunized, had it for the second time died of it. Thucydides himself had
the disease. After subsiding for a while, when the winter began, the disease reappeared and seriously diminished the strength of the Athenian
35 state.
    The plague of Athens, whatever it may have been, had a profound
effect upon historical events. It was one of the main reasons why the
Athenian armies, on the advice of Pericles, did not attempt to expel the

Lacedaemonians, who were raiding Attica. Athenian life was completely
40 demoralized, and a spirit of extreme lawlessness resulted. . . . There was
no fear of the laws of God or man. Piety and impiety came to be the same
thing, and no one expected that he would live to be called to account.
Finally, the Peloponnesians left Attica in a hurry, not for fear of the Athenians, who were locked up in their cities, but because they were afraid of
the disease.

• PROBLEM 3-71

The point of this passage is to demonstrate

(A) that "pure" outbreaks of disease were common in the ancient
world.

(B) that treatments of epidemic diseases remain relatively ineffective.

(C) the relation that exists between infectious disease and historical
events.

(D) the relatively poor health conditions in ancient Athens.

(E) the wisdom of Pericles in dealing with foreign invaders.

SOLUTION:

(C)   The first sentence of the final paragraph states, "The plague of
Athens . . . had a profound effect upon historical events." The point of this
passage is to demonstrate the relation between infectious disease and historical events (C).

(A) is incorrect because it is made clear that epidemics were complex
affairs in lines 7–10. (B) is not correct because the current level of treatment is not discussed in this passage.

The level of medical prevention in ancient Athens (D) is also incorrect because, although it may have been mentioned, it is not the main
point.

(E) is not correct because Pericles is not discussed in great detail and
is in fact only mentioned once.

• PROBLEM 3-72

One of the results of extended sickness in Athens was

(A) to put their democratic constitution in danger.

(B) to produce a moral nihilism, where death negated ethical life.

(C) to invite the Peloponnesians for a prolonged occupation of the city.

(D) to increase general belief in supernatural powers.

(E) to clarify the exact cause of the outbreak.

SOLUTION:

(B) Lines 39–41 state that " . . . There was no fear of the laws of God or man . . . no one expected he would live to be called to account." Men's morals are neutralized by the continuous presence of death; therefore, (B) is the correct answer. (A) and (D) are both incorrect because they are not justified by the text. (C) is incorrect because the Peloponnesians fled for fear of infection. (E) is also incorrect because the author discusses the lack of certainty in the cause of the epidemic.

• PROBLEM 3-73

The symptom "necrosis" (line 28) probably indicates

(A) tissue death.

(B) that victims suffered more at night.

(C) that patients could not be moved.

(D) the incompetence of doctors at that time.

(E) the incredible speed at which victims died.

SOLUTION:

(A) Lines 28–29 state that "...convalescence was often accompanied by necrosis of the fingers and the toes." Judging from this context, we can infer that necrosis means (A) "tissue death."

Fingers and toes have no relation to night and day (B). Anything that would affect fingers and toes would not make the patient difficult to move (C). The passage never mentions the incompetence of doctors (D). If "necrosis" happened during "convalescence" (recovery), it would not relate to the speed at which the victims died (E).

• PROBLEM 3-74

Two of the factors exacerbating the spread of the plague were

(A) low standards of medical practice and poor army discipline.

(B) severe overpopulation and outbreaks of several maladies.

(C) poor political judgment and failure to enforce housing codes.

(D) an influx of Ethiopians and the departure of the Lacedae-monians.

(E) the failure to identify the disease and poor nutrition.

SOLUTION:

(B)   Lines 15–17 identify the two causes of outbreak as overcrowding and coincident epidemics. (A) is incorrect because poor army discipline is not given as a factor in spreading the plague. (C) is also incorrect because housing codes are not mentioned in this passage. An influx of Ethiopians (D) would be a misreading of the author's statement that it seems the disease started in Ethiopia. Poor nutrition is not mentioned as a cause for the outbreak (E).

• PROBLEM 3-75

Which of the following symptoms IS NOT indicative of the plague the author describes?

(A) Amnesia

(B) Ulcers of the skin

(C) Delirium

(D) Death in reinfected patients

(E) Death in one week to nine days

SOLUTION:

(D)   The passage states that most people who had the plague became immune; and the rare cases of reinfection never resulted in death. Re-infected patients did not die; so this is not indicative of the plague. All the other choices are mentioned in the passage and are symptoms indicative of the plague.

• PROBLEM 3–76

The word "convalescence" in line 28 can most nearly be defined as

(A) langish.

(D) recuperation.

(B) innocuous.

(E) deterioration.

(C) contamination.

SOLUTION:

(D)   The correct answer is (D). The context clue here is "recover." "Recuperation" and "convalescence" both mean the process of becoming well after an illness, growing strong again. (A) means the opposite; (B) "innocuous" means "innocent or harmless." (C) is incorrect because it means "a process of contaminating, soiling, corrupting, or infecting." (E) is wrong because it means "to weaken" and is the opposite of "convalescence."

The age of Ancient Greece saw many different philosophies come to light. The following passage looks at the ideas and beliefs of Epicurus, Zeno, and Carneades of Cyrene.

1   The Hellenistic Age produced two major and two minor additions to the history of philosophy. Epicureanism and Stoicism represented the period's dominant philosophical movements. Skepticism and Cynicism found limited support among those unwilling to accept the Epicureans'
5   and Stoics' confidence in reason. Hellenistic philosophy marked a turning point in the Western intellectual tradition. The classical Greek philosophers linked the individual's happiness to the community's well-being. The philosophers of the Hellenistic period focused on the individual. The goal of philosophy shifted from the pursuit of knowledge for its own sake
10   to that of the individual's peace of mind and personal happiness.
        Epicurus (ca. 342–270 B.C.E.) founded a school in Athens and based his metaphysics on Democritus's atomic theory. Epicurus taught that the

goal of philosophy should be to help the individual find happiness. Unlike
15 Socrates and Plato, he did not make citizenship in a polis the basis of
happiness. Epicurus argued that a wise man eschewed public affairs and
sought self-sufficiency. Later critics accused Epicurus and his followers of
advocating a life based on pursuing the pleasures of the flesh. To
Epicurus, however, the highest pleasure was to be found in contemplation.
20   Zeno (ca. 335–263 B.C.E.) established a rival philosophical school
under the *Stoa Poikile* (painted porch) of the Athenian *Agora* (marketplace). There are a number of similarities between Stoicism and Epicureanism. Like Epicurus, Zeno emphasized the importance of the individual.
Moreover, both schools were based on a materialistic metaphysics and
25 claimed universal validity for their teachings. There were, however, significant differences between the two philosophical outlooks. Zeno taught
that the cosmos was a unified whole which was based on a universal order
(Logos or Fire). Every man carried a spark of this Logos in his reason. At
death this spark returned to its origin. The Stoics taught that each person
30 should strive to discover the natural law governing the universe and live in
accordance with it.
     The Skeptics attacked the Epicureans and the Stoics. Carneades of
Cyrene (ca. 213–129 B.C.E.) argued that all knowledge was relative. The
sensory impressions which we receive from the external world are flawed.
35 Individuals should abandon the quest for knowledge because nothing can
be known for certain. The safest course is to doubt everything. Indifference is the only philosophically defensible position.
     Diogenes of Sinope (d. 323 B.C.E.) was the most famous cynic. His
goal was to prepare the individual for any disaster. He lived as a beggar
40 and was famous for his outspoken condemnation of sham and hypocrisy.
One story has it that when he met Alexander the Great and the world-
conqueror asked him what he wanted, Diogenes replied that Alexander
should get out of his light.

• PROBLEM 3–77

Education for citizenship was a goal of

(A) Epicurus.   (D) Diogenes.

(B) Socrates.   (E) Zeno.

(C) Carneades.

SOLUTION:

(B) Education for citizenship was a goal of Socrates (B). Epicurus (A), on the other hand, emphasized individual happiness. Carneades (C) argued that all knowledge was relative; he was not concerned with society, as was Socrates; and therefore, (C) should not be chosen. Diogenes (D) was the most famous cynic; his goal was to prepare the individual for disaster. He probably would have seen education for citizenship as failure. Zeno (E) taught that the cosmos was a unified whole that was based on a universal order. His primary concern was not with citizenship.

• PROBLEM 3-78

The saying, "I am trying to find myself and my happiness," might be employed by a follower of

(A) Diogenes.

(D) Stoics.

(B) Zeno.

(E) Epicurus.

(C) Hellen.

SOLUTION:

(C) Lines 7–8 state that "The philosophers of the Hellenistic period focused on the individual." Therefore, the saying, "I am trying to find myself and my happiness," might be employed by a follower of (C) Hellen.

Diogenes (A) was the most famous cynic; his goal was to prepare the individual for disaster; so happiness would not have been a part of his philosophy.

Zeno (B) taught that the cosmos was a unified whole that was based on a universal order; so the happiness of the individual would not have been that important to him.

(D) The Stoics taught that each person should strive to discover the natural law governing the universe and live in accordance with it.

(E) Epicurus founded a school and taught that individual happiness was the goal.

• PROBLEM 3–79

The word "polis" in line 15 most nearly means

(A) a group.

(B) in a certain way.

(C) a place of one's own; a place of solitude.

(D) a tradition.

(E) a philosophical outlook.

SOLUTION:

(A)   Within the context of the passage, the word "polis," in line 15, most nearly means (A) a group. In a certain way, (B) has nothing to do with the meaning of "polis." Polis (C) does not refer to a place of one's own or a place of solitude. A (D) tradition is not the best meaning for "polis." Polis is not a philosophical outlook (E); therefore, (E) should not be selected.

• PROBLEM 3–80

The author focused on the classical Greek philosophers in order to

(A) show similarities with the Jurassic Age.

(B) contrast them with Oriental thinkers.

(C) show their relation to the earlier philosophers of the Hellenistic Age.

(D) contrast them with those of the Hellenistic Age.

(E) show his scorn of the past.

SOLUTION:

(D)   The author focused on the classical Greek philosophers in order to (D) contrast them with those of the Hellenistic Age. The purpose of the focus is not to contrast the age with a much earlier time; (A) is not the correct choice. No mention is made of the Oriental thinkers; so answer (B) is not the correct choice. Since the Hellenistic Age followed the classical Greek Age, the purpose was not to show their relation to the earlier philosophers of the Hellenistic Period; (C) should not be chosen. The author exhibits no scorn of the past in his writing; (E) is, therefore, not an appropriate answer.

• PROBLEM 3–81

The most important element of Stoic thought was

(A) its similarity to Epicureanism.

(B) the universal validity of its teaching.

(C) the idea that each person carried a spark of Logos in his reason.

(D) its establishment under the painted porch of the Athenian marketplace.

(E) its emphasis on the individual.

SOLUTION:

(E) The most important element of Stoic thought was its emphasis on the individual—not on the group, as earlier schools of thought had emphasized. The Stoic taught that each person carried a spark of Logos in his reason, but (C) is not the best choice because this was not the most important element of the philosophy. (D) is also a true statement, but it has little to do with "thought." (A) Stoic thought was similar to Epicurus's thought, but that was not the most important element of Stoic thought. The writing *claims* universal validity; but since this has not been proven, (B) is not the best choice.

• PROBLEM 3–82

Carneades taught that

(A) all knowledge was relative.

(B) the goal of philosophy should be to help the individual find happiness.

(C) a wise man eschewed public affairs and sought self-sufficiency.

(D) the individual should be prepared for any disaster.

(E) the highest pleasure was to be found in contemplation.

SOLUTION:

(A) Carneades taught that all knowledge was relative; (A) is the correct answer. It was Epicurus (B) that taught that the goal of philosophy should be to help the individual find happiness and that (C) a wise man eschewed public affairs and sought self-sufficiency. He also stated that the highest pleasure was to be found in contemplation (E). Diogenes taught that the individual should be prepared for any disaster; (D) is not the correct answer.

This passage discusses the life of Dwight D. Eisenhower and the development of a coin commemorating him.

1   The new Eisenhower Dollar coin was first issued in 1971 amid national excitement over the appearance of a new coin design. The coin also signaled the resumption of the silver dollar-size coin after a lapse of 36 years. It was created by Chief Engraver Frank Gasparro as a result of
5 nearly two years of study and work. Gasparro stood at the curb on New York's 5th Avenue in 1945 during a victory parade for General Eisenhower and glimpsed the famous military hero as he passed by. Carrying that image in his memory Gasparro returned to Philadelphia and began sketching a design of "Ike" as he remembered the General. Gasparro was
10 elated when, in 1969, he was asked to design a dollar-size coin with Eisenhower's portrait.

      The Dollar coin is the greatest achievement of Gasparro's life to date, although he has already created the reverse designs for the 1959 Lincoln Memorial Cent and the 1964 Kennedy Half Dollar. At the age of 14,
15 Gasparro was apprenticed to a famous Philadelphia sculptor. The young boy learned by watching and doing, and often swept floors and ran errands for the old master for 15¢ a day during the Depression years. After more study, some of it in Europe, he joined the United States Mint as a junior engraver in 1942. He has since created many coin designs for foreign
20 countries and numerous commemorative medals for the U.S. Mint's medallic series. He was appointed Chief Engraver in 1965.

      The coin portrait of Eisenhower, our 34th President, shows him as the crusading Supreme Allied Commander during World War II. Reared in Abilene, Kansas, "Ike" graduated from West Point Military Academy in
25 1915 and held many important military posts in the United States, the Panama Canal Zone, and in the Philippines. After the attack on Pearl Harbor, he joined the staff of the War Department in Washington. In 1942, Ike was sent to England as the American Theater Commander where he planned and conducted military campaigns in North Africa and Italy.
30   Named Supreme Commander, Allied Expeditionary Force by President Roosevelt, Eisenhower planned and directed the enormous Normandy Invasion of June 6, 1944 which led to the destruction of the German Nazi Army and the liberation of Western Europe from many long years of captivity. After the war, he became President of Columbia University and
35 later was called back into uniform to direct the North Atlantic Treaty

Organization forces in 1950. In 1952 he was elected to the first of two terms as President of the United States and entered the Capital with the stirring words: "We must be willing, individually and as a Nation, to accept whatever sacrifices may be required of us. A people that values its
40 privileges above its principles soon loses both."

Eisenhower stood for the highest kind of honesty and frankness, qualities that endeared him to the American people. His winning smile, outwardness and reputation as a man who could get the job done, enabled him to win friends all over the world in the cause of global peace. In spite
45 of his military background, he was dedicated to the search for peace in the world: "Americans, indeed all free men, remember that in the final choice a soldier's pack is not so heavy a burden as a prisoner's chains."

Halfway around the world, in an underground cavern in England where the Allied Commanders directed the battles of World War II, there
50 is a bronze plaque attached to a wall in the War Strategy Room. On the plaque is one of the finest tributes a grateful people could pay to any man. The inscription says simply, "A great man passed this way in defense of freedom." Soldier, Statesman, Author, President—Dwight Eisenhower died on March 28, 1969 at Walter Reed Army Hospital and was buried in
55 a chapel near his home in Abilene, Kansas. He had written five best-selling books in his lifetime.

The reverse of the Eisenhower Dollar celebrates the Apollo 11 Moon Landing by use of the space crew's mission patch—the American eagle landing on the Moon. Carrying through the theme of peace and freedom,
60 the design reminds us of the historic words engraved on a special plate attached to one of the legs of the Lunar Landing Module: "Here Men From The Planet Earth First Set Foot Upon The Moon—July 1969 A.D.— We Came In Peace For All Mankind." It was President Eisenhower who signed the National Aeronautics and Space Act in 1958 which created
65 NASA and started America's space program.

• PROBLEM 3–83

The primary purpose of the passage is to

(A) praise both Gasparro and Eisenhower.

(B) show the personal link between Gasparro and Eisenhower.

(C) describe the design on the Eisenhower Dollar.

(D) remind Americans of the symbolic nature of the nation's coins in general and of the Eisenhower Dollar in particular.

(E) provide background information that enhances appreciation of the Eisenhower Dollar.

SOLUTION:

(E) The passage deals with the various circumstances of the Eisenhower Dollar—its designer, what appears on it, the life of the man depicted on it—to increase understanding and appreciation of the coin. The other choices provide only partial explanations of the passage's purposes.

• PROBLEM 3–84

The passage contains information that answers which of the following questions?

I. What was Eisenhower's first military assignment?

II. In what country was Eisenhower when he planned and directed the Normandy Invasion?

III. Where was Eisenhower during the attack on Pearl Harbor?

(A) I only.   (D) I and II only.

(B) II only.   (E) I, II, and III.

(C) III only.

SOLUTION:

(B) The passage says that the Allied Commanders were headquartered in England; Eisenhower planned the Normandy Invasion while serving as Allied Supreme Commander. It is not clear from the passage where

Eisenhower was during the bombing of Pearl Harbor or what his first military assignment was, as neither event is specifically mentioned in the text.

• PROBLEM 3-85

According to the passage, Gasparro had first seen Eisenhower how many years before he was asked to design the Eisenhower Dollar?

(A) 2

(B) 14

(C) 24

(D) 26

(E) 36

SOLUTION:

(C) Gasparro saw Eisenhower in 1945; he was asked to design the coin in 1959.

• PROBLEM 3-86

According to the passage, the design on the reverse is especially appropriate for the Eisenhower Dollar because

(A) the designer was personally connected to Eisenhower.

(B) the words reflect those on the Lunar Landing Module.

(C) the coin depicts an eagle and the Lunar Landing Module was named Eagle.

(D) Eisenhower signed the bill that created NASA.

(E) Americans were the first to land on the moon.

SOLUTION:

(D) The design is appropriate for the Eisenhower Dollar because Eisenhower signed the bill that created NASA and started America's space program, one of the fruits of which (the lunar landing) is alluded to on the coin's reverse. (A) is not actually true as the two men never met. (B), (C), and (E) may contain actual truths about the moon landing, but they don't connect it to Eisenhower in such a way that it would be appropriate to appear on his coin; only (D) demonstrates this relationship.

• **PROBLEM 3-87**

The passage stresses Eisenhower's

I. intellectual qualities.

II. forthrightness.

III. effectiveness.

(A) I only.

(B) II only.

(C) III only.

(D) II and III only.

(E) I, II, and III.

SOLUTION:

(D) The passage points out that Eisenhower had the reputation of one who "could get the job done;" and much of his popularity rested on his honesty and "frankness." The passage does not stress his intellectual qualities.

• **PROBLEM 3-88**

According to the passage, Eisenhower was all of the following EXCEPT

(A) a university president.

(B) a writer.

(C) an actor.

(D) a statesman.

(E) a General.

SOLUTION:

(C) Eisenhower wrote five books and was a statesman, General, and university president (Columbia). The "theater" alluded to is, of course, a scene of military operations.

• PROBLEM 3-89

It can be inferred from the passage that Eisenhower's greatest military achievement occurred in

(A) North Africa.

(D) Southern Europe.

(B) Western Europe.

(E) Germany.

(C) the Pacific.

SOLUTION:

(B) The passage describes the invasion of Normandy as "enormous" and describes how it led to the destruction of the Nazi army and the liberation of Western Europe. These glowing praises are not equalled anywhere else in the passage in describing a specific military achievement; so it could be inferred that this would be considered Eisenhower's "greatest." The invasion of Normandy took place in Western Europe.

• PROBLEM 3-90

Which of the following statements most accurately reflects the chief idea in Eisenhower's remark that "in the final choice a soldier's pack is not so heavy a burden as a prisoner's chains"?

(A) War can seldom be justified.

(B) We must sometimes go to war to protect vital national interests.

(C) It is better to fight than to submit to brute force.

(D) We should engage in war only as a last resort.

(E) It is better to go to war than to lose one's freedom if a choice is necessary.

SOLUTION:

(E) Although the other choices capture some sense of Eisenhower's comment, none of them take into account the second half of the sentence, which describes the "heavy burden" of "prisoner's chains." Only choice (E) contains this implication of the importance of freedom.

• PROBLEM 3-91

The author looks upon the life of Eisenhower with

(A) reverence.   (D) amusement.

(B) ambivalence.   (E) apathy.

(C) disdain.

SOLUTION:

(A) Choice (A) is correct because the author writes this passage with a tone of reverence and admiration. (B) is incorrect because the author takes a positive position and does not approach this in an uncertain way. The tone is positive; so (C) disdain is not correct. The author is not amused (D) nor apathetic (E) toward this subject.

• PROBLEM 3-92

According to the passage, the silver dollar-size coin had not been minted in how many years?

(A) 15   (D) 14

(B) 36   (E) 34

(C) 24

SOLUTION:

(B) Thirty-six years is correct according to the first paragraph. (A) is incorrect, although the number was mentioned as the wage for which Gasparro worked during the Depression. (C), (D), and (E) are all numbers mentioned in the passage, but do not answer the question.

• PROBLEM 3-93

How is the passage structured?

(A) Comparison

(B) Cause and effect

(C) Statement and clarification

(D) Generalization and example

(E) Chronological

SOLUTION:

(E)   The passage is structured in chronological order because it details the lies of two men from childhood to old age or death. The first chronological sequence is Gasparro's life and the second is Eisenhower's story. (A) is incorrect because the two lives are not compared. Nothing is shown to be a cause-and-effect situation (B). A main statement is not made and then clarified (C); nor is a generalization supported by examples (D).

• PROBLEM 3-94

What is the main idea behind the plaque's inscription of "A great man passed this way in defense of freedom"?

(A) Eisenhower upheld the American value of freedom in many ways.

(B) Eisenhower defended his country on foreign soil.

(C) Eisenhower spent much time in the War Strategy Room.

(D) Eisenhower was a valiant soldier.

(E) Eisenhower was a popular President.

SOLUTION:

(A)   Through military service and his presidency, Eisenhower always held on to the value of freedom. Yes, Eisenhower did fight in foreign countries (B), but this is not what the inscription means. (C) This is not why the plaque was placed in the War Strategy Room. (D) Although this might reflect the author's opinion of Eisenhower, it does not fully explain the inscription. (E) Eisenhower's popularity might have been caused by his "defense of freedom," but this was not important to the plaque's inscription.

In the following passage, Thomas Henry Huxley argues that science is an integral part of culture and should be studied along with traditional courses, which include the classics and other liberal arts.

1   How often have we not been told that the study of physical science is incompetent to confer culture; that it touches none of the higher problems of life; and, what is worse, that the continual devotion to scientific studies tends to generate a narrow and bigoted belief in the applicability of scien-
5   tific methods to the search after truth of all kinds? How frequently one has reason to observe that no reply to a troublesome argument tells so well as calling its author a "mere scientific specialist." And, as I am afraid it is not permissible to speak of this form of opposition to scientific education in the past tense; may we not expect to be told that this, not only omission,
10 but prohibition, of "mere literary instruction and education" is a patent example of scientific narrow-mindedness?

I am not acquainted with Sir Josiah Mason's reasons for the action which he has taken; but if, as I apprehend is the case, he refers to the ordinary classical course of our schools and universities by the name of
15 "mere literary instruction and education," I venture to offer sundry reasons of my own in support of that action.

For I hold very strongly by two convictions: The first is, that neither the discipline nor the subject-matter of classical education is of such direct value to the student of physical science as to justify the expenditure of
20 valuable time upon either; and the second is, that for the purpose of attaining real culture, an exclusively scientific education is at least as effectual as an exclusively literary education.

I need hardly point out to you that these opinions, especially the latter, are diametrically opposed to those of the great majority of educated
25 Englishmen, influenced as they are by school and university traditions. In their belief, culture is obtainable only by a liberal education; and a liberal education is synonymous, not merely with education and instruction in literature, but in one particular form of literature, namely, that of Greek and Roman antiquity. They hold that the man who has learned Latin and
30 Greek, however little, is educated; while he who is versed in other branches of knowledge, however deeply, is a more or less respectable

specialist, not admissible into the cultured caste. The stamp of the educated man, the University degree, is not for him.

I am too well acquainted with the generous catholicity of spirit, the true sympathy with scientific thought, which pervades the writings of our
35 chief apostle of culture to identify him with these opinions; and yet one may cull from one and another of those epistles to the Philistines, which so much delight all who do not answer to that name, sentences which lend them some support.

Mr. Arnold tells us that the meaning of culture is "to know the best
40 that has been thought and said in the world." It is the criticism of life contained in literature. That criticism regards "Europe as being, for intellectual and spiritual purposes, one great confederation, bound to a joint action and working to a common result; and whose members have, for their common outfit, a knowledge of Greek, Roman, and Eastern antiquity,
45 and of one another. Special, local, and temporary advantages being put out of account, that modern nation will in the intellectual and spiritual sphere make most progress, which most thoroughly carries out this programme. And what is that but saying that we too, all of us, as individuals, the more thoroughly we carry it out, shall make the more progress?"

50 We have here to deal with two distinct propositions. The first, that a criticism of life is the essence of culture; the second, that literature contains the materials which suffice for the construction of such criticism.

I think that we must all assent to the first proposition. For culture certainly means something quite different from learning or technical skill.
55 It implies the possession of an ideal, and the habit of critically estimating the value of things by comparison with a theoretic standard. Perfect culture should supply a complete theory of life, based upon a clear knowledge alike of its possibilities and of its limitations.

But we may agree to all this, and yet strongly dissent from the as-
60 sumption that literature alone is competent to supply this knowledge. After having learnt all that Greek, Roman, and Eastern antiquity have thought and said, and all that modern literatures have to tell us, it is not self-evident that we have laid a sufficiently broad and deep foundation for that criticism of life, which constitutes culture.

65 Indeed, to anyone acquainted with the scope of physical science, it is not at all evident. Considering progress only in the "intellectual and spiritual sphere," I find myself wholly unable to admit that either nations or individuals will really advance, if their common outfit draws nothing from the stores of physical science. I should say that an army, without weapons
70 of precision and with no particular base of operations, might more hopefully enter upon a campaign on the Rhine, than a man, devoid of a knowledge of what physical science has done in the last century, upon a criticism of life.

• PROBLEM 3–95

Which best describes what the author is doing in the sentence, "And, as I am afraid . . . narrow-mindedness" (lines 7–11)?

(A) Stating the terms of his argument

(B) Arguing for scientific training

(C) Stating common beliefs of his opponents

(D) Redefining the term "culture"

(E) Establishing the central analogy of the passage

SOLUTION:

(C) He is actually exaggerating his opponents' views through conventional irony. The argument *per se* (A) is not developed here. The section occurs within (B) the broader plea for scientific training. Culture is taken up much later in the passage (D). There is no *central* analogy in this passage (E).

• PROBLEM 3–96

From the first four paragraphs, we can infer that the college has decided to

(A) include classical studies in its curriculum.

(B) exclude classical studies from its curriculum.

(C) establish Latin and Greek as required subjects.

(D) define university education as exclusively scientific.

(E) incorporate scientific studies within the curriculum.

SOLUTION:

(E) From the displeasure of Huxley's opponents, we can infer that scientific studies have gained some ground. Classical studies have long been within the curriculum (A). There is no suggestion of their abolition (B). Classical studies continue to be (C) required subjects, though Huxley questions their utility in scientific education. Despite his opponents' fears, exclusively scientific education (D) hardly appears possible.

• PROBLEM 3-97

In line 15, the term "sundry" most nearly means

(A) significant.   (D) related.

(B) various.   (E) dependent.

(C) convincing.

SOLUTION:

(B) The term has the neutral meaning of number, with a slight connotation of offhandedness. It does not include connotations of significance (A). Nor are his views *necessarily* sound arguments (C). There is no necessary relationship among them (D). Further, the specific relation of dependence is not contained in the word "sundry."

• PROBLEM 3-98

The author's use of the term "cultured caste" (line 31) suggests

(A) distinctive merit.   (D) superiority of the wealthy.

(B) exclusion of merit.   (E) inclusion of the poor.

(C) social inequity.

SOLUTION:

(B) Huxley is referring to an unfair system of intellectual judgment in which only those with a knowledge of Latin and Greek (which Huxley regards as fairly useless) are considered "cultured." Understanding of this term depends upon appreciation of Huxley's subtle irony. Many with distinctive merit, but little Greek, are excluded from the "caste" (A). The question of social—as opposed to educational—inequality does not arise here (C). The "caste" includes only those with classical educations, which probably—but not necessarily—includes the wealthy. (D). Huxley does not address class considerations in this passage (E).

• PROBLEM 3-99

In the sentence, "I am too well acquainted ... some support" (lines 33–38), the author argues that "our chief apostle"

(A) unintentionally reinforces prejudices.

(B) has contributed valuable insights.

(C) holds views contrary to those of the author.

(D) does not deserve his current reputation.

(E) is a valuable supporter of the author.

SOLUTION:

(A)   Cited out of context, Arnold, the "chief apostle," lends support to those with biases against science. He *may* well have contributed insights (B); Huxley makes no explicit comment. Arnold probably holds some views contrary to those of the author (C); but this point is not made explicitly in the paragraph. Huxley implies that Arnold certainly deserves his current reputation (D), even if he is not a valuable ally of the author (E).

• PROBLEM 3-100

The word "outfit" in line 44 most nearly means

(A) company.   (D) tools.

(B) uniform.   (E) beliefs.

(C) gathering.

SOLUTION:

(B)   Huxley is using a metaphor in which his opponents' clothing is made up of their areas of knowledge. Here the word means regalia or costuming. Huxley later (line 69) modifies it to suggest weaponry. The company again forms a gathering which means the uniform, but is not itself the uniform (C). The idea of "tools" might be conceivable in the later usage (line 69) (D), but does not fit here. Beliefs are only one element in the group's common uniform (E).

Appendix

ESSENTIAL VOCABULARY

GROUP 1

abase – *v.* – to degrade; humiliate; disgrace

aberration – *n.* – departure from what is right, true, correct

abeyance – *n.* – a state of temporary suspension

abhor – *v.* – to hate

abominate – *v.* – to loathe; to hate

absolve – *v.* – to forgive; to acquit

abstemious – *adj.* – sparingly used or used with temperance

abstinence – *n.* – the act or practice of voluntarily refraining from any action

abstract – *adj.* – not easy to understand; theoretical

abstruse – *adj.* – 1. hidden, concealed; 2. difficult to be comprehended

acclaim – *n.* – loud approval; applause

accolade – *n.* – approving or praising mention

accomplice – *n.* – co-conspirator; a partner; partner-in-crime

accretion – *n.* – growth in size by addition or accumulation

accrue – *v.* – collect; build up

acquiesce – *v.* – agree or consent to an opinion

acrid – *adj.* – sharp; bitter; foul smelling

adamant – *adj.* – not yielding; firm

adversary – *n.* – an enemy; foe

advocate – 1. *v.* – to plead in favor of; 2. *n.* – supporter; defender

aesthetic – *adj.* – showing good taste; artistic

aghast – *adj.* – 1. astonished; amazed; 2. horrified; terrified; appalled

alacrity – *n.* – 1. enthusiasm; fervor; 2. liveliness; sprightliness

alleviate – *v.* – to lessen or make easier

allocate – *v.* – set aside; designate; assign

allusion – *n.* – an indirect reference to something

aloof – *adj.* – distant in interest; reserved; cool

altercation – *n.* – controversy; dispute

altruistic – *adj.* – unselfish

amass – *v.* – to collect together; accumulate

ambiguous – *adj.* – not clear; uncertain; vague

ambivalent – *adj.* – undecided

ameliorate – *v.* – to make better; to improve

amiable – *adj.* – friendly

amorphous – *adj.* – having no determinate form

analogy – *n.* – similarity; correlation; parallelism; simile; metaphor

anarchist – *n.* – one who believes that a formal government is unnecessary

anomaly – *n.* – abnormality; irregularity; deviation from the regular arrangement

anonymous – *adj.* – nameless; unidentified

antagonism – *n.* – hostility; opposition

antipathy – *n.* – inherent aversion or antagonism of feeling

antiseptic – *adj.* – preventing infection or decay

apathy – *n.* – lack of emotion or interest

appease – *v.* – to make quiet; to calm

apprehensive – *adj.* – fearful; aware; conscious

arbiter – *n.* – one who is authorized to judge or decide

arbitrary – *adj.* – based on one's preference or judgment

arduous – *adj.* – difficult; laborious

arid – *adj.* – 1. dry; parched; 2. barren; 3. uninteresting; dull

arrogant – *adj.* – acting superior to others; conceited

articulate – 1. *v.* – to speak distinctly; 2. *adj.* – eloquent; fluent; 3. *adj.* – capable of speech; 4. *v.* – to hinge; to connect; 5. *v.* – to convey; to express effectively

assess – *v.* – to estimate the value of

astute – *adj.* – cunning; sly; crafty

atrophy – *v.* – to waste away through lack of nutrition

audacious – *adj.* – fearless; bold

augment – *v.* – to increase or add to; to make larger

Drill 1

DIRECTIONS: Match each word in the left column with the word in the right column that is most **opposite** in meaning.

Word		Match	
1.	J articulate	A.	hostile
2.	___ apathy	B.	concrete
3.	A amiable	C.	selfish
4.	C altruistic	D.	reasoned
5.	___ ambivalent	E.	ally
6.	B abstract	F.	disperse
7.	___ acquiesce	G.	enthusiasm
8.	___ arbitrary	H.	certain
9.	F amass	I.	resist
10.	___ adversary	J.	incoherent
11.	M audacious	K.	fragrant
12.	___ aberration	L.	conformity
13.	___ acrid	M.	unadventurous

DIRECTIONS: Match each word in the left column with the word in the right column that is most **similar** in meaning.

Word		Match	
14.	___ adamant	A.	afraid
15.	___ aesthetic	B.	disagreement
16.	A apprehensive	C.	tasteful
17.	___ antagonism	D.	insistent
18.	___ altercation	E.	hostility

GROUP 2

auspicious – *adj.* – 1. having omens of success; 2. prosperous; 3. favorable; kind

austere – *v.* – harsh; severe; strict

authentic – *adj.* – real; genuine; trustworthy

authoritarian – *n.* – acting as a dictator; demanding obedience

awry – *adv.* – 1. crooked(ly); uneven(ly); 2. *adj.* – wrong, askew

axiom – *n.* – an established principle or statement accepted as true

azure – *n.* – the clear blue color of the sky

baleful – *adj.* – sinister; threatening; evil; deadly

banal – *adj.* – common; petty; ordinary

baroque – *adj.* – extravagant; ornate

bauble – *n.* – 1. that which is gay or showy; 2. a baby's toy

beget – *v.* – to produce, as an effect

behoove – *v.* – to be advantageous; to be necessary

belittle – *v.* – to make small; to think lightly of

benefactor – *n.* – one who helps others; a donor

beneficent – *adj.* – doing good

benevolent – *adj.* – kind; generous

benign – *adj.* – mild; harmless

berate – *v.* – scold; reprove; reproach; criticize

bereave – *v.* – to deprive

bereft – *adj.* – deprived; left sad because of someone's death

beseech – *v.* – 1. to ask or pray with urgency; 2. to beg eagerly for

biased – *adj.* – prejudiced; influenced; not neutral

biennial – *adj.* – 1. happening every two years; 2. *n.* – a plant which blooms every two years

blasphemous – *adj.* – irreligious, away from acceptable standards

blatant – *adj.* – 1. obvious; unmistakable; 2. crude; vulgar

blithe – *adj.* – happy; cheery, merry

bombastic – *adj.* – pompous; wordy; turgid

brevity – *n.* – briefness; shortness

brusque – *adj.* – abrupt, blunt, or short in manner or speech bumptious – *adj.* – impertinent; conceited

burnish – *v.* – to make or become smooth, bright, and glossy

cabal – *v.* – to intrigue or plot; usually in a small group

cache – *n.* – 1. stockpile; store; heap; 2. hiding place for goods

cacophony – *n.* – a jarring or disagreeable sound of words

cajole – *v.* – to flatter; to coax

candid – *adj.* – honest; truthful; sincere

capricious – *adj.* – changeable; fickle

cascade – *n.* – 1. waterfall; 2. *v.* – pour; rush; fall

caustic – *adj.* – burning; sarcastic; harsh

censor – *v.* – to examine and delete objectionable material

censure – *v.* – to criticize or disapprove of

chagrin – *n.* – mortification or disappointment

charisma – *n.* – appeal; magnetism; presence

charlatan – *n.* – an imposter; fake

chastise – *v.* – punish; discipline; admonish; rebuke

chronology – *n.* – the arrangement of events, dates, etc. in a certain order of occurrence

circumlocution – *n.* – an indirect or lengthy way of expressing something

coalesce – *v.* – to combine; come together

coda – *n.* – a musical passage which brings a composition to its definite close

cognizant – *adj.* – being informed or aware

cohesion – *n.* – the act of holding together

collaborate – *v.* – to work together; cooperate

Drill 2

DIRECTIONS: Match each word in the left column with the word in the right column that is most **opposite** in meaning.

Word	Match
1. ____ augment	A. permit
2. ____ biased	B. heroine
3. ____ banal	C. praise
4. ____ benevolent	D. diminish
5. ____ censor	E. dishonest
6. ____ authentic	F. malicious
7. ____ candid	G. neutral
8. ____ belittle	H. mournful
9. ____ charlatan	I. unusual
10. ____ blithe	J. fake
11. ____ bombastic	K. directness
12. ____ circumlocution	L. modest

DIRECTIONS: Match each word in the left column with the word in the right column that is most **similar** in meaning.

Word	Match
13. ____ collaborate	A. harmless
14. ____ benign	B. cunning
15. ____ astute	C. changeable
16. ____ censure	D. cooperate
17. ____ capricious	E. criticize
18. ____ baleful	F. reprimand
19. ____ berate	G. ominous

GROUP 3

colloquial – *adj.* – casual; common; conversational; idiomatic

compatible – *adj.* – in agreement with; harmonious

complacent – *adj.* – content; self-satisfied; smug

compliant – *adj.* – yielding; obedient

comprehensive – *adj.* – all-inclusive; complete; thorough

compromise – *v.* – to settle by mutual adjustment

concede – 1. *v.* – to acknowledge; admit; 2. to surrender; to abandon one's position

conciliatory – *adj.* – tending to make peace between persons at variance

concise – *adj.* – in few words; brief; condensed

condescend – *v.* – to come down from one's position or dignity

condone – *v.* – to overlook; to forgive

conglomeration – *n.* – mixture; collection

conjoin – *v.* – to unite; to combine

conjure – *v.* – 1. to call upon or appeal to; 2. to cause to be, appear, come

connoisseur – *n.* – expert; authority (usually refers to a wine or food expert)

consecrate – *v.* – to sanctify; make sacred; immortalize

consensus – *n.* – unanimity; agreement

conspicuous – *adj.* – easy to see; noticeable

consternation – *n.* – amazement or terror that causes confusion

consummation – *n.* – the completion; finish

contemporary – *adj.* – living or happening at the same time; modern

contempt – *n.* – scorn; disrespect

contentious – *adj.* – argumentative; quarrelsome

contrite – *adj.* – regretful; sorrowful

contumacious – *adj.* – insubordinate; rebellious; disobedient

conundrum – *n.* – any question or thing of a perplexing nature

conventional – *adj.* – traditional; common; routine

correlate – *v.* – to bring one thing into mutual relation with another thing

corroborate – *v.* – 1. to strengthen; 2. to confirm; to make more certain cower – *v.* – crouch down in fear or shame

craven – *adj.* – cowardly; fearful

culpable – *adj.* – blameworthy

cynic – *n.* – one who believes that others are motivated entirely by selfishness

dais – *n.* – a raised platform in a room where tables for honored guests are placed

dank – *adj.* – disagreeably damp or humid

dearth – *n.* – scarcity; shortage

debacle – *n.* – disaster; ruination

debauchery – *n.* – extreme indulgence of one's appetites, especially for sensual pleasure

debilitate – *v.* – deprive of strength

decorous – *adj.* – characterized by good taste

defamation – *n.* – the malicious uttering of falsehood respecting another

deference – *adj.* – yielding to the opinion of another

deference – *n.* – a yielding in opinion to another

deign – *v.* – condescend

deleterious – *adj.* – harmful to health, well-being

deliberate 1. – *v.* – to consider carefully; weigh in the mind; 2. *adj.* – intentional

delineate – *v.* – to outline; to describe

demur – *v.* – to object, to take issue

denounce – *v.* – to speak out against; condemn

depict – *v.* – to portray in words; present a visual image

deplete – *v.* – to reduce; to empty

depravity – *n.* – moral corruption; badness

deride – *v.* – to ridicule; laugh at with scorn

derision – *n.* – ridicule; mockery

derogatory – *adj.* – belittling; uncomplimentary

desecrate – *v.* – to violate a holy place or sanctuary

desiccate – *v.* – to dry completely

destitute – *adj.* – poor; poverty-stricken

Drill 3

DIRECTIONS: Match each word in the left column with the word in the right column that is most **opposite** in meaning.

	Word		Match
1.	_____ deplete	A.	unintentional
2.	_____ contemporary	B.	disapprove
3.	_____ concise	C.	invisible
4.	_____ deliberate	D.	respect
5.	_____ depravity	E.	fill
6.	_____ condone	F.	support
7.	_____ conspicuous	G.	beginning
8.	_____ consummation	H.	ancient
9.	_____ denounce	I.	virtue
10.	_____ contempt	J.	verbose
11.	_____ colloquial	K.	submissive
12.	_____ contumacious	L.	innocent
13.	_____ culpable	M.	success
14.	_____ demur	N.	agree
15.	_____ debacle	O.	sophisticated

DIRECTIONS: Match each word in the left column with the word in the right column that is most **similar** in meaning.

	Word		Match
16.	_____ compatible	A.	portray
17.	_____ depict	B.	content
18.	_____ conventional	C.	harmonious
19.	_____ comprehensive	D.	thorough
20.	_____ complacent	E.	common

GROUP 4

detached – *adj.* – separated; not interested; standing alone

deter – *v.* – to prevent; to discourage; hinder

devoid – *adj.* – lacking; empty

dichotomy – *n.* – division of things by pairs

didactic – *adj.* – 1. instructive; 2. dogmatic; preachy

digress – *v.* – stray from the subject; wander from topic

diligence – *n.* – hard work

disavow – *v.* – to deny; to refuse

discerning – *adj.* – distinguishing one thing from another

discomfit – *v.* – 1. to overthrow the plans or expectations of; 2. to confuse

discord – *n.* – disagreement; lack of harmony

discourse – *n.* – a communication of thoughts by words

discriminating 1. – *v.* – distinguishing one thing from another; 2. *v.* – demonstrating bias; 3. *adj.* – able to distingush

disdain 1. – *n.* – intense dislike; 2. *v.* – look down upon; scorn

disheartened – *adj.* – discouraged; depressed

disinterested – *adj.* – impartial; unbiased

disparage – *v.* – to belittle; undervalue

disparity – *n.* – difference in form, character, or degree

dispassionate – *adj.* – lack of feeling; impartial

disperse – *v.* – to scatter; separate

disseminate – *v.* – to circulate; scatter

dissent – *v.* – to disagree; differ in opinion

dissonance – *n.* – harsh contradiction

diverge – *v.* – separate; split

diverse – *adj.* – different; dissimilar

docile – *adj.* – manageable; obedient

document – 1. *n.* – official paper containing information; 2. *v.* – to support; substantiate; verify

doggerel – *adj.* – trivial; inartistic

dogmatic – *adj.* – stubborn; biased, opinionated

dowdy – *adj.* – drab; shabby

dubious – *adj.* – doubtful; uncertain; skeptical; suspicious duress – *n.* – force; constraint

earthy – *adj.* – 1. not refined; coarse; 2. simple and natural

ebullient – *adj.* – showing excitement

eccentric – *adj.* – odd; peculiar; strange

eclectic – *adj.* – choosing or selecting from various sources

economical – *adj.* – not wasteful

educe – *v.* – draw forth

efface – *v.* – wipe out; erase

effeminate – *adj.* – having qualities generally attributed to a woman

effervescence – *n.* -1. liveliness; spirit; enthusiasm; 2. bubbliness

effigy – *n.* – the image or likeness of a person

effluvium – *n.* – an outflow in the form of a vapor

egocentric – *adj.* – self-centered

elaboration – *n.* – act of clarifying; adding details

eloquence – *n.* – the ability to speak well

elusive – *adj.* – hard to catch; difficult to understand

eminence – *n.* – 1. high or lofty place; 2. superiority in position or rank

emulate – *v.* – to imitate; copy; mimic

endorse – *v.* – support; to approve of; recommend

engender – *v.* – to create; bring about

enhance – *v.* – to improve; complement; make more attractive

enigma- *n.* – mystery; secret; perplexity

ennui – *n.* – boredom; apathy

ephemeral – *adj.* – temporary; brief; short-lived

epitome – *n.* – model; typification; representation

equivocal – *adj.* – doubtful; uncertain

errant – *adj.* – wandering

erratic – *adj.* – unpredictable; strange

erroneous – *adj.* – untrue; inaccurate; not correct

erudite – *adj.* – having extensive knowledge; learned

esoteric – *adj.* – incomprehensible; obscure

ethnic – *adj.* – native; racial; cultural

euphony – *n.* – pleasant sound

evanescent – *adj.* – vanishing; fleeting

Drill 4

DIRECTIONS: Match each word in the left column with the word in the right column that is most **opposite** in meaning.

	Word		Match
1.	____ detached	A.	agree
2.	____ deter	B.	certain
3.	____ dissent	C.	lethargy
4.	____ discord	D.	connected
5.	____ efface	E.	assist
6.	____ dubious	F.	respect
7.	____ diligence	G.	compliment
8.	____ disdain	H.	sanctify
9.	____ desecrate	I.	harmony
10.	____ disparage	J.	restore
11.	____ dowdy	K.	excitement
12.	____ erudite	L.	acknowledge
13.	____ ennui	M.	chic
14.	____ evanescent	N.	uninformed
15.	____ disheartened	O.	wild
16.	____ disavow	P.	appearing
17.	____ docile	Q.	uplifted

DIRECTIONS: Match each word in the left column with the word in the right column that is most **similar** in meaning.

	Word		Match
18.	____ effervescence	A.	stubborn
19.	____ dogmatic	B.	distribute
20.	____ disseminate	C.	substantiate
21.	____ document	D.	liveliness
22.	____ eccentric	E.	odd
23.	____ ethnic	F.	native
24.	____ discomfit	G.	confuse

GROUP 5

evoke – *v.* – call forth; provoke

exculpate – *v.* – to declare or prove guiltless

execute – *v.* – 1. put to death; kill; 2. to carry out; fulfill

exemplary – *adj.* – serving as an example; outstanding

exhaustive – *adj.* – thorough; complete

exigent – *n.* – an urgent occasion

exonerate – *v.* – to unload; to release from burden

exorbitant – *adj.* – going beyond what is reasonable; excessive

exotic – *adj.* – unusual; striking

expedient – *adj.* – helpful; practical; worthwhile

expedite – *v.* – speed up

explicit – *adj.* – specific; definite

exposition – *n.* – a setting forth of facts or ideas

extol – *v.* – praise; commend

extraneous – *adj.* – irrelevant; not related; not essential

exuberant – *adj.* – overflowing; lavish; superabundant

facade – *n.* – front view; false appearance

facetious – *adj.* – lightly joking

facilitate – *v.* – make easier; simplify

fallacious – *adj.* – misleading

fanatic – *n.* – enthusiast; extremist

fastidious – *adj.* – fussy; hard to please

feasible – *adj.* – reasonable; practical

fecund – *adj.* – fruitful in children; productive

ferret – *v.* – drive or hunt out of hiding

fervent – *adj.* – passionate; intense

fervor – *n.* – passion; intensity

fickle – *adj.* – changeable; unpredictable

figment – *n.* – product; creation

finesse – *n.* – the ability to handle situations with skill and diplomacy

finite – *adj.* – measurable; limited; not everlasting

flag – *v.* – 1. to send a message by signaling; 2. to become limp fledgling – *n.* – inexperienced person; beginner

flippant – *adj.* – 1. speaking with ease and rapidity; 2. impertinent

flout – *v.* – to mock; to sneer

fluency – *n.* – smoothness of speech

flux – *n.* – current; continuous change

forbearance – *n.* – patience; self-restraint

fortuitous – *adj.* – accidental; happening by chance; lucky

foster – *v.* – encourage; nurture; support

frenetic – *adj.* – frantic; frenzied

frivolity – *adj.* – giddiness; lack of seriousness

frugality – *n.* – thrift

fulsome – *adj.* – offensive, especially because of excess

fundamental – *adj.* – basic; necessary

furtive – *adj.* – secretive; sly

fustian – *n.* – an inflated style of talking or writing

futile – *adj.* – worthless; unprofitable

gaffe – *n.* – a blunder

gainsay – *v.* – to deny or contradict

garbled – *adj.* – mixed up

garner – *v.* – to accumulate

garrulous – *adj.* – talking much about unimportant things

genial – *adj.* – 1. contributing to life and growth; 2. amiable; cordial

genre – *n.* – a kind, sort, or type

germane – *adj.* – pertinent; related; to the point

gerrymander – *v.* – to manipulate unfairly

Drill 5

DIRECTIONS: Match each word in the left column with the word in the right column that is most **opposite** in meaning.

	Word		Match
1.	_____ extraneous	A.	incomplete
2.	_____ ephemeral	B.	delay
3.	_____ exhaustive	C.	dependable
4.	_____ expedite	D.	comprehensible
5.	_____ erroneous	E.	dissonance
6.	_____ erratic	F.	eternal
7.	_____ explicit	G.	condemn
8.	_____ euphony	H.	relevant
9.	_____ elusive	I.	indefinite
10.	_____ extol	J.	accurate
11.	_____ facetious	K.	combat
12.	_____ extol	L.	considerate
13.	_____ foster	M.	rude
14.	_____ fastidious	N.	quiet
15.	_____ flippant	O.	denounce
16.	_____ germane	P.	calm
17.	_____ garrulous	Q.	solemn
18.	_____ genial	R.	immaterial
19.	_____ frenetic	S.	neglectful

DIRECTIONS: Match each word in the left column with the word in the right column that is most **similar** in meaning.

	Word		Match
20.	_____ endorse	A.	enable
21.	_____ expedient	B.	recommend
22.	_____ facilitate	C.	create
23.	_____ fallacious	D.	worthwhile
24.	_____ engender	E.	deceptive
25.	_____ furtive	F.	stealthy
26.	_____ fickle	G.	unpredictable

GROUP 6

gibber – *v.* – speak foolishly

gloat – *v.* – brag; glory over

glutton – *n.* – overeater

goad – *v.* – to arouse or incite

grandiose – *adj.* – extravagant; flamboyant

gravity – *n.* – seriousness

guile – *n.* – slyness; deceit

gullible – *adj.* – easily fooled

hackneyed – *adj.* – commonplace; trite

haggard – *adj.* – tired-looking; fatigued

hamper – *v.* – interfere with; hinder

haphazard – *adj.* – disorganized; random

haughty – *adj.* – proud and disdainful

hedonistic – *adj.* – pleasure seeking

heed – *v.* – obey; yield to

heresy – *n.* – opinion contrary to popular belief

hierarchy – *n.* – body of people, things, or concepts divided into ranks

hindrance – *n.* – blockage; obstacle

homeostasis – *n.* – the maintenance of stability or equilibrium

hone – *v.* – sharpen

humility – *n.* – lack of pride; modesty

hypocritical – *adj.* – two-faced; deceptive

hypothetical – *adj.* – assumed; uncertain

iconoclast – *n.* – a breaker or destroyer of images

ideology – *n.* – set of beliefs; principles

idyllic – *adj.* – pleasing and simple

ignoble – *adj.* – shameful; dishonorable

illuminate – *v.* – make understandable

illusory – *adj.* – unreal; false; deceptive

imbue – *v.* – inspire; arouse

immune – *adj.* – protected; unthreatened by

immutable – *adj.* – unchangeable; permanent

impale – *v.* – fix on a stake; stick; pierce

impartial – *adj.* – unbiased; fair

impede – *v.* – to stop in progress

imperious – *adj.* – authoritative

impervious – *adj.* – 1. incapable of being penetrated; 2. not affected or influenced by

impetuous – *adj.* – 1. rash; impulsive; 2. forcible; violent

implement – *v.* – to carry into effect

implication – *n.* – suggestion; inference

implicit – *adj.* – to be understood though not fully expressed

impromptu – *adj.* – without preparation

improvident – *adj.* – lacking foresight and thrift

impudent – *adj.* – shameless; immodest

impugn – *v.* – to contradict

inadvertent – *adj.* – not on purpose; unintentional

inarticulate – *adj.* – speechless; unable to speak clearly

incessant – *adj.* – constant; continual

inchoate – *adj.* – existing in elementary or beginning form

incidental – *adj.* – extraneous; unexpected

incisive – *adj.* – cutting into

inclined – *adj.* – 1. apt to; likely to; 2. angled

incognito – *adj.* – unidentified; disguised; concealed

incoherent – *adj.* – illogical; rambling

incompatible – *adj.* – disagreeing; disharmonious

incredulous – *adj.* – unwilling to believe; skeptical

incursion – *n.* – 1. a running in; 2. invasion; raid

indict – *v.* – charge with a crime

indifferent – *adj.* – unconcerned

indignant – *adj.* – to consider as unworthy or improper

indolent – *adj.* – lazy; inactive

indulgent – *adj.* – lenient: patient

Drill 6

DIRECTIONS: Match each word in the left column with the word in the right column that is most **opposite** in meaning.

Word		Match	
1.	____ heresy	A.	predictable
2.	____ fickle	B.	dispassionate
3.	____ illusory	C.	simple
4.	____ frivolity	D.	extraneous
5.	____ grandiose	E.	real
6.	____ fervent	F.	beneficial
7.	____ fundamental	G.	orthodoxy
8.	____ furtive	H.	organized
9.	____ futile	I.	candid
10.	____ haphazard	J.	seriousness
11.	____ ignoble	K.	vigorous
12.	____ haggard	L.	cynical
13.	____ gloat	M.	deter
14.	____ hedonist	N.	belittle
15.	____ gullible	O.	admirable
16.	____ goad	P.	puritan

DIRECTIONS: Match each word in the left column with the word in the right column that is most **similar** in meaning.

Word		Match	
17.	____ glutton	A.	hinder
18.	____ heed	B.	obstacle
19.	____ hamper	C.	trite
20.	____ hackneyed	D.	overeater
21.	____ hindrance	E.	obey
22.	____ impale	F.	principles
23.	____ ideology	G.	transfix

GROUP 7

ineluctable – *adj.* – not to be avoided or escaped

inept – *adj.* – incompetent; unskilled

inert – *adj.* – without power to move or to resist an opposite force

inevitable – *adj.* – sure to happen; unavoidable

infamous – *adj.* – having a bad reputation; notorious

infer- *v.* – form an opinion; conclude

ingenious – *adj.* – gifted with genius; innate or natural quality

inherent – *adj.* – innate; basic; inborn

initiate – 1. *v.* – begin; admit into a group; 2. *n.* – a person who is in the process of being admitted into a group

innate – *adj.* – natural; inborn

innocuous – *adj.* – harmless; innocent

innovate – *v.* – introduce a change; depart from the old

innuendo – *n.* – an indirect remark, gesture or reference

insipid – *adj.* – uninteresting; bland

insolvent – *adj.* – bankrupt; not able to pay debts

instigate – *v.* – start; provoke

intangible – *adj.* – incapable of being touched; immaterial

intermittent – *adj.* – 1. stopping and starting again at intervals; 2. *n.* – a disease which entirely subsides or ceases at certain intervals

intransigent – *adj.* – refusing to compromise

invective – *n.* – a violent verbal attack

ironic – *adj.* – contradictory; inconsistent; sarcastic

irrational – *adj.* – not logical

jaded – *adj.* – 1. tired or worn-out; 2. dulled

jeopardy – *n.* – danger

judicious – *adj.* – possessing sound judgement

ken – *n.* – range of knowledge

kindle – *v.* – ignite; arouse

kinship – *n.* – family relationship

kith – *n.* – acquaintances and relations

knavery – *n.* – dishonesty

labyrinth – *n.* – maze

laconic – *n.* – a brief, pithy expression

laggard – *n.* – a lazy person; one who lags behind

lament – *v.* – to mourn or grieve

languid – *adj.* – weak; fatigued

lascivious – *adj.* – indecent; immoral

latency – *n.* – the condition of being hidden or undeveloped

laud – *v.* – praise

lax – *adj.* – careless; irresponsible

lecherous – *adj.* – impure in thought and act

lethal – *adj.* – deadly

lethargic – *adj.* – lazy; passive

levee – *n.* – the act or time of rising

levity – *n.* – silliness; lack of seriousness

liaison – *n.* – connection; link

ligneous – *adj.* – consisting of or resembling wood

litigate – *v.* – to contest in a lawsuit

livid – *adj.* – 1. black-and-blue; discolored; 2. enraged; irate

lucid – *adj.* -1. shining; 2. easily understood

lucrative – *adj.* – profitable; gainful

luminous – *adj.* – giving off light; bright

lustrous – *adj.* – bright; radiant

macerate – *v.* – 1. to soften by soaking; 2. to cause to waste away; 3. to torment

magnanimous – *adj.* – forgiving; unselfish

malediction – *n.* – curse; evil spell

malicious – *adj.* – spiteful; vindictive

malleable – *adj.* – that which can be pounded without breaking; adaptable

Drill 7

DIRECTIONS: Match each word in the left column with the word in the right column that is most **opposite** in meaning.

Word		Match	
1. _____	innate	A.	proper
2. _____	incredulous	B.	injurous
3. _____	inevitable	C.	responsible
4. _____	intangible	D.	honor
5. _____	lamentable	E.	blissful
6. _____	livid	F.	encouraging
7. _____	lascivious	G.	compromising
8. _____	innocuous	H.	prudish
9. _____	lecherous	I.	gravity
10. _____	levity	J.	resentful
11. _____	lax	K.	gullible
12. _____	intransigent	L.	material
13. _____	invective	M.	avoidable
14. _____	magnanimous	N.	learned

DIRECTIONS: Match each word in the left column with the word in the right column that is most **similar** in meaning.

Word		Match	
15. _____	infer	A.	bewail
16. _____	instigate	B.	radiant
17. _____	luminous	C.	fatigued
18. _____	knave	D.	alliance
19. _____	liaison	E.	rogue
20. _____	languid	F.	provoke
21. _____	lament	G.	conclude

GROUP 8

mandatory – *adj.* – authoritatively commanded or required

manifest – *adj.* – obvious; clear

marred – *adj.* – damaged

maverick – *n.* – person who acts independent of a group

meander – *v.* – wind on a course; go aimlessly

melancholy – *n.* – depression; gloom

mellifluous – *adj.* – flowing sweetly and smoothly

mentor – *n.* – teacher

mercenary – *n.* – working or done for payment only

metamorphosis – *n.* – change of form

meticulous – *adj.* – exacting; precise

minute – *adj.* – extremely small; tiny

miser – *n.* – penny pincher; stingy person

mitigate – *v.* – alleviate; lessen; soothe

molten – *adj.* – melted

morose – *adj.* – moody; despondent

motif – *n.* – theme

motility – *n.* – the quality of exhibiting spontaneous motion

mundane – *adj.* – ordinary; commonplace

munificent – *adj.* – very generous in giving; lavish

myriad – *adj.* – innumerable; countless

nebulous – *adj.* – 1. cloudy; hazy; 2. unclear; vague

negligence – *n.* – carelessness

neophyte – *n.* – beginner; newcomer

nettle – *v.* – annoy; irritate

neutral – *adj.* – impartial; unbiased

nostalgic – *adj.* – longing for the past; filled with bittersweet memories

notorious – *adj.* – infamous; renowned

novel – *adj.* – new

nullify – *v.* – cancel; invalidate

oaf – *n.* – 1. a misshapen child; 2. a stupid, clumsy fellow

obdurate – *adj.* – stubborn; inflexible

objective – 1. *adj.* – open-minded; impartial; 2. *n.* – goal obliterate – *v.* – destroy completely

obscure – *adj.* – not easily understood; dark

obsequious – *adj.* – slavishly attentive; servile

obsolete – *adj.* – out of date; passé

occult – *adj.* – mystical; mysterious

ominous – *adj.* – threatening

omniscient – *adj.* – having universal knowledge

opaque – *adj.* – dull; cloudy; nontransparent

optimist – *n.* – person who hopes for the best; sees the good side

opulence – *n.* – wealth; fortune

ornate – *adj.* – elaborate; lavish; decorated

orthodox – *adj.* – traditional; accepted

oscillate – *v.* – 1. to swing to and fro; 2. to be indecisive; to fluctuate

ossify – *v.* – to settle or fix rigidly in a practice, custom, attitude, etc.

ostensible – *adj.* – 1. proper to be shown; 2. apparent; declared

ostracize – *v.* – to cast out or banish

pagan – 1. n – polytheist; 2. *adj.* – polytheistic

palliate – *v.* – 1. to alleviate or ease; 2. to make appear less serious

pallid – *adj.* – sallow; colorless

palpable – *adj.* – tangible; apparent

panegyric – *n.* – a formal speech written in praise of a distinguished person

paradox – *n.* – 1. a statement that seems contradictory but that may actually be true in fact; 2. something inconsistent with common experience

parallel – *adj.* – extending in the same direction and at the same distance apart at every point

paraphernalia – *n.* – equipment; accessories

partisan – 1. *n* – supporter; follower; 2. *adj.* – biased; one-sided

passive – *adj.* – submissive; unassertive

pathology – *n.* – part of medicine dealing with the nature of diseases, their causes and symptoms, and the structural and functional changes

pedagogue – *n.* – a dogmatic teacher

penchant – *n.* – a strong liking or fondness

pensive – *adj.* – reflective; contemplative

Drill 8

DIRECTIONS: Match each word in the left column with the word in the right column that is most **opposite** in meaning.

	Word		Match
1.	____ ostensible	A.	aversion
2.	____ obsolete	B.	flexible
3.	____ nebulous	C.	unnoticeable
4.	____ penchant	D.	actual
5.	____ neophyte	E.	opponent
6.	____ partisan	F.	domineering
7.	____ obdurate	G.	distinct
8.	____ obsequious	H.	assertive
9.	____ palpable	I.	modern
10.	____ passive	J.	veteran
11.	____ meticulous	K.	jovial
12.	____ morose	L.	sloppy
13.	____ minute	M.	huge
14.	____ novel	N.	stale

DIRECTIONS: Match each word in the left column with the word in the right column that is most **similar** in meaning.

	Word		Match
15.	____ nullify	A.	invalidate
16.	____ ominous	B.	irritate
17.	____ nettle	C.	dull
18.	____ palliate	D.	threatening
19.	____ opaque	E.	alleviate
20.	____ marred	F.	lessen
21.	____ mitigate	G.	damaged
22.	____ negligence	H.	carelessness

GROUP 9

perceptive – *adj.* – full of insight; aware

percussion – *n.* – the striking of one object against another

peripheral – *adj.* – marginal; outer

perjury – *n.* – the practice of lying

permeable – *adj.* – porous; allowing to pass through

pernicious – *adj.* – dangerous; harmful

perpetual – *adj.* – enduring for all time

pertinent – *adj.* – related to the matter at hand

pervade – *v.* – to occupy the whole of

pessimism – *n.* – seeing only the gloomy side; hopelessness

petulant – *adj.* – 1. forward; immodest; 2. impatient or irritable

phenomenon – *n.* – 1. miracle; 2. occurrence

philanthropy – n.- charity; unselfishness

phlegmatic – *adj.* – without emotion or interest

pinnacle – *n.* – 1. a small turret that rises above the roof of a building; 2. the highest point

pious – *adj.* – religious; devout; dedicated

piquant – *adj.* – 1. agreeably pungent or stimulating to the taste; 2. exciting interest or curiosity

pittance – *n.* – small allowance

placate – *v.* – pacify

placid – *adj.* – serene; tranquil

plausible – *adj.* – probable; feasible

plethora – *n.* – condition of going beyond what is needed; excess; overabundance

plumb – *v.* – 1. to fall or sink straight down; 2. to hang vertically

polemic – *adj.* – controversial; argumentative

pragmatic – *adj.* – matter-of-fact; practical

prattle – *v.* – to speak in a childish manner; babble

precipitate – *v.* – 1. to throw headlong; 2. to cause to happen

preclude – *v.* – inhibit; make impossible

predecessor – *n.* – one who has occupied an office before another

pristine – *adj.* – still pure or untouched

privy – *adj.* – private; confidential

probity – *n.* – true virtue or integrity; complete honesty

problematic – *adj.* – uncertain

prodigal – *adj.* – wasteful; lavish

prodigious – *adj.* – exceptional; tremendous

prodigy – *n.* – 1. an extraordinary happening; 2. something so extraordinary as to inspire wonder

profound – *adj.* – deep; knowledgeable; thorough

profusion – *n.* – great amount; abundance

progeny – *n.* – children; offspring

propinquity – *n.* – nearness in time or place, relationship, or nature

prosaic – *adj.* – tiresome; ordinary

proselytize – *v.* – to make a convert of

provincial – *adj.* – regional; unsophisticated

provocative – *adj.* – 1. tempting; 2. irritating

prudent – *adj.* – wise; careful; prepared

pundit – *n.* – a person of great learning

pungent – *adj.* – sharp; stinging

qualified – *adj.* – experienced; indefinite

qualify – *v.* – 1. to render fit; 2. to furnish with legal power; 3. to modify

quandary – *n.* – dilemma

quiescent – *adj.* – inactive; at rest

quirk – *n.* – peculiar behavior; startling twist

rabid – *adj.* – furious; with extreme anger

rampart – *n.* – 1. anything that protects or defends; 2. an embankment of earth that surrounds a fort or castle

rancid – *adj.* – having a bad odor

rant – *v.* – to speak in a loud, pompous manner; rave

Drill: Group 9

DIRECTIONS: Match each word in the left column with the word in the right column that is most **opposite** in meaning.

	Word		Match
1.	____ pristine	A.	inexperienced
2.	____ phlegmatic	B.	anger
3.	____ profound	C.	central
4.	____ qualified	D.	cheerful
5.	____ placid	E.	shallow
6.	____ placate	F.	joyous
7.	____ pensive	G.	extraordinary
8.	____ peripheral	H.	contaminated
9.	____ petulant	I.	excited
10.	____ prosaic	J.	turbulent
11.	____ placate	K.	dearth
12.	____ profusion	L.	facilitate
13.	____ peripheral	M.	superficial
14.	____ plausible	N.	improbable
15.	____ preclude	O.	minute
16.	____ prodigious	P.	anger
17.	____ profound	Q.	central

DIRECTIONS: Match each word in the left column with the word in the right column that is most **similar** in meaning.

	Word		Match
18.	____ provocative	A.	nearness
19.	____ pungent	B.	tempting
20.	____ propinquity	C.	reverent
21.	____ pious	D.	flavorsome
22.	____ pragmatic	E.	practical
23.	____ pernicious	F.	lavish
24.	____ prodigal	G.	harmful

GROUP 10

rationalize – *v.* – to offer reasons for; account for

raucous – *adj.* – disagreeable to the sense of hearing; harsh

realm – *n.* – an area; sphere of activity

rebuff – *n.* – an abrupt, blunt refusal

recession – *n.* – withdrawal; depression

reciprocal – *adj.* – mutual; having the same relationship to each other

recluse – *n.* – solitary and shut off from society

recondite – *adj.* – beyond the grasp of ordinary understanding

rectify – *v.* – correct

redundant – *adj.* – repetitious; unnecessary

refute – *v.* – challenge; disprove

regal – *adj.* – royal; grand

reiterate – *v.* – repeat; to state again

relegate – *v.* – banish; put to a lower position

relevant – *adj.* – of concern; significant

relinquish – *v.* – to let go; abandon

remorse – *n.* – guilt; sorrow

renascence – *n.* – a new birth; revival

render – *v.* – deliver; provide; to give up a possession

replica – *n.* – copy; representation

reprehensible – *adj.* – wicked; disgraceful

reprobate – *adj.* – 1. vicious; unprincipled; 2. *v.* – to disapprove with detestation

repudiate – *v.* – reject; cancel

repugnant – *adj.* – inclined to disobey or oppose

rescind – *v.* – retract; discard

resignation – *n.* – 1. quitting; 2. submission

resolution – *n.* – proposal; promise; determination

respite – *n.* – recess; rest period

reticent – *adj.* – silent; reserved; shy

retroaction – *n.* – an action elicited by a stimulus

reverent – *adj.* – respectful

reverie – *n.* – the condition of being unaware of one's surroundings; trance

rhetorical – *adj.* – having to do with verbal communication

ribald – *adj.* – characterized by coarse joking or mocking

rigor- *n.* – severity

rivet – *v.* – to fasten, fix, or hold firmly

rummage – *v.* – search thoroughly

saga – *n.* – a legend; story

sagacious – *adj.* – wise; cunning

salient – *adj.* – noticeable; prominent

salubrious – *adj.* – favorable to health

salvage – *v.* – rescue from loss

sanction – *n.* – 1. support; encouragement; 2. something which makes a rule binding

sanguine – *adj.* – 1. optimistic; cheerful; 2. red

sardonic – *adj.* – bitterly ironical

satiric – *adj.* – indulging in the use of ridicule or sarcasm to expose or attack vice, folly, etc.

saturate – *v.* – soak thoroughly; drench

saturnine – *adj.* – heavy; grave; gloomy

saunter – *v.* – walk at a leisurely pace; stroll

savor – *v.* – to receive pleasure from; enjoy

scanty – *adj.* – inadequate; sparse

scrupulous – *adj.* – honorable; exact

scrutinize – *v.* – examine closely; study

seethe – *v.* – to be in a state of emotional turmoil; to become angry

serrated – *adj.* – having a sawtoothed edge

servile – *adj.* – slavish, groveling

shoddy – *adj.* – of inferior quality; cheap

Drill 10

DIRECTIONS: Match each word in the left column with the word in the right column that is most **opposite** in meaning.

Word		Match	
1.	____ salient	A.	forward
2.	____ reticent	B.	promote
3.	____ raucous	C.	pleasant
4.	____ redundant	D.	minor
5.	____ relegate	E.	affirm
6.	____ repugnant	F.	unprincipled
7.	____ repudiate	G.	necessary
8.	____ rebuff	H.	pleasant
9.	____ scrupulous	I.	welcome
10.	____ sanguine	J.	pessimistic
11.	____ reticent	K.	joy
12.	____ prudent	L.	pessimistic
13.	____ relegate	M.	unrelated
14.	____ remorse	N.	careless
15.	____ repudiate	O.	affirm
16.	____ sanguine	P.	forward
17.	____ relevant	Q.	promote

DIRECTIONS: Match each word in the left column with the word in the right column that is most **similar** in meaning.

Word		Match	
18.	____ rescind	A.	deliver
19.	____ reprehensible	B.	blameworthy
20.	____ render	C.	retract
21.	____ sagacious	D.	drench
22.	____ saturate	E.	wise
23.	____ rigor	F.	drench
24.	____ saturate	G.	retract
25.	____ rescind	H.	severity
26.	____ reprehensible	I.	disgraceful

GROUP 11

sinuous – *adj.* – winding; crooked

skeptic – *n.* – doubter

skrumble – *v.* – to toss about haphazardly

skulk – *v.* – to move secretly

slander – *v.* – defame; maliciously misrepresent

sojourn – *n.* – temporary stay; visit

solemnity – *n.* – seriousness

solicit – *v.* – ask; seek

soliloquy – *n.* – a talk one has with oneself (esp. on stage)

spendthrift – *n.* – one who spends money carelessly or wastefully

sporadic – *adj.* – rarely occurring or appearing; intermittent

spurious – *adj.* – false; counterfeit

squalid – *adj.* – foul; filthy

stagnant – *adj.* – motionless; uncirculating

stamina – *n.* – endurance

stanza – *n.* – group of lines in a poem having a definite pattern

static – *adj.* – inactive; changeless

sterile – *adj.* – 1. incapable of producing others; 2. lacking in interest or vitality; 3. free from living microorganisms

stipend – *n.* – payment for work done

stoic – *adj.* – detached; unruffled; calm

stupor – *n.* – a stunned or bewildered condition

suave – *adj.* – effortlessly gracious

subsidiary – *adj.* – subordinate

substantive – *adj.* – 1. existing independently; 2. having a real existence

subtlety – *n.* – 1. understatement; 2. propensity for understatement; 3. sophistication; 4. cunning

succinct – *adj.* – consisting of few words; concise

suffuse – *v.* – to overspread

sullen – *adj.* – 1. showing resentment; 2. gloomy; dismal

sunder – *v.* – break; split in two

superficial – *adj.* – on the surface; narrow-minded; lacking depth

superfluous – *adj.* – unnecessary; extra

surmise – *v.* – draw an inference; guess

surpass – *v.* – go beyond; outdo

surreptitious – *adj.* – done without proper authority

sychophant – *adj.* – flatterer

sycophant – *n.* – a person who seeks favor by flattering people of wealth or influence

syllogism – *n.* – reasoning from the general to the particular

symmetry – *n.* – correspondence of parts; harmony

synthesis – *n.* – 1. the putting together of two or more things; 2. a whole made up of parts put together

taciturn – *adj.* – reserved; quiet; secretive

tantalize – *v.* – to tempt; to torment

taut – *adj.* – 1. stretched tightly; 2. tense

tedious – *adj.* – time-consuming; burdensome; uninteresting

temerity – *n.* – foolish boldness

temper – *v.* – soften; pacify; compose

temperament – *n.* – 1. a middle course reached by mutual concession; 2. frame of mind

tenacious – *adj.* – persistently holding to something

tentative – *adj.* – not confirmed; indefinite

tepid – *adj.* – lacking warmth, interest, enthusiasm; lukewarm

terse – *adj.* – concise; abrupt

thrifty – *adj.* – economical; pennywise

thwart – *v.* – prevent from accomplishing a purpose; frustrate

timbre – *n.* – the degree of resonance of a voiced sound

torpid – *adj.* – lacking alertness and activity; lethargic

toxic – *adj.* – poisonous

tractable – *adj.* – easily led or managed

tranquility – *n.* – peace; stillness; harmony

transitory – *adj.* – of a passing nature; speedily vanishing

transpire – *v.* – to take place; come about

travesty – *n.* – a crude and ridiculous representation

trek – *v.* – to make a journey

trepidation – *n.* – apprehension; uneasiness

tribute – *n.* – expression of admiration

Drill 11

DIRECTIONS: Match each word in the left column with the word in the right column that is most **opposite** in meaning.

	Word		**Match**
1.	____ scrutinize	A.	frivolity
2.	____ skeptic	B.	enjoyable
3.	____ solemnity	C.	prodigal
4.	____ static	D.	chaos
5.	____ tedious	E.	give
6.	____ tentative	F.	skim
7.	____ thrifty	G.	turbulent
8.	____ tranquility	H.	active
9.	____ solicit	I.	believer
10.	____ stagnant	J.	confirmed

DIRECTIONS: Match each word in the left column with the word in the right column that is most **similar** in meaning.

	Word		**Match**
11.	____ symmetry	A.	understated
12.	____ superfluous	B.	unnecessary
13.	____ sycophant	C.	balance
14.	____ subtle	D.	fear
15.	____ trepidation	E.	flatterer

GROUP 12

trite – *adj.* – commonplace; overused

trivial – *adj.* – unimportant; small; worthless

truculent – *adj.* – aggressive; eager to fight

tumid – *adj.* – swollen; inflated

tumult – *n.* – great commotion or agitation

turbulence – *n.* – condition of being physically agitated; disturbance

turpitude – *n.* – shameful wickedness

ubiquitous – *adj.* – ever present in all places; universal

ulterior – *adj.* – buried; concealed

uncanny – *adj.* – of a strange nature; weird

undermine – *v.* – weaken; ruin

unequivocal – *adj.* – clear; definite

uniform – *adj.* – consistent; unvaried; unchanging

unique – *adj.* – without equal; incomparable

universal – *adj.* – concerning everyone; existing everywhere

unobtrusive – *adj.* – inconspicuous; reserved

unprecedented – *adj.* – unheard of; exceptional

unpretentious – *adj.* – simple; plain; modest

unruly – *adj.* – not submitting to discipline; disobedient

untoward – *adj.* – 1. hard to manage or deal with; 2. inconvenient

unwonted – *adj.* – not ordinary; unusual

urbane – *adj.* – cultured; suave

usury – *n.* – the act of lending money at illegal rates of interest

vacillation – *n.* – fluctuation

vacuous – *adj.* – containing nothing; empty

valid – *adj.* – acceptable; legal

vantage – *n.* – position giving an advantage

vaunted – *v.* – boasted of

vehement – *adj.* – intense; excited; enthusiastic

venerate – *v.* – revere

veracious – *adj.* – conforming to fact; accurate

veracity – *n.* – 1. honesty; 2. accuracy of statement

verbose – *adj.* – wordy; talkative

versatile – *adj.* – having many uses; multifaceted

vertigo – *n.* – dizziness

vex – *v.* – to trouble the nerves; annoy

viable – *adj.* – 1. capable of maintaining life; 2. possible; attainable

vigor – *n.* – energy; forcefulness

vilify – *v.* – slander

vindicate – *v.* – to free from charge; clear

virile – *adj.* – manly, masculine

virtuoso – *n.* – highly skilled artist

virulent- *adj.* – deadly; harmful; malicious

viscous – *adj.* – thick, syrupy, and sticky

visionary – *adj.* – 1. characterized by impractical ideas; 2. not real

vital – *adj.* – important; spirited

vivacious – *adj.* – animated; gay

vogue – *n.* – modern fashion

volatile – *adj.* – changeable; undependable

voluble – *adj.* – fluent

vulnerable – *adj.* – open to attack; unprotected

waive – *v.* – to give up possession or right

wane – *v.* – grow gradually smaller

wanton – *adj.* – unruly; excessive

welter – *v.* – 1. to roll about or wallow; 2. to rise and fall

wheedle – *v.* – try to persuade; coax

whet – *v.* – sharpen

whimsical – adj.- fanciful; amusing

winsome – *adj.* – agreeable; charming; delightful

wither – *v.* – wilt; shrivel; humiliate; cut down

zealot- *n.* – believer, enthusiast; fan

zenith – *n.* – point directly overhead in the sky

zephyr – *n.* – a gentle wind; breeze

Drill 12

DIRECTIONS: Match each word in the left column with the word in the right column that is most **opposite** in meaning.

	Word		Match
1.	____ uniform	A.	amateur
2.	____ virtuoso	B.	trivial
3.	____ vital	C.	visible
4.	____ wane	D.	placid
5.	____ unobtrusive	E.	unacceptable
6.	____ vigor	F.	support
7.	____ volatile	G.	constancy
8.	____ vacillation	H.	lethargy
9.	____ undermine	I.	wax
10.	____ valid	J.	varied

DIRECTIONS: Match each word in the left column with the word in the right column that is most **similar** in meaning.

	Word		Match
11.	____ wither	A.	intense
12.	____ whimsical	B.	deadly
13.	____ viable	C.	amusing
14.	____ vehement	D.	possible
15.	____ virulent	E.	shrivel

ADDITIONAL VOCABULARY

The following words comprise additional vocabulary terms which are commonly found on the SAT I.

abaft – *adv.* – on or toward the rear of a ship

abandon – 1. *v.* – to leave behind; 2. *v.* – to give something up;

abbreviate – *v.* – to shorten; compress; diminish

abdicate – *v.* – to reject, denounce, or abandon

aberrant – *adj.* – abnormal

abjure – *v.* – to renounce upon oath

abnegation – *n.* – a denial

abridge – *v.* – 1. to shorten; 2. to limit; to take away

abscond – *v.* – to go away hastily or secretly; to hide

abysmal – *adj.* – bottomless; immeasurable

accede – *v.* – to comply with; to consent to

accomplice – *n.* – co-conspirator; partner; partner-in-crime

acerbity – *n.* – harshness or bitterness

acrimony – *n.* – sharpness

addle – *adj.* – barren; confused

adept – *adj.* – skilled; practiced

adjure – *v.* – to entreat earnestly and solemnly

adulation – *n.* – praise in excess

adulterate – *v.* – to corrupt, debase, or make impure

adverse – *adj.* – negative; hostile; antagonistic; inimical

affable – *adj.* – friendly; amiable; good-natured

agrarian – *adj.* – relating to land and the equal divisions of land

alchemy – *n.* – any imaginary power of transmitting one thing into another

allegory – *n.* – symbolic narration or description

allure – *v.* – 1. to attract; entice; 2. *n.* – attraction; temptation; glamour

amiss – 1. *adj.* – wrong; awry; 2. *adv.* – wrongly; mistakenly

anachronism – *n.* – representation of something existing at other than its proper time annihilate – *v.* – to reduce to nothing

anoint – *v.* – 1. to crown; ordain; 2. to smear with oil

apocalyptic – *adj.* – pertaining to revelation or discovery

arrogate – *v.* – to claim or demand unduly

artifice – *n.* – skill; ingenuity; craft

askance – *adv.* – sideways; out of one corner of the eye

assay – *n.* – the determination of any quantity of a metal in an ore or alloy

attenuate – *v.* – 1. to make thin or slender; 2. to lessen or weaken

avarice – *n.* – inordinate desire of gaining and possessing wealth

batten – *v.* – to grow fat; to thrive

beholden – *adj.* – obliged; indebted

bellicose – *adj.* – warlike; disposed to quarrel or fight

berate – *v.* – scold; reprove; reproach; criticize

bereft – *adj.* – hurt by someone's death

besmirch – *v.* – to soil or discolor

bestial – *adj.* – having the qualities of a beast

betroth – *v.* – to promise or pledge in marriage

blighted – *adj.* – destroyed; frustrated

bode – *v.* – to foreshow something

boorish – *adj.* – rude; ill-mannered

brindled – *adj.* – streaked or spotted with a darker color

broach – *v.* – 1. to pierce; 2. to introduce into conversation

bucolic – *adj.* – pastoral

burlesque – *v.* – to imitate comically

burly – *adj.* – strong; bulky; stocky

cadaver – *n.* – a dead body

calamity – *n.* – disaster

caliber – *n.* – 1. the diameter of a bullet or shell; 2. quality

callow – *adj.* – immature

calumny – *n.* – slander

canard – *n.* – a false statement or rumor

captious – *adj.* – disposed to find fault

carnage – *n.* – slaughter

carte blanche – *n.* – unlimited power to decide

castigate – *v.* – to chastise

cataclysm – *n.* – 1. an overflowing of water; 2. an extraordinary change

catalyst – *n.* – anything which creates a situation in which change can occur

catharsis – *n.* – purgation

cavil – *v.* – to find fault without good reason

celibate – *adj.* – unmarried, single; chaste

cessation – *n.* – a ceasing; a stop

chafe – *v.* – to rage; to fret

chaffing – *n.* – banter

chaste – *adj.* – virtuous; free from obscenity

choleric – *adj.* – cranky; cantankerous

circumvent – *v.* – to go around

clandestine – *adj.* – secret; private; hidden

cogent – *adj.* – urgent; compelling; convincing

cohort – *n.* – a group; a band

collusion – *n.* – secret agreement for a fraudulent or illegal purpose

comport – *v.* – to agree; to accord

conclave – *n.* – any private meeting or close assembly

conglomeration – *n.* – mixture; collection

connivance – *n.* -passive co-operation

consort – *n.* -1. a companion; 2. *v.* – to be in harmony or agreement

contravene – *v.* – to go against; to oppose

contusion – *n.* – a bruise; an injury where the skin is not broken

copious – *adj.* – abundant; in great quantities

covenant – *n.* – a binding and solemn agreement

coy – *adj.* – 1. modest; bashful; 2. pretending shyness to attract

crass – *adj.* – gross; thick; coarse

cursory – *adj.* – hasty; slight

dally – *v.* – to delay; to put off

dauntless – *adj.* – fearless; not discouraged

debonair – *adj.* – having an affable manner; courteous

decadence – *n.* – a decline in force or quality

deciduous – *adj.* – falling off at a particular season or stage of growth

decry – *v.* – to denounce or condemn openly

defunct – *adj.* – no longer living or existing

deliquesce – *v.* – to melt away

delusion – *n.* – a false statement or opinion

deposition – *n.* – 1. a removal from a position or power; 2. a testimony

depredation – *n.* – a plundering or laying waste

descant – *v.* – to talk at length

despoil – *v.* – to strip; to rob

despotism – *n.* – 1. tyranny; 2. absolute power or influence

desultory – *adj.* – without order or natural connection

dexterous – *adj.* – having or showing mental skill

diffidence – *n.* – 1. lack of self-confidence; 2. distrust

dilapidated – *n.* – falling to pieces or into disrepair

dilettante – *n.* – an admirer of the fine arts; a dabbler

dint – *n.* – a blow; a stroke

disarray – *n.* – 1. disorder; confusion; 2. incomplete or disorderly attire

divulge – *v.* – to become public; to become known

dormant – *adj.* – as if asleep

doting – *adj.* – excessively fond

doughty – *adj.* – brave; valiant

dregs – *n.* – waste or worthless manner

ecclesiastic – *adj.* – pertaining or relating to a church

edify – *v.* – 1. to build or establish; 2. to instruct and improve the mind

effrontery – *n.* – impudence; assurance

effusive – *adj.* – pouring out or forth; overflowing

egregious – *adj.* – eminent; remarkable

egress – *v.* – to depart; to go out

elegy – *n.* – a poem of lament and praise for the dead

elucidate – *v.* – to make clear or manifest; to explain

emanate – *v.* – to send forth; to emit

embellish – *v.* – to improve the appearance of

enamored – *adj.* – filled with love and desire

encroach – *v.* – to trespass or intrude

encumber – *v.* – to hold back; to hinder

endue – *v.* – to put on; to cover

enrapture – *v.* – to fill with pleasure

epilogue – *n.* – closing section of a play or novel providing further comment

epiphany – *n.* – an appearance of a supernatural being

epitaph – *n.* – an inscription on a monument, in honor or memory of a dead person

equinox – *n.* – precise time when the day and night everywhere is of equal length

equivocate – *v.* – to be purposely ambiguous

eschew – *v.* – to escape from; to avoid

estranged – *adj.* – kept at a distance; alienated

ethereal – *adj.* – 1. very light; airy; 2. heavenly; not earthly

euphemism – *n.* – the use of a word or phrase in place of one that is distasteful

euphoria – *n.* – a feeling of well-being

exhume – *v.* – to unearth; to reveal

expunge – *v.* – to blot out; to delete

exude – *v.* – to flow slowly or ooze in drops

facsimile – *n.* – copy; reproduction; replica

faction – *n.* – a number of people in an organization having a common end view

fallible – *adj.* – liable to be mistaken or erroneous

fathom – *v.* – comprehend; uncover

fatuous – *adj.* – silly; inane; unreal

fealty – *n.* – fidelity; loyalty

feign – *v.* – to invent or imagine

ferment – *v.* – to excite or agitate

fervid – *adj.* – very hot; burning

fester – *v.* – to become more and more virulent and fixed

fetish – *n.* – anything to which one gives excessive devotion or blind adoration

fidelity – *n.* – faithfulness; honesty

fissure – *n.* – a dividing or breaking into parts

flaccid – *adj.* – 1. hanging in loose folds or wrinkles; 2. lacking force; weak

flamboyant – *adj.* – ornate; too showy

flinch – *v.* – wince; draw back; retreat

foible – *n.* – a slight frailty in character

foist – *v.* – to put in slyly or stealthily

foray – *v.* – to raid for spoils, plunder

forensic – *adj.* – pertaining to legal or public argument

fortitude – *n.* – firm courage; strength

fractious – *adj.* – rebellious; apt to quarrel

fraught – *adj.* – loaded; charged

froward – *adj.* – not willing to yield or comply with what is reasonable

fulminate – *v.* – to explode with sudden violence

galvanize – *v.* – to stimulate as if by electric shock; startle; excite

gamut – *n.* – 1. a complete range; 2. any complete musical scale

garish – *adj.* – gaudy; showy

gauche – *adj.* – awkward; lacking grace

gauntlet – *n.* – a long glove with a flaring cuff covering the lower part of the arm

generic – *adj.* – common; general; universal

glib – *adj.* – smooth and slippery; speaking or spoken in a smooth manner

gnarled – *adj.* – full of knots

gormand – *n.* – a greedy or ravenous eater; glutton

gregarious – *adj.* – fond of the company of others

grisly – *adj.* – frightful; horrible

guffaw – *n.* – a loud, coarse burst of laughter

guise – *n.* – 1. customary behavior; 2. manner of dress; 3. false appearance

halcyon – *adj.* – calm; quiet; peaceful

hapless – *adj.* – unlucky; unfortunate

harangue – *v.* – to speak in an impassioned and forcible manner

heretic – *n.* – one who holds opinion contrary to that which is generally accepted

hiatus – *n.* – interval; break; period of rest

hoary – *adj.* – very aged; ancient

homage – *n.* – honor; respect

homily – *n.* – discourse or sermon read to an audience

hubris – *n.* – arrogance

hybrid – *n.* – anything of mixed origin

idiosyncrasy – *n.* – any personal peculiarity, mannerism, etc.

igneous – *adj.* – having the nature of fire

ignominious – *adj.* – 1. contemptible; 2. degrading

immaculate – *adj.* – 1. perfectly clean; perfectly correct; 2. pure

imminent – *adj.* – appearing as if about to happen

impasse – *n.* – a situation that has no solution or escape

impenitent – *adj.* – without regret, shame, or remorse

impiety – *n.* – 1. irreverence toward God; 2. lack of respect

impolitic – *adj.* – unwise; imprudent

imprecate – *v.* – to pray for evil; to invoke a curse

imputation – *n.* – attribution

incarcerate – *v.* – to imprison or confine

incommodious – *adj.* – uncomfortable; troublesome

incorporeal – *adj.* – not consisting of matter

incorrigible – *adj.* – not capable of correction or improvement

incubate – *v.* – to sit on and hatch (eggs)

inculcate – *v.* – to impress upon the mind by frequent repetition or urging

indemnify – *v.* – to protect against or keep free from loss

indigenous – *adj.* – innate; inherent; inborn

indomitable – *adj.* – not easily discouraged or defeated

indubitably – *adv.* – unquestionably; surely

inept – *adj.* – incompetent; unskilled

inimical – *adj.* – unfriendly; adverse

iniquitous – *adj.* – unjust; wicked

inordinate – *adj.* – not regulated; excessive

intrepid – *adj.* – fearless; brave

inured – *adj.* – accustomed

invoke – *v.* – ask for; call upon

irascible – *adj.* – easily provoked or inflamed to anger

irreparable – *adj.* – that which cannot be repaired or regained

itinerary – *n.* – travel plan; schedule; course

jettison – *n.* – a throwing overboard of goods to lighten a vehicle in an emergency

jocund – *adj.* – merry; gay; cheerful

jovial – *adj.* – cheery; jolly; playful

juncture – *n.* – critical point; meeting

juxtapose – *v.* – place side-by-side

knead – *v.* – mix; massage

lacerate – *v.* – 1. to tear or mangle; 2. to wound or hurt

lambent – *adj.* – giving off a soft radiance

larceny – *n.* – theft; stealing

lassitude – *n.* – a state or feeling of being tired or weak

lewd – *adj.* – lustful; wicked

libertine – *n.* – one who indulges his desires without restraint

licentious – *adj.* – disregarding accepted rules and standards

limber – *adj.* – flexible; pliant

lithe – *adj.* – easily bent; pliable

loquacious – *adj.* – talkative

lucent – *adj.* – shining; translucent

lugubrious – *adj.* – mournful; very sad

lurid – *adj.* – ghastly pale; gloomy

magnate – *n.* – a very influential person in any field of activity malefactor – *n.* – one who commits a crime

malign – *v.* – to defame; speak evil of

mandate – *n.* – order; charge

marauder – *n.* – a rover in search of booty or plunder

maudlin – *adj.* – foolishly and tearfully sentimental

mendacious – *adj.* – addicted to deception

mercurial – *adj.* – quick, volatile; changeable

meretricious – *adj.* – alluring by false, showy charms; fleshy

mesmerize – *v.* – hypnotize

mettle – *n.* – high quality of character

mien – *n.* – manner; external appearance

mimicry – *n.* – imitation

misanthropy – *n.* – hatred of mankind

mite – *n.* – 1. very small sum of money; 2. very small creature

modulate – *v.* – 1. to regulate or adjust; 2. to vary the pitch of the voice

mollify – *v.* – to soften; to make less intense

moot – *adj.* – subject to or open for discussion or debate

mordant – *adj.* – biting. cutting, or caustic

mutinous – *adj.* – inclined to revolt

narcissistic – *adj.* – egotistical; self-centered

nautical – *adj.* – of the sea

nefarious – *adj.* – very wicked; abominable

nemesis – *n.* – just punishment; retribution

nexus – *n.* – a connection

nostrum – *n.* – a quack medicine

noxious – *adj.* – harmful to health or morals

nugatory – *adj.* – trifling; futile; insignificant

obeisance – *n.* – a gesture of respect or reverence

obfuscate – *v.* – to darken; to confuse

objurgate – *v.* – to chide vehemently

obligatory – *adj.* – mandatory; necessary

obloquy – *n.* – verbal abuse of a person or thing

obsequious – *adj.* – slavishly attentive; servile

obstinate – *adj.* – stubborn

obtrude – *v.* – to thrust forward; to eject

odious – *adj.* – hateful; disgusting

oligarchy – *n.* – form of government in which the supreme power is placed in the hands of a small exclusive group

opalescent – *adj.* – iridescent

opprobrious – *adj.* – reproachful or contemptuous

oust – *v.* – drive out; eject

painstaking – *adj.* – thorough; careful; precise

palatial – *adj.* – large and ornate, like a palace

palindrome – *n.* – a word, verse or sentence that is the same when read backward or forward

paltry – *adj.* – worthless; trifling

pandemonium – *n.* – a place of wild disorder, noise, or confusion

paradigm – *n.* – model; example

parapet – *n.* – a wall or railing to protect people from falling

pariah – *n.* – an outcast; someone despised by others

parity – *n.* – state of being the same in power, value, or rank

parley – *v.* – to speak with another; to discourse

parochial – *adj.* – religious; narrow-minded

parry – *v.* – to ward off; to avoid

parsimonious – *adj.* – miserly; stingy

paucity – *n.* – scarcity; small number

peculate – *v.* – to embezzle

pecuniary – *adj.* – relating to money

pedestrian – *adj.* – mediocre; ordinary

pellucid – *adj.* – transparent

penury – *n.* – lack of money or property

perdition – *n.* – complete and irreparable loss

peremptory – *adj.* – 1. barring future action; 2. that cannot be denied, changed, etc.

perfidious – *adj.* – violating good faith or vows

perquisite – *n.* – a fee, profit, etc. in addition to the stated income of one's employment

peruse – *v.* – to read carefully and thoroughly

petty – *adj.* – unimportant; of subordinate standing

phobia – *n.* – morbid fear

pied – *adj.* – spotted

pinioned – *adj.* – 1. having wings; 2. having wings or arms bound or confined

pittance – *n.* – small allowance

platonic – *adj.* – 1. idealistic or impractical; 2. not amorous or sensual

plenary – *adj.* – full; entire; complete

pommel – *n.* – the rounded, upward-projecting front of a saddle

portend – *v.* – to foreshadow

potable – *adj.* – drinkable

potent – *adj.* – having great power or physical strength

prate – *v.* – to talk much and foolishly

precept – *n.* – a rule or direction of moral conduct

precocious – *adj.* – developed or matured earlier than usual

prefatory – *adj.* – introductory

preponderate – *adj.* – to outweigh

prerogative – *n.* – a prior or exclusive right or privilege

prevaricate – *v.* – to evade the truth

prognosis – *n.* – a forecast, especially in medicine

prolific – *adj.* – fruitful

propagate – *v.* – to reproduce or multiply

propitiate – *v.* – to win the good will of

protocol – *n.* – an original draft or record of a document

provident – *adj.* – prudent; economical

proviso – *n.* – conditional stipulation to an agreement

provoke – *v.* – to stir action or feeling; arouse

pseudonym – *n.* – a borrowed or fictitious name

puerile – *adj.* – childish; immature

pungent – *adj.* – sharp; stinging

purloin – *v.* – to steal

purview – *n.* – the range of control, activity, or understanding

quaff – *v.* – to drink or swallow in large quantities

quagmire – *n.* – a difficult position, as if on shaky ground

quaint – *adj.* – old-fashioned; unusual; odd

qualm – *n.* – sudden feeling of uneasiness or doubt

quarantine – *n.* – isolation of a person to prevent spread of disease

quintessence – *n.* – 1. the ultimate substance; 2. the pure essence of anything

quixotic – *adj.* – extravagantly chivalrous

quizzical – *adj.* – odd; comical

ramification – *n.* – the arrangement of branches; consequence

rampant – *adj.* – violent and uncontrollable action

rancor – *n.* – a continuing and bitter hate or ill will

ratify – *v.* – to make valid; confirm

raze – *v.* – to scrape or shave off

rebuttal – *n.* – refutation

recalcitrant – *adj.* – refusing to obey authority

recidivism – *n.* – habitual or chronic relapse

recumbent – *adj.* – leaning or reclining

recusant – *adj.* – disobedient of authority

redolent – *adj.* – sweet-smelling; fragrant

refurbish – *v.* – to make new

reminiscence – *n.* – a remembering

remonstrate – *v.* – to exhibit strong reasons against an act

rendition – *n.* – a performance or interpretation

repertoire – *n.* – stock of plays which can be readily performed by a company

reprehend – *v.* – to reprimand; to find fault with

reprieve – *v.* – to give temporary relief

resilient – *adj.* – flexible; capable of withstanding stress

resonant – *adj.* – resounding; re-echoing

resplendent – *adj.* – dazzling; splendid

resurgent – *adj.* – rising or tending to rise again

revile – *v.* – to be abusive in speech

risible – *adj.* – able or inclined to laugh

roseate – *adj.* – bright, cheerful, or optimistic

rote – *n.* – a fixed, mechanical way of doing something

rotundity – *n.* – condition of being rounded out or plump

rudimentary – *adj.* – elementary

ruminate – *v.* – to muse on

rummage – *v.* – search thoroughly

rustic – *adj.* – plain and unsophisticated; homely

salutatory – *adj.* – of or containing greetings

sapid – *adj.* – having a pleasant taste

sarcasm – *n.* – ironic; bitter humor designed to wound

satire – *n.* – a novel or play that uses humor or irony to expose folly

savant – *n.* – a learned person

schism – *n.* – a division in an organized group

scourge – *v.* – to whip severely

scurrilous – *adj.* – using low and indecent language

sedentary – *adj.* – 1. characterized by sitting; 2. remaining in one locality

seethe – *v.* – to be in a state of emotional turmoil; to become angry

serendipity – *n.* – an apparent aptitude for making fortunate discoveries accidentally

shoal – *n.* – a great quantity

sloth – *n.* – disinclination to action or labor

slovenly – *adv.* – careless in habits. behavior, etc.; untidy

solace – *n.* – hope; comfort during a time of grief

somber – *adj.* – dark and depressing; gloomy

sordid – *adj.* – filthy; base; vile

specious – *adj.* – appearing just and fair without really being so

spelunker – *n.* – one who explores caves

splenetic – *adj.* – bad-tempered; irritable

staid – *adj.* – sober; sedate

stamina – *n.* – endurance

stanch – *v.* – to stop or check the flow of blood

steadfast – *adj.* – loyal

stigma – *n.* – a mark of disgrace

stigmatize – *v.* – to characterize or make as disgraceful

stipend – *n.* – payment for work done

stolid – *adj.* – unexcitable; dull

striated – *adj.* – marked with fine parallel lines

strident – *adj.* – creaking; harsh; grating

stymie – *n.* – 1. to hinder or obstruct; 2. in golf, an opponent's ball lying in direct line between the player's ball and the hole

succor – *n.* – aid; assistance

succumb – *v.* – give in; yield; collapse

sumptuous – *adj.* – involving great expense

sundry – *adj.* – 1. various; miscellaneous; 2. separate; distinct

supplant – *v.* – to take the place of

suppliant – *adj.* – asking earnestly and submissively

suppress – *v.* – to bring to an end; hold back

surfeit – *v.* – to feed or supply in excess

susceptible – *adj.* – easily imposed; inclined

swathe – *v.* – to wrap around something; envelop

symmetry – *n.* – equal in form on either side of a dividing line

tacit – *adj.* – not voiced or expressed

tarry – *v.* – to go or move slowly; delay

tawdry – *n.* – a gaudy ornament

teem – *v.* – 1. to be stocked to overflowing; 2. to pour out; to empty

tenet – *n.* – any principle, doctrine, etc. which a person, school, etc. believes or maintains

termagant – *n.* – a boisterous, scolding woman; a shrew

terrestrial – *adj.* – pertaining to the earth

tether – *n.* – the range or limit of one's abilities

thrall – *n.* – a slave

throe – *v.* – to put in agony

thwart – *v.* – prevent from accomplishing a purpose; frustrate

timorous – *adj.* – fearful

tortuous – *adj.* – pertaining to or involving excruciating pain

traduce – *v.* – 1. to exhibit; 2. to slander

transmute – *v.* – to transform

traumatic – *adj.* – causing a violent injury

travail – *v.* – to harass; to torment

trenchant – *adj.* – 1. keen; penetrating; 2. clear-cut; distinct

tribunal – *n.* – the seat of judgment

troth – *n.* – belief; faith; fidelity

turbid – *adj.* – 1. thick; dense; 2. confused; perplexed

turmoil – *n.* – unrest; agitation

tutelage – *n.* – the condition of being under a guardian or a tutor

tycoon – *n.* – wealthy leader

tyranny – *n.* – absolute power; autocracy

umbrage – *n.* – shade; shadow

uncouth – *adj.* – uncultured; crude

unfeigned – *adj.* – genuine; real; sincere

usurpation – *n.* – act of taking something for oneself; seizure

utopia – *n.* – imaginary land with perfect social and political systems

uxoricide – *n.* – the murder of a wife by her husband

vagabond – *n.* – wanderer; one without a fixed place

vagary – *n.* – 1. an odd action or idea; 2. a wandering

vagrant – 1. *n.* – homeless person; 2. *adj.* – rambling; wandering; transient

valance – *n.* – short drapery hanging over the window frame

valor – *n.* – bravery

vaunt – *v.* – to brag or boast

velocity – *n.* – speed

venal – *adj.* – that can be readily bribed or corrupted

vendetta – *n.* – feud

veneer – *n.* – 1. a thin surface layer; 2. any attractive but superficial appearance

venue – *n.* – location

verbatim – *adj.* – employing the same words as another; literal

verbiage – *n.* – wordiness

verity – *n.* – truthfulness

vestige – *n.* – a trace of something that no longer exists

vicarious – *adj.* – taking the place of another person or thing

vicissitude – *n.* – charges or variation occurring irregularly in the course of something

vigilance – *n.* – watchfulness

vigorous – *adj.* – energetic; strong

visage – *n.* – appearance

vitriolic – *adj.* – extremely biting or caustic

vociferous – *adj.* – making a loud outcry

volition – *n.* – the act of willing

voracious – *adj.* – greedy in eating

vouchsafe – *v.* – 1. to be gracious enough to grant; 2. to guarantee as safe

waft – *v.* – move gently by wind or breeze

wan – *adj.* – pale; pallid

warrant – *v.* – justify; authorize

wily – *adj.* – cunning; sly

wither – *v.* – to shrivel up; to die

wizened – *adj.* – withered; shrunken

wrath – *n.* – violent or unrestrained anger; fury

wreak – *v.* – to give vent or free play

wrest – *v.* – 1. to turn or twist; 2. usurp; 3. to distort or change the true meaning of

wry – *adj.* – mocking; cynical

xenophobia – *n.* – fear of foreigners

yoke – *n.* – harness; collar; bond

yore – *n.* – former period of time

PREFIXES

Prefix	Meaning	Example
ab –, a –, abs –	away, without, from	absent – away, not present apathy – without interest abstain – keep from doing, refrain
ad –	to, toward	adjacent – next to address – to direct towards
ante –	before	antecedent – going before in time anterior – occurring before
anti –	against	antidote – remedy to act against an evil antibiotic – substance that fights against bacteria
be –	over, thoroughly	bemoan – to mourn over belabor – to exert much labor upon
bi –	two	bisect – to divide biennial – happening every two years
cata –, cat –, cath –	down	catacombs – underground passageways catalogue – descriptive list catheter – tubular medical device
circum –	around	circumscribe – to draw a circle around circumspect – watchful on all sides
com –	with	combine – to join together communication – to have dealings with
contra –	against	contrary – opposed contrast – to stand in opposition
de –	down, from	decline – to bend downward decontrol – to release from government control

Prefix	Meaning	Example
di –	two	dichotomy – cutting in two diarchy – system of government with two authorities
dis –, di–	apart, away	discern – to distinguish as separate dismiss – to send away digress – to turn aside
epi –, ep –, eph –	upon, among	epidemic – happening among many people epicycle – circle whose center moves round in the circumference of a greater circle epaulet – decoration worn to ornament or protect the shoulder ephedra – any of a large genus of desert shrubs
ex –, e –	from, out	exceed – go beyond the limit emit – to send forth
extra –	outside, beyond	extraordinary – beyond or out of the common method extrasensory – beyond the senses
hyper –	beyond, over	hyperactive – over the normal activity level hypercritic – one who is critical beyond measure
hypo –	beneath, lower	hypodermic – parts beneath the skin hypocrisy – to be under a pretense of goodness
in –, il –, im –, ir –	not	inactive – not active illogical – not logical imperfect – not perfect irreversible – not reversible
in –, il –, im –, ir –	in, on, into	instill – to put in slowly illation – action of bringing in impose – to lay on irrupt – to break in

Prefix	Meaning	Example
inter –	among, between	intercom – to exchange conversations between people interlude – performance given between parts in a play
intra –	within	intravenous – within a vein intramural – within a single college or its students
meta –	beyond, over, along with	metamorphosis – change over in form or nature metatarsus – part of foot beyond the flat of the foot
mis –	badly, wrongly	misconstrue – to interpret wrongly misappropriate – to use wrongly
mono –	one	monogamy – to be married to one person at a time monotone – a single, unvaried tone
multi –	many	multiple – of many parts multitude – a great number
non –	no, not	nonsense – lack of sense nonentity – not existing
ob –	against	obscene – offensive to modesty obstruct – to hinder the passage of
para –, par –	beside	parallel – continuously at equal distance apart parenthesis – sentence inserted within a passage
per –	through	persevere – to maintain an effort permeate – to pass through
poly –	many	polygon – a plane figure with many sides or angles polytheism – belief in the existence of many gods
post –	after	posterior – coming after postpone – to put off until a future time

Prefix	Meaning	Example
pre –	before	premature – ready before the proper time premonition – a previous warning
pro –	in favor of, forward	prolific – bringing forth offspring project – throw or cast forward
re –	back, against	reimburse – to pay back retract – to draw back
semi –	half	semicircle – half a circle semiannual – half-yearly
sub –	under	subdue – to bring under one's power submarine – to travel under the surface of the sea
super –	above	supersonic – above the speed of sound superior – higher in place or position
tele –, tel –	across	telecast – transmit across a distance telepathy – communication between mind and mind at a distance
trans –	across	transpose – to change the position of two things transmit – to send from one person to another
ultra –	beyond	ultraviolet – beyond the limit of visibility ultramarine – beyond the sea
un –	not	undeclared – not declared unbelievable – not believable
uni –	one	unity – state of oneness unison – sounding together
with –	away, against	withhold – to hold back withdraw – to take away

Drill: Prefixes

DIRECTIONS: Provide a definition for each prefix.

1. pro– _____

2. com– _____

3. epi– _____

4. ob– _____

5. ad– _____

DIRECTIONS: Identify the prefix in each word.

6. efface _____

7. hypothetical _____

8. permeate _____

9. contrast _____

10. inevitable _____

Prefix	Meaning	Example

ROOTS

Root	Meaning	Example
act, ag	do, act, drive	activate – to make active agile – having quick motion
alt	high	altitude – height alto – highest singing voice
alter, altr	other, change	alternative – choice between two things altruism – living for the good of others
am, ami	love, friend	amiable – worthy of affection amity – friendship
anim	mind, spirit	animated – spirited animosity – violent hatred
annu, enni	year	annual – every year centennial – every hundred years
aqua	water	aquarium – tank for water animals and plants aquamarine – semiprecious stone of sea-green color
arch	first, ruler	archenemy – chief enemy archetype – original pattern from which things are copied
aud, audit	hear	audible – capable of being heard audience – assembly of hearers audition – the power or act of hearing
auto	self	automatic – self-acting autobiography – story about a person who also wrote it
bell	war	belligerent – a party taking part in a war bellicose – war-like
ben, bene	good	benign – kindly disposition beneficial – advantageous

Root	Meaning	Example
bio	life	biotic – relating to life biology – the science of life
brev	short	abbreviate – make shorter brevity – shortness
cad, cas	fall	cadence – fall in voice casually – loss caused by death
capit, cap	head	captain – the head or chief decapitate – to cut off the head
cede, ceed, cess	to go, to yield	recede – to move or fall back proceed – to move onward recessive – tending to go back
cent	hundred	century – hundred years centipede – insect with a hundred legs
chron	time	chronology – science dealing with historical dates chronicle – register of events in order of time
cide, cis	to kill, to cut	homicide – one who kills incision – a cut
clam, claim	to shout	acclaim – receive with applause proclamation – announce publicly
cogn	to know	recognize – to know again cognition – awareness
corp	body	incorporate – combine into one body corpse – dead body
cred	to trust, to believe	incredible – unbelievable credulous – too prone to believe
cur, curr, curs	to run	current – flowing body of air or water excursion – short trip
dem	people	democracy – government formed for the people epidemic – affecting all people

Root	Meaning	Example
dic, dict	to say	dictate – to read aloud for another to transcribe verdict – decision of a jury
doc, doct	to teach	docile – easily instructed indoctrinate – to instruct
domin	to rule	dominate – to rule dominion – territory of rule
duc, duct	to lead	conduct – act of guiding induce – to overcome by persuasion
eu	well, good	eulogy – speech or writing in praise euphony – pleasantness or smoothness of sound
fac, fact, fect, fic	to do, to make	facilitate – to make easier factory – location of production confect – to put together fiction – something invented or imagined
fer	to bear, to carry	transfer – to move from one place to another refer – to direct to
fin	end, limit	infinity – unlimited finite – limited in quantity
flect, flex	to bend	flexible – easily bent reflect – to throw back
fort	luck	fortunate – lucky fortuitous – happening by chance
fort	strong	fortify – strengthen fortress – stronghold
frag, fract	break	fragile – easily broken fracture – break
fug	flee	fugitive – fleeing refugee – one who flees to a place of safety

Root	Meaning	Example
gen	class, race	engender – to breed generic – of a general nature in regard to all members
grad, gress	to go, to step	regress – to go back graduate – to divide into regular steps
graph	writing	telegraph – message sent by telegraph autograph – person's own handwriting or signature
ject	to throw	projectile – capable of being thrown reject – to throw away
leg	law	legitimate – lawful legal – defined by law
leg, lig, lect	to choose, gather, read	illegible – incapable of being read ligature – something that binds election – the act of choosing
liber	free	liberal – favoring freedom of ideals liberty – freedom from restraint
log	study, speech	archaeology – study of human antiquities prologue – address spoken before a performance
luc, lum	light	translucent – slightly transparent illuminate – to light up
magn	large, great	magnify – to make larger magnificent – great
mal, male	bad, wrong	malfunction – to operate incorrectly malevolent – evil
mar	sea	marine – pertaining to the sea submarine – below the surface of the sea
mater, matr	mother	maternal – motherly matriarch – government exercised by a mother

Root	Meaning	Example
mit, miss	to send	transmit – to send from one person or place to another mission – the act of sending
morph	shape	metamorphosis – a changing in shape anthropomorphic – having a human shape
mut	change	mutable – subject to change mutate – to change a vowel
nat	born	innate – inborn native – a person born in a place
neg	deny	negative – expressing denial renege – to deny
nom	name	nominate – to put forward a name nomenclature – process of naming
nov	new	novel – new renovate – to make as good as new
omni	all	omnipotent – all powerful omnipresent – all present
oper	to work	operate – to work on something cooperate – to work with others
pass, path	to feel	pathetic – affecting the tender emotions passionate – moved by strong emotion
pater, patr	father	paternal – fatherly patriarch – government exercised by a father
ped, pod	foot	pedestrian – one who travels on foot podiatrist – foot doctor
pel, puls	to drive, to push	impel – to drive forward compulsion – irresistible force
phil	love	philharmonic – loving harmony or music philanthropist – one who loves and seeks to do good for others

Root	Meaning	Example
port	carry	export – to carry out of the country portable – able to be carried
psych	mind	psychology – study of the mind psychiatrist – specialist in mental disorders
quer, ques, quir, quis	to ask	querist – one who inquires inquiry – to ask about question – that which is asked inquisitive – inclined to ask questions
rid, ris	to laugh	ridiculous – laughable derision – to mock
rupt	to break	interrupt – to break in upon erupt – to break through
sci	to know	science – systematic knowledge of physical or natural phenomena conscious – having inward knowledge
scrib, script	to write	transcribe – to write over again script – text of words
sent, sens	to feel, to think	sentimental – feel great emotion sensitive – easily affected by changes
sequ, secut	to follow	sequence – connected series consecutive – following one another in unbroken order
solv, solu, solut	to loosen	dissolve – to break up absolute – without restraint
spect	to look at	spectator – one who watches inspect – to look at closely
spir	to breathe	inspire – to breathe in respiration – process of breathing
string, strict	to bind	stringent – binding strongly restrict – to restrain within bounds

Root	Meaning	Example
stru, struct	to build	strut – a structural piece designed to resist pressure construct – to build
tang, ting, tact, tig	to touch	tangent – touching, but not intersecting patting – to touch lightly contact – touching contiguous – to touch along a boundary
ten, tent, tain	to hold	tenure – holding of office contain – to hold
term	to end	terminate – to end terminal – having an end
terr	earth	terrain – tract of land terrestrial – existing on earth
therm	heat	thermal – pertaining to heat thermometer – instrument for measuring temperature
tort, tors	to twist	contortionist – one who twists violently torsion – act of turning or twisting
tract	to pull, to draw	attract – draw toward distract – to draw away
vac	empty	vacant – empty evacuate – to empty out
ven, vent	to come	prevent – to stop from coming intervene – to come between
ver	true	verify – to prove to be true veracious – truthful
verb	word	verbose – use of excess words verbatim – word for word
vid, vis	to see	video – picture phase of television vision – act of seeing external objects

Root	Meaning	Example
vinc, vict, vang	to conquer	invincible – unconquerable victory – defeat of enemy vanguard – troops moving at the head of an army
viv, vit	life	vital – necessary to life vivacious – lively
voc	to call	vocation – a summons to a course of action vocal – uttered by voice
vol	to wish, to will	involuntary – outside the control of will volition – the act of willing or choosing

Drill: Roots

DIRECTIONS: Provide a definition for each root.

1. cede _____

2. fact _____

3. path _____

4. ject _____

5. ver _____

DIRECTIONS: Identify the root in each word.

6. acclaim _____

7. verbatim _____

8. benefactor _____

9. relegate _____

10. tension _____

SUFFIXES

Suffix	Meaning	Example
–able, –ble	capable of	believable – capable of believing legible – capable of being read
–acious, –icious, *–ous*	full of	vivacious – full of life delicious – full of pleasurable smell or taste wondrous – full of wonder
–ant, –ent	full of	eloquent – full of eloquence expectant – full of expectation
–ary	connected with	honorary – for the sake of honor disciplinary – relating to a field of study
–ate	to make	ventilate – to make public consecrate – to dedicate
–fy	to make	magnify – to make larger testify – to make witness
–ile	pertaining to, capable of	docile – capable of being managed easily infantile – pertaining to infancy
–ism	belief, ideal	conservationism – ideal of keeping safe sensationalism – matter, language designed to excite
–ist	doer	artist – one who creates art pianist – one who plays the piano
–ose	full of	verbose – full of words grandiose – striking, imposing
–osis	condition	neurosis – nervous condition psychosis – psychological condition
–tude	state	magnitude – state of greatness multitude – state of quantity

Drill: Suffixes

DIRECTIONS: Provide a definition for each suffix.

1. –ant, –ent _____

2. –tude _____

3. –ile _____

4. –fy _____

5. –ary _____

DIRECTIONS: Identify the suffix in each word.

6. audacious _____

7. expedient _____

8. gullible _____

9. grandiose _____

10. antagonism _____

ANSWER KEY

Drill 1

1.	(J)	6.	(B)	11.	(M)	16.	(A)
2.	(G)	7.	(I)	12.	(L)	17.	(E)
3.	(A)	8.	(D)	13.	(K)	18.	(B)
4.	(C)	9.	(F)	14.	(D)		
5.	(H)	10.	(E)	15.	(C)		

Drill 2

1.	(D)	6.	(J)	11.	(L)	16.	(E)
2.	(G)	7.	(E)	12.	(K)	17.	(C)
3.	(I)	8.	(C)	13.	(D)	18.	(G)
4.	(F)	9.	(B)	14.	(A)	19.	(F)
5.	(A)	10.	(H)	15.	(B)		

Drill 3

1.	(E)	6.	(B)	11.	(O)	16.	(C)
2.	(H)	7.	(C)	12.	(K)	17.	(A)
3.	(J)	8.	(G)	13.	(L)	18.	(E)
4.	(A)	9.	(F)	14.	(N)	19.	(D)
5.	(I)	10.	(D)	15.	(M)	20.	(B)

Drill 4

1.	(D)	7.	(C)	13.	(K)	19.	(A)
2.	(E)	8.	(F)	14.	(P)	20.	(B)
3.	(A)	9.	(H)	15.	(Q)	21.	(C)
4.	(I)	10.	(G)	16.	(L)	22.	(E)
5.	(J)	11.	(M)	17.	(O)	23.	(F)
6.	(B)	12.	(N)	18.	(D)	24.	(B)

Drill 5

1.	(H)	8.	(E)	15.	(L)	22.	(A)
2.	(F)	9.	(D)	16.	(R)	23.	(E)
3.	(A)	10.	(G)	17.	(N)	24.	(C)
4.	(B)	11.	(Q)	18.	(M)	25.	(F)
5.	(J)	12.	(O)	19.	(P)	26.	(G)
6.	(C)	13.	(K)	20.	(B)		
7.	(I)	14.	(S)	21.	(D)		

Drill 6

1.	(G)	7.	(D)	13.	(N)	19.	(A)
2.	(A)	8.	(I)	14.	(P)	20.	(C)
3.	(E)	9.	(F)	15.	(L)	21.	(B)
4.	(J)	10.	(H)	16.	(M)	22.	(G)
5.	(C)	11.	(O)	17.	(D)	23.	(F)
6.	(B)	12.	(K)	18.	(E)		

Drill 7

1.	(N)	7.	(A)	13.	(D)	19.	(D)
2.	(K)	8.	(B)	14.	(J)	20.	(C)
3.	(M)	9.	(H)	15.	(G)	21.	(A)
4.	(L)	10.	(I)	16.	(F)		
5.	(F)	11.	(C)	17.	(B)		
6.	(E)	12.	(G)	18.	(E)		

Drill 8

1.	(D)	7.	(B)	13.	(M)	19.	(C)
2.	(I)	8.	(F)	14.	(N)	20.	(G)
3.	(G)	9.	(C)	15.	(A)	21.	(F)
4.	(A)	10.	(H)	16.	(D)	22.	(H)
5.	(J)	11.	(L)	17.	(B)		
6.	(E)	12.	(K)	18.	(E)		

Drill 9

1.	(H)	7.	(F)	13.	(Q)	19.	(D)
2.	(I)	8.	(C)	14.	(N)	20.	(A)
3.	(E)	9.	(D)	15.	(L)	21.	(C)
4.	(A)	10.	(G)	16.	(O)	22.	(E)
5.	(J)	11.	(P)	17.	(M)	23.	(G)
6.	(B)	12.	(K)	18.	(B)	24.	(F)

Drill 10

1.	(D)	8.	(I)	15.	(O)	22.	(D)
2.	(A)	9.	(F)	16.	(L)	23.	(H)
3.	(H)	10.	(J)	17.	(M)	24.	(F)
4.	(G)	11.	(P)	18.	(C)	25.	(G)
5.	(B)	12.	(N)	19.	(B)	26.	(I)
6.	(C)	13.	(Q)	20.	(A)		
7.	(E)	14.	(K)	21.	(E)		

Drill 11

1.	(F)	5.	(B)	9.	(E)	13.	(E)
2.	(I)	6.	(J)	10.	(G)	14.	(A)
3.	(A)	7.	(C)	11.	(C)	15.	(D)
4.	(H)	8.	(D)	12.	(B)		

Drill 12

1.	(J)	5.	(C)	9.	(F)	13.	(D)
2.	(A)	6.	(H)	10.	(E)	14.	(A)
3.	(B)	7.	(D)	11.	(E)	15.	(B)
4.	(I)	8.	(G)	12.	(C)		

Drill: Prefixes

1. forward
2. with
3. upon, among
4. against
5. to, toward
6. ef–
7. hypo–
8. per–
9. con–
10. in–

Drill: Roots

1. to go, to yield
2. to do, to make
3. to feel
4. to throw
5. true
6. claim
7. verb
8. ben(e)
9. leg
10. ten

Drill: Suffixes

1. full of
2. state
3. pertaining to, capable of
4. to make
5. connected with
6. (a)cious
7. ent
8. ible
9. ose
10. ism

Index

Numbers on this page refer to <u>PROBLEM NUMBERS</u>, not page numbers.

INDEX

SENTENCE COMPLETIONS

One-Word Completions

Negative Value Words — 1–8, 1–17, 1–29, 1–35, 1–36, 1–38, 1–41, 1–43, 1–52, 1–53, 1–57, 1–58, 1–68, 1–83, 1–84, 1–85, 1–93, 1–95, 1–99

Neutral Value Words — 1–20, 1–34, 1–92, 1–96

Positive Value Words — 1–10, 1–11, 1–12, 1–14, 1–24, 1–25, 1–26, 1–32, 1–37, 1–49, 1–56, 1–60, 1–71, 1–77, 1–79, 1–86, 1–98

Two-Word Completions

Mixed Value Words — 1–2, 1–18, 1–27, 1–30, 1–39, 1–40, 1–44, 1–55, 1–64, 1–66, 1–70, 1–72, 1–73, 1–78, 1–80, 1–88, 1–90, 1–100

Negative Value Words — 1–1, 1–4, 1–5, 1–6, 1–13, 1–19, 1–22, 1–23, 1–31, 1–33, 1–45, 1–46, 1–48, 1–50, 1–54, 1–62, 1–76, 1–82, 1–97

Neutral Value Words — 1–3, 1–16, 1–21, 1–63, 1–65, 1–67, 1–69, 1–74, 1–75, 1–87, 1–89, 1–91

Positive Value Words — 1–7, 1–9, 1–15, 1–28, 1–42, 1–47, 1–51, 1–59, 1–61, 1–81, 1–94

ANALOGIES

Cause and Effect — 2–14, 2–21, 2–23, 2–30, 2–49, 2–50, 2–53, 2–75, 2–78, 2–86

Group to Member — 2–11, 2–17, 2–60, 2–61, 2–74, 2–90

Object to Material — 2–7, 2–22

Part to Whole — 2–6, 2–10, 2–17 2–25, 2–26, 2–27, 2–28, 2–37, 2–38, 2–40, 2–48, 2–52, 2–56, 2–59, 2–71, 2–85

Trait to Example — 2–29, 2–34, 2–51, 2–54, 2–55, 2–63, 2–67, 2–68, 2–69, 2–70, 2–79, 2–81, 2–83, 2–84, 2–88, 2–89, 2–100

User to Tool — 2–1, 2–3, 2–8, 2–9, 2–15, 2–33, 2–43, 2–64, 2–66, 2–72

Numbers on this page refer to **PROBLEM NUMBERS**, not page numbers.

THE BEST TEST PREPARATION FOR THE
SAT* II:
Subject Test
LITERATURE

6 Full-Length Practice Exams

Based on official exam questions released by the College Board

Detailed explanations to every exam question

Far more comprehensive than any other test preparation book

Includes a **COMPREHENSIVE REVIEW COURSE** of Chemistry covering all major topics found on the exam

REA **Research & Education Association**

* SAT is a registered trademark of the College Entrance Examination Board, which does not endorse this book.

Available at your local bookstore or order directly from us by sending in coupon below.

THE BEST TEST PREPARATION FOR THE

SAT* II:
Subject Test
WRITING

6 Full-Length Practice Exams

Based on official exam questions released by the College Board

Detailed explanations to every exam question

Far more comprehensive than any other test preparation book

Includes a **COMPREHENSIVE REVIEW COURSE** of Standard Written English & Essay Writing Skills covering all major topics found on the exam.

REA *Research & Education Association*

* SAT is a registered trademark of the College Entrance Examination Board, which does not endorse this book.

Available at your local bookstore or order directly from us by sending in coupon below.

Available at your local bookstore or order directly from us by sending in coupon below.

REA's **Problem Solvers**

The "PROBLEM SOLVERS" are comprehensive supplemental text-books designed to save time in finding solutions to problems. Each "PROBLEM SOLVER" is the first of its kind ever produced in its field. It is the product of a massive effort to illustrate almost any imaginable problem in exceptional depth, detail, and clarity. Each problem is worked out in detail with a step-by-step solution, and the problems are arranged in order of complexity from elementary to advanced. Each book is fully indexed for locating problems rapidly.

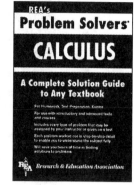

ACCOUNTING
ADVANCED CALCULUS
ALGEBRA & TRIGONOMETRY
AUTOMATIC CONTROL
   SYSTEMS/ROBOTICS
BIOLOGY
BUSINESS, ACCOUNTING, & FINANCE
CALCULUS
CHEMISTRY
COMPLEX VARIABLES
DIFFERENTIAL EQUATIONS
ECONOMICS
ELECTRICAL MACHINES
ELECTRIC CIRCUITS
ELECTROMAGNETICS
ELECTRONIC COMMUNICATIONS
ELECTRONICS
FINITE & DISCRETE MATH
FLUID MECHANICS/DYNAMICS
GENETICS
GEOMETRY
HEAT TRANSFER

LINEAR ALGEBRA
MACHINE DESIGN
MATHEMATICS for ENGINEERS
MECHANICS
NUMERICAL ANALYSIS
OPERATIONS RESEARCH
OPTICS
ORGANIC CHEMISTRY
PHYSICAL CHEMISTRY
PHYSICS
PRE-CALCULUS
PROBABILITY
PSYCHOLOGY
STATISTICS
STRENGTH OF MATERIALS &
   MECHANICS OF SOLIDS
TECHNICAL DESIGN GRAPHICS
THERMODYNAMICS
TOPOLOGY
TRANSPORT PHENOMENA
VECTOR ANALYSIS

If you would like more information about any of these books,
complete the coupon below and return it to us or visit your local bookstore.

RESEARCH & EDUCATION ASSOCIATION
61 Ethel Road W. • Piscataway, New Jersey 08854
Phone: (732) 819-8880   **website: www.rea.com**

Please send me more information about your Problem Solver books

Name _____

Address _____

City _____ State _____ Zip _____

REA's Test Preps
The Best in Test Preparation

- REA "Test Preps" are **far more** comprehensive than any other test preparation series
- Each book contains up to **eight** full-length practice tests based on the most recent exams
- **Every** type of question likely to be given on the exams is included
- Answers are accompanied by **full** and **detailed** explanations

REA has published over 60 Test Preparation volumes in several series. They include:

Advanced Placement Exams (APs)
Biology
Calculus AB & Calculus BC
Chemistry
Computer Science
English Language & Composition
English Literature & Composition
European History
Government & Politics
Physics
Psychology
Statistics
Spanish Language
United States History

College-Level Examination Program (CLEP)
Analyzing and Interpreting Literature
College Algebra
Freshman College Composition
General Examinations
General Examinations Review
History of the United States I
Human Growth and Development
Introductory Sociology
Principles of Marketing
Spanish

SAT II: Subject Tests
American History
Biology E/M
Chemistry
English Language Proficiency Test
French
German

SAT II: Subject Tests (cont'd)
Literature
Mathematics Level IC, IIC
Physics
Spanish
Writing

Graduate Record Exams (GREs)
Biology
Chemistry
Computer Science
Economics
Engineering
General
History
Literature in English
Mathematics
Physics
Psychology
Sociology

ACT - ACT Assessment

ASVAB - Armed Services Vocational Aptitude Battery

CBEST - California Basic Educational Skills Test

CDL - Commercial Driver License Exam

CLAST - College-Level Academic Skills Test

ELM - Entry Level Mathematics

ExCET - Exam for the Certification of Educators in Texas

FE (EIT) - Fundamentals of Engineering Exam

FE Review - Fundamentals of Engineering Review

GED - High School Equivalency Diploma Exam (U.S. & Canadian editions)

GMAT - Graduate Management Admission Test

LSAT - Law School Admission Test

MAT - Miller Analogies Test

MCAT - Medical College Admission Test

MSAT - Multiple Subjects Assessment for Teachers

NJ HSPT- New Jersey High School Proficiency Test

PPST - Pre-Professional Skills Tests

PRAXIS II/NTE - Core Battery

PSAT - Preliminary Scholastic Assessment Test

SAT I - Reasoning Test

SAT I - Quick Study & Review

TASP - Texas Academic Skills Program

TOEFL - Test of English as a Foreign Language

TOEIC - Test of English for International Communication

RESEARCH & EDUCATION ASSOCIATION
61 Ethel Road W. • Piscataway, New Jersey 08854
Phone: (732) 819-8880   **website: www.rea.com**

Please send me more information about your Test Prep books

Name _____

Address _____

City _____ State _____ Zip _____

MAXnotes®

REA's Literature Study Guides

MAXnotes® are student-friendly. They offer a fresh look at masterpieces of literature, presented in a lively and interesting fashion. **MAXnotes®** offer the essentials of what you should know about the work, including outlines, explanations and discussions of the plot, character lists, analyses, and historical context. **MAXnotes®** are designed to help you think independently about literary works by raising various issues and thought-provoking ideas and questions. Written by literary experts who currently teach the subject, **MAXnotes®** enhance your understanding and enjoyment of the work.

Available **MAXnotes®** include the following:

Absalom, Absalom!	Henry IV, Part I	Othello
The Aeneid of Virgil	Henry V	Paradise
Animal Farm	The House on Mango Street	Paradise Lost
Antony and Cleopatra	Huckleberry Finn	A Passage to India
As I Lay Dying	I Know Why the Caged	Plato's Republic
As You Like It	Bird Sings	Portrait of a Lady
The Autobiography of	The Iliad	A Portrait of the Artist
Malcolm X	Invisible Man	as a Young Man
The Awakening	Jane Eyre	Pride and Prejudice
Beloved	Jazz	A Raisin in the Sun
Beowulf	The Joy Luck Club	Richard II
Billy Budd	Jude the Obscure	Romeo and Juliet
The Bluest Eye, A Novel	Julius Caesar	The Scarlet Letter
Brave New World	King Lear	Sir Gawain and the
The Canterbury Tales	Leaves of Grass	Green Knight
The Catcher in the Rye	Les Misérables	Slaughterhouse-Five
The Color Purple	Lord of the Flies	Song of Solomon
The Crucible	Macbeth	The Sound and the Fury
Death in Venice	The Merchant of Venice	The Stranger
Death of a Salesman	Metamorphoses of Ovid	Sula
The Divine Comedy I: Inferno	Metamorphosis	The Sun Also Rises
Dubliners	Middlemarch	A Tale of Two Cities
The Edible Woman	A Midsummer Night's Dream	The Taming of the Shrew
Emma	Moby-Dick	Tar Baby
Euripides' Medea & Electra	Moll Flanders	The Tempest
Frankenstein	Mrs. Dalloway	Tess of the D'Urbervilles
Gone with the Wind	Much Ado About Nothing	Their Eyes Were Watching God
The Grapes of Wrath	Mules and Men	Things Fall Apart
Great Expectations	My Antonia	To Kill a Mockingbird
The Great Gatsby	Native Son	To the Lighthouse
Gulliver's Travels	1984	Twelfth Night
Handmaid's Tale	The Odyssey	Uncle Tom's Cabin
Hamlet	Oedipus Trilogy	Waiting for Godot
Hard Times	Of Mice and Men	Wuthering Heights
Heart of Darkness	On the Road	Guide to Literary Terms

RESEARCH & EDUCATION ASSOCIATION
61 Ethel Road W. • Piscataway, New Jersey 08854
Phone: (732) 819-8880   **website: www.rea.com**

Please send me more information about MAXnotes®.

Name _____

Address _____

City _____ State _____ Zip _____